WHEN THE MOCKING BIRD
SANG AT MIDNIGHT

WHEN THE MOCKING BIRD SANG AT MIDNIGHT

J. FRANK ROLLINS

To order additional copies of this book, contact:
Xlibris Corporation
1-888-795-4274
www.Xlibris.com
Orders@Xlibris.com
39881

In this story I will use the word "I" sometimes and "Frank" sometimes. It seems to me to be more informative this way, and in writing as story the writer is the boss. And there are a lot of "happenings" that I cannot write about because it may hurt someone or get upset with me writing about them or their relatives. Remember that life is only a long series of "happenings," whether they be good or bad. Your life is no different. It happened that you got up this morning; it happened that you went about doing "your thing" for the rest of the day. Each thing you do and every place is just another "happening." With all this in mind, I will get on with the story as I believe that the Lord has brought back to my memory, and maybe I have taken the liberty to "puff the goods" a little for clarity's sake. With this said and written, I must get on with the story . . .

Frank had been working all day long for D & R Sheet Metal Company in Decatur, Georgia. He had cried all day on the job. His heart was broken because of a failing marriage. The girl that he had trusted, cherished, and was married to for seven years had left him a few weeks earlier. She told him that she didn't love him anymore; she had found a different play ground somewhere else and with someone else. Frank's love for her and the bitter loneliness were becoming more than he could bear. He was considering ending his life for good. However, since he was a Christian and a licensed preacher in the Baptist church, he could not afford to bring disgrace upon the church by doing a thing like that. That night he cried and prayed until about midnight, finally falling to sleep.

At a little time after falling to sleep, Frank was awakened by something very strange to him, something that he had never heard before. He had been living in the country and on the farm all his life, but he had never heard a mockingbird singing outside in the total darkness at the hour of midnight. The mockingbird was perched on a small branch of a maple tree just a few feet outside his bedroom window. He opened the window but could not see the bird in the darkness only a few feet away from his window. That was the sweetest tone he had ever heard coming from a bird of any kind. It was the most joyous sound that he had ever heard in his life. He had heard many birds sing in his lifetime but never one that put all its soul and being into the melodious notes and sounds like this bird. Frank suddenly sat on the side of the bed and asked himself, "Why did this bird sing to me? Then he suddenly realized that God had heard his prayers and had sent the bird as a message bearer for him to me. If that mockingbird could sing to me in total darkness, it was time for Frank to break away from the total darkness and loneliness in his own life and come from total darkness, sadness and despair and come into the light that God had given him and begin living again. Then Frank fell on his knees and began talking to his Lord. Then it seemed that a voice said, "Frank, who are you?"

"Lord, you know who I am." "I am Frank Rollins."

"But, Frank, who are you really?"

"Lord, I am Frank Rollins, whom you have called and licensed to bear your name to many."

"You are a chosen vessel ordained and commissioned to bear my word to many people. Just what are you doing here?" the Lord said.

"I'm working, grieving, and trying to get on with my life."

"Frank, am I not more important than your wife? I have said that I would never leave you nor forsake you. Now get up from your knees and set your eyes on me and the work that I have given you to do, and you will find peace, love, and great joy in following me and doing my bidding. Frank, I knew you before you were born, yea, before you were conceived in thy mother's womb. Get the up and go to a place that I will prepare for you to learn my word and teaching. Be not troubled with the *ones that have tried to block you from doing my work, for it would have been better for them if they had never been born.*"

Then Frank fell into a deep sleep and trance. His mind began to go back, way back in time, way back and even further back to when he was only a baby—then he began remembering the past years that he had long forgotten.

So many people cannot remember much about their young life or ever being a baby. Well my memory of being a baby was before I was a year old. I remember my mother, father, and two brothers, Irra and Neal, living in a big circuslike tent out in the big woods near a sawmill. Our dining table was a huge oak stump about two feet high in the middle of the tent. I crawled up to the table, pulled myself up, and got some food off the stump table.

As I grew up, Mom and Daddy told us kids how they lived in Anniston, Alabama, until I was two weeks old. At that time Mom said that she looked into my little dark beady eyes and couldn't see anything good in them; to her they looked like the beady eyes of a criminal or an outlaw. It was at that time she had my daddy quit a good job working in a foundry making seven or eight dollars per day and move fifteen miles out of town so I would not be influenced by the "wrong crowd" in the big city. Boy, she didn't waste any time getting me out of there and completely away from the rest of the world. The world around us mainly sawmill folk, wild animals, and snakes. We were so surrounded by the trees that we even tipped our hat to the wildlife that surrounded us on all sides and from above, and from all the birds that fly above. That was the beginning of our love for nature and the common things around us. When we kids became old enough to walk around by ourselves, we became nature lovers.

That old tent became home for us for several months while my father kept logging for the mill that was really in our side yard, only a few yards from the sawmill. This was a very noisy place to live, but it was better than letting little Frank wind up being a beady-eyed outlaw in his future life.

The old circus-type tent wasn't real bad to live in. It was a good cool place to live in the summer and real cold in the winter. However, we had a woodstove to cook on and an old army cast-iron heater to warm us in winter. And we had plenty of wood to use for fuel for heating and cooking. It was a joy to live out there in godforsaken woodland and enjoy all the natural things that so many people never learn about.

Our family followed the sawmill for about two years living in a tent. During this time I had a new baby brother. They named him Lewis, and he was only fourteen months younger than me. After about two years living in a tent and moving it about fourteen times following the sawmill from one location to another and over two counties, Mom and Daddy rented a small house. It was about one-half mile from Mr. Jim Webb's sawmill. His mill was stationary and was under a huge tin roof. This way he didn't lose time if it was raining or even snowing. All his employees loved him, for he was a good man and he made free caskets in his woodworking shop for the dead ones in his community, even for miles around. He said that we should always respect the dead and their families. He made free caskets for all races, both black and white. People began coming from many miles away to get good quality coffins given to them. Daddy rented the house from him and began logging for his mill. One thing Daddy liked about Mr. Webb was he always paid all his workers in cash at the end of the week.

The next thing that I remembered was visiting the Webb family when I was about one year old. The womenfolks were inside quilting and I crawled out on the front porch and pulled up to an old bedside chamber that had not been completely emptied, and I managed to get the chamber up to my mouth and began to drink the urine from the chamber. It was salty and the most awful stuff that I ever tasted. Mom finally saw me and washed that awful-tasting stuff out of my mouth and gave me some good water to drink. However, that awful taste remains with me until this day. Even today every time I see an old chamber along the roadside with flowers growing in it brings back haunting memories of very early childhood.

This first house was an old farmhouse with four small rooms and a front porch all across the front of the house. I can remember feeding the chickens through the cracks in the porch floor. By the time I was about three years old we moved to another larger three-room house about a mile from where we were living. It was in much better repair than the other one. It even had a brick fireplace in the east end of the large living room. There was a large bedroom, a large kitchen and dining room combination, and a smaller side room for storage. There was no front porch, but it had a large back porch built inside the L-shaped house. There was a large mantle over the fireplace, big enough for Mom and Daddy's big Bruton snuff boxes, a kerosene lamp, matchboxes, and various other items. Here we all had room enough to live in comfort and pleasure. There was a large yard with shade trees and a large garden with a wire fence to keep the rabbits and other critters from eating our salad greens and other stuff. There were several fruit trees full of young fruit. Boy, this seemed like heaven on earth to the entire family. It was nothing like living in a canvas tent out in the backwoods. Here we had real beds, with cotton mattresses. The new house even had real lumber ceiling overhead.

Our new home was across the dirt road from the Liberty Hill schoolhouse. The Liberty Hill School was a little one room schoolhouse with one large schoolroom and a cloakroom running all the way across the end of the building. This room was where the students hung their coats, caps and hats, and put their lunch buckets on a shelf running all the way down the room. It was also where Mrs. Getty Gable would take the unruly students and wear out their behinds for unruly things that they had done. Someone in the room would pay her a visit to the cloakroom about every day. It was mostly for fighting and talking, and cussing out loud in the schoolroom or out on the play ground. She would use a hickory switch sized to fit the crime. If you had done something real bad you got a real big whipping in the front of the classroom in plain view of all *the other students*. She had one real bad boy that she had to whip about every day. He was the most unruly kid in the school district. Mrs. Jetty, as everyone called her, would have expelled him, but she wanted to reform him and make teaching him worth all her efforts. However, that was not possible for her to do since he seemed to be just the makings of an unhung outlaw. Irra started his education at this school. Neal was not old enough to attend school at that time. Frank was only three years old, and he couldn't go to school at that age, however he wanted to.

Frank was always subject to having the croup, an ailment that kept one from breathing well. His throat would swell and hinder his breathing. When Frank would play outside in damp weather, he would get croup and have difficulty breathing. His mother would give a spoonful of sugar wet down with kerosene. On one morning he came down with what Mom thought was the croup. The kerosene and sugar didn't do any good. As the day went by, Frank only got worse. Mom sent Daddy over to a neighbor's house to call Dr. Caffey who lived and had his office a little east of Anniston. Dr. Caffey realized the urgency of the call and came quickly. He hurried unto the house and looked in his throat and quickly announced that Frank had diphtheria, and there was only one thing to do, and that was give him a shot. The doctor said that he didn't have the medication with him and Frank would be dead within four hours if I didn't get the proper shot. He told one of my cousins to go to Heflin, which was about ten miles away and get the medication from Dr. Wright who was the Cleburne County health officer. The old dirt roads were very washed out and almost impossible to drive on in a car. But my cousin Ebb Haywood said that he would go to Heflin and get the drug from Dr. Wright, the Cleburnee health officer. Dr. Caffey agreed to stay with Frank and try to keep him alive until Ebb returned with the medicine. When Ebb got to Dr. Wright's home, he was eating supper. When Ebb told the doctor what he wanted, the doctor refused to go to his office for the drug and told Ebb to come back the next morning about eight o'clock. That didn't set well with Ebb at all. After a cuss fight with the doctor, Ebb ran outside and came back with a large tire-changing tool and began swinging at the doctor. At that time Dr. Wright agreed to go to his office and give Ebb the proper drug. Ebb opened the old Model T Ford as fast as he could drive on that old muddy dirt road. After driving with only one headlight, Ebb finally arrived at the Rollins house with the medication and gave it to Dr. Caffey. The doctor laid Frank on the bed and gave him a shot in his hip. Within about ten minutes Frank was breathing almost normally again. By the next morning he was very much better. If Frank had not got the injection that night, this story would not be written. There will always be a place in my heart for the really dedicated medical personnel and doctors. Some of them are willing to risk all and go the last mile for someone whom they had never seen before. And I shall always feel a great deal of gratitude for my cousin, Ebb Haywood. If he had not become violent and angry with a doctor, my life would have ended that night before my fourth birthday.

Some of the students in the school came to visit me when I was very sick with diphtheria. The Cleburnee County health officer sent a nurse to our house to quarantine our house for a given amount of days, and the nurse sent all the children that had visited me home for the same amount of time. However, none of the other children came down with the deadly disease. Since we lived just across the road from the school, the school was closed for about ten to fourteen days. But it was for their good. All the fear was over and the school began classes again.

Our family got great pleasure in living near the school. Neal, Frank, and Lewis could watch the children playing in the school yard, and on certain occasions we could see a good fight, and even Mrs. Jetty get her switch and beat the tar out of a couple of bullies that kept on fighting. One boy named Edgar just had to get in a fight at least one or twice each week, and the teacher got her thrills each time by taking him out beside the schoolhouse and wearing him out with a larger stick than she used on the other ones. That was because he was determined to fight someone smaller than himself. The cloakroom was to narrow for her to give him the kind of beating she was to give him. Finally she got tired of trying to get him to strengthen up, so she finally expelled him and sent one of the other boys to go fetch Edgar's father to take Edgar home, and she didn't spare the father either. That day I believe she would have been willing to hang a father and son if she could have, but there wasn't a low limb on the large oak tree big enough to hold up the two of them to hang on. And she would have to remove the well rope to hang them with, and that would mean that the other students would not have cold fresh water from the well until someone would come and cut them down and haul their bodies off to the bone yard or burial place. Besides, the rope might be too short to draw water after cutting off some that was around their dirty necks. And she knew that to use a dirty rope to draw water with may be bad luck or something like that. That was very thoughtful of her to consider the welfare of the other students. She may have thought that both of them would give her a little trouble while she put the hangman's noose around their dirty necks. And she might have thought that the devil might send her another student as mean as or even meaner than Edgar.

While living there we always had a hog, a good-looking cow, and a lot of frying chickens, and some laying ones too. Daddy always wanted a fine looking cow because he didn't want anyone seeing him milking an old scrawny cow if Mom was sick or something and he had to milk. He always said that a man should not milk because it may be bad luck to take what you could not give; therefore, it was always a woman's place to do all the milking. However, my mom and daddy had some interesting discussions about this matter. My daddy was not only a log cutter, he also was a seemingly wise man when it came to milking or something that it didn't seem right for him to do. No matter what someone wanted him to do, he could "bad luck" his way out of it. Daddy had two old hound dogs that people wanted to buy, but he always said that it was bad luck to sell a dog, so we kept the mangy things. Mom had several hen's nesting boxes nailed along the barn wall where the hens would go to lay their eggs and occasionally set on about a dozen eggs to have her a little family of her own that she could see grow up until the preacher saw all the little tender broilers and hinted for an invite over for a Sunday dinner and maybe a Sunday supper too. On Saturday she began catching three or four young roosters about five or six weeks old and putting them in a special chicken-holding box. We knew not to cuss very much that day for the preacher was sure to be there after church the next day. And I'm not lying; I think a preacher and his family could eat a whole coopful of chickens in just one Sunday. And if he came for a two-week revival, your flock of frying-size chicken would be digested before the two weeks was over. My grandma once told us that a traveling preacher came to visit them a few years earlier. She went out and got the oldest and poorest rooster she had and prepared it for his dinner. She burned the chicken on one side and half cooked the other side and fed him with leftover biscuits from the day before. After struggling with the meal for a half hour, he said he had to be somewhere else soon, and he left whittling a strong toothpick from a piece of kindling pine he got from the stove wood box on his way out. She said she never saw him again, that she reckoned that he was still picking that tough rooster from between his teeth until that day. But that ain't no way to treat a visiting preacher. She should have fed him one of Uncle Green's possums that she had skinned, dried, and smoked. Boy, we all looked forward to her dried smoked possum with homemade biscuit and red-eyed gravy.

Someone told me that their pastor sometimes ate so much chicken that when he got in the pulpit on Sunday night, he flapped his arms like wings and crowed like a rooster. We lived in this house for about two years.

Then it was time to move again. This time we moved into a small one-room shack of a house, if one could call it a house. It was about eighteen feet by twenty feet in size, and it was the worst house that we ever lived in. The tin roof was full of holes, and when it rained we have enough buckets and pans to catch all the rainwater that came through the holes in the rusty metal roof. It seemed that the family living there before us must have been shooting at the rats that ran across the rafters and the bullets went up through the roof. They must have missed a few when they were shooting, judging from all the holes in the roof and all the huge rats that invaded the house after we moved in. There was a large hole left somewhere because we found a large possum in Mommy's flower sack one morning when she ran her hand down in the sack to dip some flour out to make some biscuits for breakfast. After she stopped screaming, she dipped the flour out, sifted out the possum hairs, or at least most of them, she made us some of the most harry biscuits that we ever had. While we ate them, we could close our eyes and imagine how good they would taste if the possum was baked inside them. However, sometimes one misses the very best things that could have been on the breakfast table. The walls of the old house had cracks between the boards large enough for lizards and small snakes to crawl between them in some places, but that was not so bad because the small snakes were more afraid of us than we were of them. Momma said that she was afraid of only four kinds of snakes—big ones, little ones, dead ones and live ones. And that was about all we ever had up in the woody area where we lived in those days. We didn't need air-conditioning much in summer because the wind came through all the cracks to keep us somewhat cooler than we thought possible. Our problem was trying to keep warm in winter with only one fireplace and the air-conditioning running when the winter winds kept blowing freezing air through the cracks in the walls, floor and roof. We always wished that the former occupants had done less shooting or took better aim at the rats.

There was a large spring about thirty yards from our back door where we dipped up our water supply. The water was very cold and clear. Below the spring was a large spillway branch that was lined with watercress. We gathered it and ate it from time to time. We also had three sweet or sugar apple trees in our backyard. One tree had small red apples, and the other two trees had large white mellow sweet apples. That was our late-summer and early-fall treat. The other fruit was good but nothing to compare with the sugar apples we had. Grandpa gave us his old newspapers to use as bathroom tissue; however, we never had a toilet or outhouse. We just went up in the thickly wooded area all around our house. We had a garden here and let our cow run in Grandpa's pasture with his cows and mules.

One might wonder how a family living in a one-room house, and arranged their furniture and furnishings. Well, it was very hard to make everything fit into the space of twenty foot by eighteen foot house go into the proper place. The house had three doors, a front door on the end of the house in the center, and two side doors one on either side. The fireplace was on the other end of the house. This left little room for the furnishings However, with one bed on either side of the front door and the kitchen cabinet and stove set up in the left hand back corner, and with the kitchen table set at the end of one bed it wasn't very difficult. We used the four kitchen chairs in front of the fireplace for our living area. Our beds served as our couches. There was a closeness in our family especially when it was raining or bad weather during the day.

Living in this condition must have been very hard on Momma and Dad. Sometimes they would sit and cry as they discussed moving back to Anniston and finding some kind of work so the family could live a normal life again. They had moved out of Anniston and into total poverty because of my little dark beady eyes, perhaps the eyes of a future outlaw

13

or future John Dillinger or maybe something worse. One thing was for certain, there was not any bank out in those backwoods for me to start robbing at that time in my early life. By leaving the city, life had become very hard for the family. In Anniston, we had a very nice home to live in, city water, and one two-hole outhouse with an inside latch on the door. There the family had electric lights and gas heat or a coal heater to keep warm. Man, it would have been much better if I had been born with larger and softer-colored eyes. Some people say that you can look a person in the eyes and tell a lot about their nature and character. But does this apply to a two-week-old baby? About the only thing you've ever robbed or stolen was eggs from a bird's nest or eggs from under Mom's old setting hen to sell to the peddler truckman to buy candy for Irra, Neal, Lewis, and myself. And maybe steal a rotten-ended watermelon from my grandpa's melon patch.

After about a year the sawmill bunch decided to move to another location miles and miles away. Mom and Daddy decided not to go with the mill this time. Daddy got a contract job cutting railroad cross ties in the forest about a mile from where we were living. He was to cut the cross ties for a Mr. Burkhalter who owned several hundred acres of woodland near where we were living. Momma would help Daddy saw down the huge oak trees and saw them in eight-foot lengths. Daddy would then split the trees into four sections using hard dogwood wedges that he had handmade from seasoned dogwood trees.

Dogwood was the hardest woodman could find to make the splitting wedges from, and it would not split easily when driven into the trees to make them split apart. Daddy would take his Blue Grass double-blade ax and shape each quarter section of the log into a straight seven-inch-by-nine-inch cross tie. This took a lot of skill and hard chopping and splitting away the wood until it had square corners. He could hew out about eight or ten ties each day. I think he was paid about twenty cents per cross tie if it was sound wood with no rotten spots visible to the naked eye. Sometimes a rotten hole would be filled with a wood peg hammered in, cut smooth and covered with a little mud, to make it appear that it had been drug on the ground. It was very hard to do all that chopping and splitting and let your labor lie in the woods and rot. Why not let it rot away while heavy trains passed over it? This was much more money than he could make cutting logs. And I think Daddy was getting great pleasure in making Mama help him saw the trees and get back at her for making him quit a good job in the pipe foundry just to get my little dark beady eyes out in the woods so I would not become another outlaw and be hung from a huge oak tree limb in the Calhoun County courtyard. God, how she must have loved me! Just think of all the torment and poverty the family went through just to keep me from swinging on a big oak tree limb. Daddy said many times that he wished I had been a girl or that I had big blue eyes.

After Daddy started cutting ties, he was able to rent a larger three-room house with a large side room and a long front porch. The main living and bedroom had ceiling overhead. Now we didn't have the pleasure of watching old big tomcat jump from rafter to rafter chasing the big slick-tailed rats. You know, we all kind of missed the cat and mouse chase on the rafters after we went to bed and while the fireplace gave off a soft glowing light. Gosh, how we all missed the life-and-death chase after we went to bed and got quiet. We even would leave chicken bones on the table or some other smelly food so the rats would smell it and attempt to retrieve it for their little rat family. Sometimes we would throw another log on the fire so we could see the combat begin. Mama scolded us for such cruelty. She thought that Daddy should shoot the rats with his old twelve-gauge shotgun, but if he had done that he would have blown holes in the tin roof about the size of a nearly grown green apple or maybe the size of a half-grown rutabaga turnip, and besides, look at all the rat parts that would be splattered over the underside of the tin roof and falling all over the beds and stuff. And if Daddy had done that ole tom would not get his pleasure chasing them rats. In our new home we could hear the rats playing in the attic space, but they very seldom came down. Our worries about the rats stopped when Mama saw a large spotted chicken snake about six feet long and as big around as Uncle Green's pickax handle slither up under the house. If we could have compared it to a fire alarm, it would have been at least a five alarmer. She made Daddy take up half the living room floor looking for that snake. However, the snake was never found as long as we lived there. The new home had a cow stall, a hog pen, and a large garden fenced in with chicken-proof wire about six feet high. We could step out the kitchen door and into the garden. This was very convenient for us to gather veggies and stuff from the garden.

Since we were renting the house from our mother's father, he was always on us kids to do things for him, like picking up apples, pulling weed, and hoeing his garden. We boys didn't think that this was part of the deal. However, Mom and Dad and Grandpa thought differently, so we picked up apples, pulled weeds, and hoed the garden. It became hard for us to get more than eight or ten hours' rest and play time during the average day.

Now that we had an outdoor outhouse with two places for resting and other things, we felt that we were climbing the ladder of success. Although we were a mile from our nearest neighbor except Grandma and Grandpa, we felt that we were climbing the social ladder at last. We even decided to clean up and go about ten miles to Heflin to buy groceries, and to get a chance to wear our Sunday clothes. The peddling truck had been bringing us our supplies, but not this time. We felt proud and wanted folk along the road to see us in Grandpa's wagon living like other people. Well, they might think that we were riding in our own wagon and that the fine looking mules were also ours. Mama put on her best feed-sack dress and Daddy put on his newest overalls, and we kids put on our best overalls and long-sleeve shirts. We even washed up pretty good for the trip. Since we had not been to town in several months, we were warned to be on our best behavior. We took this trip about twice each year from then on for a few years. I can almost feel the old wagon bed bumping my tail as we rode down the old dirt road that was washed out and full of small ditches and rocks. Soon we learned to stuff a sack with grass hay to sit on to save our backsides from such a bumping. For a few trips I had rather been whooped with a dogwood brush broom than to be bumped all the way to town and back.

It was one of these trips a year or so earlier that when we arrived in Heflin that Daddy took Lewis and me over to a stack of fresh-cut lumber and set us upon the lumber stack. He went inside and came out with a large paper bag filled with golden ripe bananas. He told us to eat them while he took Irra and Neal inside to try on some shoes. He seemed to be gone forever or perhaps longer. When the three arrived, he told Irra and Neal to eat some bananas. Well, it was too late. Lewis and I had eaten six bananas each and were fighting over the thirteenth one. In those days the storekeeper would always throw in the thirteenth one for good measure. Well, Daddy didn't tell us to eat just so many, so we ate them all. He went back in the store and bought another dozen for Irra and Neal. Mama came out with Daddy this time with her arms full of groceries and other stuff. I don't know what they had eaten, but they looked like that they didn't want any bananas. When Mom and Daddy asked why we ate all the bananas, we told him that he forgot to tell us where to stop. Mama was so mad about the banana eating that she threatened to give Lewis and me a big dose of castor oil. But the bumpy ride home made her forget to give it to us.

The new house we were now living in was Grandpa's second house he had built for his family. The old run-down shack of a house was his first and that was where my mother was born along with eight other kids. After running out of space to bed all the children down, Grandpa had to build the fourth house—the one we now lived in. As the children grew up and were old enough to work, Grandpa built the large house about two hundred yards up on a little hill. It was a beautiful home with four large rooms with two on either side of a large hallway running all the way from front to back. There was three large porches, a front, back, and side porch. The thing that we grandchildren liked most about the house was a stairway leading up into the large attic space that was supposed to become two large bedrooms but was never finished. It was floored, and two large domers were built to let in light in the future rooms. This space was used for a storage area. Grandpa had Mr. Webb build his coffin and line it with fine linen and it had beautiful heart pine carrying handles on each side. It was delivered and carried up the stairs and placed in the attic awaiting his departure from this life. I could hardly go up there and play in the attic and that coffin right there in the middle of the play area. After a few years Uncle Green, Grandpa's bachelor brother who lived with them decided to store his seed peanuts in Grandpa's coffin so the rats couldn't eat them during the winter. Well, that worked for a winter or two. But finally the rats outsmarted Uncle Green. The rats went to one of the back corners and ate and chewed a large hole in the lower back corner of the fine casket and ate all his seed peanuts and cut up most of the lining. They also brought in bits of straw, leaves, bits of paper and anything nasty and build a large rat bed inside the beautiful coffin. That was the first time most of us saw Granddad get angry, swear, and cry. He was more proud of that pine coffin than anything that he owned. After the discovery of the damage they had a carpenter come and repair the woodwork in such a way that one couldn't tell that it was ever rat eaten and damaged. The lining was not replaced because the family wanted to buy fine silk to replace it but somehow their fear of the rats doing it again kept them from doing it. Sometime in the later years they sold the coffin to a poor family for two weeks' work in Grandpa's field and two gallons of elderberry wine. I think Grandma was glad to see it go because it depressed her to know that thing was resting over her bedroom.

In the summer of the first year that we lived in the big house a Mr. Dempsey saw Daddy in town one Saturday and contacted for Daddy to make him ten gallons of blackberry wine. He told Daddy it was so he could take a little for his stomach trouble. To order ten gallons of pure blackberry wine, his stomach pain must have been bad. The next day we all began picking blackberries to fill the order. I want you to know my daddy was not a bootlegger or anything like that. But we needed money, and Mr. Dempsey agreed to pay Daddy two dollars a gallon for ten gallons of wine. And we all could pitch in and help. We picked two large washtubs full of berries and set them out on the front porch and covered the berries with creek water and threw an old quilt over each tub to keep the chickens out. Mama told us boys that she was going to can the berries in a few days and for us not to even look at them, for it might make them spoil after she canned them for our winter use. In a few days they got to smelling powerfully good to us. We would ask her wren she was going to can them and she told us that we had to wait for the peddling truck to bring her some fruit jars. But we didn't believe her because the peddling truck had quit coming over there because Grandma owed him thirteen dollars and we owed him about eight dollars. In a few more days while we boys went to the small creek, fishing and hunting frogs something happened to the berries and the tubs were put back on the wash bench. We thought Mama had canned them and put them in the storm shelter or storm pit that Daddy had dug in the little bank by our front porch. The storm pit was about eight feet by ten feet and was covered over with logs and about two feet of dirt over the logs. That is where we kept our canned stuff for winter. In about two weeks, Mama and Daddy borrowed Grandpa's mules and wagon, drove off to Heflin to buy a few things and left us boys to fend for ourselves until they returned in about six or seven hours.

We had a large barn just above our house. It had a corn crib, two stables with a hallway between them, and also a large hay loft above all this with a ladder going straight up into the hay loft. We decided to play in the hay loft while they were gone to Heflin. While we were rolling and sliding on the hay, one of us discovered two five gallon jugs buried in the hay with corn cob stoppers sticking up through the hay. Irra removed one corn cob and looked in the jug. Boy, the aroma coming from the jug was maybe the sweetest smell that we ever smelled. It reminded us of the smell of the berries that we had set out on the porch and covered with the old quilts but it smelled much better than that. Irra told Neal to climb down the ladder and get him a hollow weed that was growing in the cow lot behind the barn. When Neal brought Irra the hollow weed, Irra broke off a section about a foot and a half long and stuck it down in the jug and pulled it out and stuck it to his tongue. He liked what he had tasted. He stuck it back in the jug and began to drink the wine, not really knowing what it was. He thought it was the juice from the berries that had disappeared from our porch. After Irra drank all the good-tasting juice, he wanted he let Neal take his turn at it. Then it was my turn, and Lewis got his turn at the straw or hollow weed. After the first round of drinking the heavenly nectar, we all took another round from the other jug. After an hour or a little longer swinging down the good berry juice, we all became very dizzy and decided to climb down and go get on the porch. While climbing down, Neal fell about halfway down and landed in the soft hay and manure that covered the ground under the ladder. Irra helped him get to his feet, and we all staggered to the front porch and lay down and became very disoriented and dizzy. Well, we were real drunk on Mr. Dempsey's blackberry wine. Somehow Irra had caught Daddy's favorite big red rooster. He was plucking all the feathers out of the rooster's tail and wings, and over the rooster's body. Irra had about half the feathers plucked out when Mama and Daddy arrived home from their trip to Heflin. When Daddy saw Irra picking the feathers from his beautiful red rooster, it made him very angry. And when they saw all of us rolling around on the porch laughing and hollering at each other and acting silly, they knew something was badly wrong. They ran up to the porch and Mama said, "Wess, these little devils have been into something. Just look at them. Their eyes are all red and they look and act like they are drunk. And just look at what Irra is doing to that rooster."

"Irra, just what in the devil are you doing to that poor old rooster?" Daddy asked.

"Well you don't want me to cook him with these red feathers on him, do you? We are going to have red rooster for dinner and we think his feathers wouldn't taste real good."

"Wess, just look at them. They look drunk or something! Do you think they found Dempsey's wine jugs up in the hay loft?"

"I'll run up there and see."

While Daddy was checking the jugs Mom got the old dogwood brush broom and started to whip the boys, but they couldn't stand up long enough To do any whipping. Daddy came running back and with a loud voice said, "Them little hellions and outlaws have been up in the barn loft drinking poor old Dempsey's wine and I believe they have drunk about a gallon from each jug. Don't hit them with that brush broom anymore. It is my fault that they drunk the wine, I found the hollow weed and I got a good drink myself, don't you want to climb up there with me and get a little snort before Dempsey comes after it?"

"Do you recon that I could climb the ladder to get a little drink myself?"

"No, you might fall and break yourself. When Mr. Dempsey comes after it tonight I will pour you out a jar full. No, I will pour out a big jar full for us and replace it with creek water before Dempsey gets here."

Somehow Daddy poured out a half-gallon fruit jar full of that good-tasting wine and hid it in the hay pile for Mom and him to celebrate that night. We boys had our celebration already and were still celebrating. That was about two-thirty in the afternoon. Daddy replaced the wine with good creek water and put the corn cob stopper back in each jug. About seven O'clock that day Dempsey arrived in a good-looking buggy pulled by a beautiful spotted horse. He helped Daddy get the wine down from the barn loft and on to the buggy. He paid Daddy two nice new ten-dollar bills. That was the most money that Daddy and Mama had ever had at one time since leaving Anniston. After loading the jugs on the buggy, Dempsey wanted a large cup so he could pour himself a little snort. He had two, then three cups full of that good stuff. Then he borrowed our wash pan so he could treat his horse to some. He then poured maybe about a gallon in the wash pan and held it up to the horse, Old Spot, as he called him. Old Spot readily took a liking to the wine and drank down the whole panful and turned his head around as to suggest another panful. Dempsey gave him almost another panful and said to Daddy, "I don't know about old Spot, but it is getting dark and I have miles to go."

Dempsey then climbed on to the buggy and slashed the horse with the buggy whip. Old Spot started running out across Aunt May's cotton patch as fast as he could run. Then Dempsey managed to get the horse and buggy back in the road and stayed on the road until they came to a large creek that you had to drive through the water to cross. Old Spot put on his brakes and stopped suddenly to get a drink from the creek. He stopped so quickly that one jug that was loaded on the seat with Dempsey plunged off the seat and into the creek. Old Spot smelled the wine and backed up a few feet and began drinking the water and wine mixture among the pieces of the broken jug. When he had had enough, he reared up on his back legs, and down the road he went until he came to Mr. Dewberry's cornfield, at which time he left the road and cut across the cornfield for several hundred yards. He circled back and across Mrs. Dewberry's garden which had a five-foot wire fence until this time. When leaving the garden the horse and buggy came across the Dewberry's yard pulling about fifty feet of Mrs. Dewberry's garden fence behind the buggy. The Dewberrys were setting on the front porch when the horse and buggy came by in the darkness, almost hitting the porch. They had been drinking a little strong wine mixed with some of Mr. Dewberry's white lightning whisky, and they were just about departed from reality when the horse and buggy came by across the yard and hit the front porch steps. Mr. Dewberry turned to his wife and asked, "Did you hear some train or tornado come through our yard? And you didn't see what I didn't see, did you?"

"No, I didn't see or hear something running and dragging something up behind it either, there ain't no trains or storms running around here tonight. It must be that you poured too much whisky in the wine jug. From now on let me do the mixing." Dewberry got up from the old rocking chair and said to his wife, "I know I didn't see a big old horse pulling a buggy through our garden and taking the new wire fence with them, and scaring our tomatoes, beans, and stuff half to death. And don't go around telling our neighbors what we didn't see because they will think that we were drinking again, and you know we haven't touched stuff an at least a few minutes." Laughing, they staggered into the house.

Dempsey, the horse and buggy got in the road again dragging the wire fence behind the buggy while Dempsey was bouncing around the seat and trying to control a drunken horse. You just don't control a drunken horse very well when he is as big and as Old Spot. He went down the dirt road hitting mailboxes, flower bed and anything that got in his way. They kept going until they got about a mile from Dempsey's house. There the horse decided to take a shortcut through a pine forest of large pines. The horse could go through between the trees but the buggy wouldn't fit. It was there that Dempsey's son found him the next day. He had three broken ribs, a broken arm, and cuts and bruises over most of his body. Old Spot came back to the barn dragging the buggy shaves and harness with him. That was the time the search for Dempsey began by his son and wife. When they found him and the remainder of the buggy, they took him to the doctor in Heflin to get him patched up and ready to go again. He told his family that he had not had that much fun on a buggy ride in his life, and he saved one jug of the blackberry wine. Dempsey told his son, "If Old Spot don't die from that bump on his head he got from running into that low-hanging pine limb and I get a new buggy, I'm agonna try it again, but I won't let old Spot drink as much wine the next go around. I don't want him to get that drunk again. If I do he may become a wino or an alcoholic or something."

From time to time I have the occasion to pass the old Dempsey home and always remember the time Daddy sold him the wine and what happened to him on the way home. Daddy and Mama used to sit and laugh and talk about it. I don't believe Daddy ever made any more wine for anyone, and certainly not for himself. We were brought up in a godly home although we didn't attend church very much. Our lives were shaped, influenced and molded by those events and the people living around us. When I see the old Dempsey home, I am reminded that all things around me will pass away in time and something new will replace them.

Our family did much growing up during the time that we lived in Grandpa's house. We helped him on the little farm. His children cut cross ties for the railroad people and carried them to Heflin on his wagon and sold them direct to the railroad people represented by Mr. Owens who owned a dry goods and hardware store in the north corner of Heflin next to the railroad and train station. This way Grandpa cut the middle man and was paid more for his ties. He tried to make his living by being smart and taking advantage of every deal he made. That is how he became our grandpa. Some people said that he bought our grandma from a little offspring Indian tribe for a few sacks of corn, some home grown tobacco. An old muzzle loader shotgun, a bony cow, a half-grown pig and some cornstalk fodder to winter the cow on. The Indians were trying to become civilized, and they didn't believe that was possible while they had Grandma in their small tribe. She was a small woman, and they needed a big woman that could hunt, clear land, and plow crops. So they traded her off to Grandpa to get something to help them make crop, but didn't have anyone left to do the work. However, Grandpa got the best of the trade. If Grandpa had not made the trade, Mama would not have been born and I would not be here today. Now, that is the story; however, some of us believed something else was the reason for the Indians to trade her off. It was because she never stopped talking long enough for anyone around her to get in a word sideways. If you didn't want to talk for hours, you should stay away from Grandma. Daddy always said that she could talk the horns off a billy goat and make him throw in his beard and tail to boot. Grandma was always a great help to Grandpa. She cooked, washed, grew the garden, plowed the fields, cut cross tied, cut firewood, kept the house clean, and gathered vegetables and produce for him to sell. I just don't know how he would have survived without her for his squaw or wife. Grandpa would get the crowd out working and he would go to the woods to hunt for a bee tree or find something else to do. None of us could remember ever seeing him do any work other than going to town to sell something to get his hands on some money that the others had *worked their fingers to the bone to get*. That is one reason I think was

WHEN THE MOCKING BIRD SANG AT MIDNIGHT

a smart man. The rest of the family and generation would like the opportunity to do the same. But the rest of us didn't buy an Indian squaw for a slaving wife. The others just had to go and hunt one for free.

Grandpa's farm was small and was mainly made up of farmland and fruit trees. There were almost a hundred apple and pear trees and a few grapevines. He grew several varieties of apples and peaches that he would gather the fruit and carry to Anniston and sell during the fruit bearing season. We would help gather the fruit and load it on the wagon and get ready for the trip the next day. Sometimes the steel wagon wheel rims would become loose because the wood part of the wheel would dry out. We often removed the wheels and soaked them in the creek overnight so the steel rim would be tight and not come off during the trip. Many times the load was green corn, turnip greens, green peas and beans, collards, cucumbers, and kindling pine. The kindling pine was split into splinters and bundles with old inner-tube rubber bands cut from old inner-tubes off a truck or car. Grandpa would gather up and sell almost anything that the city people would buy. There was always a ready market for fruit and vegetables and kindling pine. In the winter months, we would go to the woods and gather up a wagonload of good heart kindling pine knots and the rich hearts of the dead rotten pine trees. We gathered about two or three loads per week. It was gathered on one day and hauled to Anniston to sell the next day. Sometimes he would hire Daddy to go with him to do most of the selling and unloading. At times it would be so late that they would tie up the mules and feed and water them after pulling the wagon in the wagon yard behind the hotel and the hardware store. Grandpa would always go to the hotel and let Daddy sleep in the wagon so he could make sure no one would steal them. However, one night Daddy was so tired that he went to sleep, and about midnight someone came along and didn't see Daddy sleeping under some feed sacks and hitched up the mules and took off down Noble Street with the wagon while Daddy was fast asleep. Daddy woke up and rose up behind the wagon seat, grabbed the thief and hollered real loud and shoved him to one side. The man screamed and jumped off the wagon on to the hard street and ran away. Daddy told a police officer what had happened and the man was caught and locked up. It was not the first time he tried to get away with steeling a wagon from the wagon yard. Grandpa read in the paper that he had two more wagons and three stolen mules out on his farm a few miles out.

Most of the times when they had to stay overnight, Grandpa would come down grinning and tell Daddy about the sweet little girl that he met in the hotel. Sometimes as they were selling produce over on the west side of the railroad tracks, he would go into certain homes and return a half hour later and have Daddy help him fill boxes, buckets, and sacks full of corn, tomatoes, squash, beans, peas, corn, and anything else the poor widow woman might want. There was never any money exchanged in such deals. He would always say that he could not bear to see someone in need of food and not do something to help out. He usually told Daddy that he was in the house drinking coffee and talking about what the woman wanted him to bring her the next trip. Somehow as we talked about it at times that if Grandma had ever found out about the other woman she would skelp him and then bury him in that rat-eaten coffin that was up in the attic over their bedroom.

21

After spending the night in Anniston, Daddy and Grandpa would finish selling the rest of the load and get going home to tell his family how much money he had made on that load. He always paid Daddy well to keep him from telling all the story of why Grandpa didn't come home with more money. He would sometimes tell them that he had to unload some of the stuff along the road because it didn't sell well or that someone brought a load of produce ahead of him. But the truth was that he squandered some of his money and produce on lovely old gals along the way. I always liked Grandpa, but I kind of wanted to see her scalp him and hang his gray hair on her bedpost at the foot of their bed like she said many times that she would liked to do. One time when he was whipping me for stealing his only straight razor to cut me a fishing pole down by the creek and putting a large gap in the blade, I tried to get Grandma to scalp him for me while I help her hold him down. She refused but said, "Frank, he will get it someday when I am not so tired and not so late in the day. I might not be able to eat these turnip greens that I have cooked with possum grease and pig ears, and I might not sleep very well with his ball headed body in that coffin up in the attic."

"After you eat the turnip green, maybe we can take your rusty butcher knife and go to work on his white hair, could we?"

"No, I'm just too tired after cutting the bushes off the creek bank all day. Maybe I'll feel better by morning and you'll feel more like holding him down for me to do the scalping. Do you think that you can stand all the hollering and screaming he might do while we do that to him? This might go on for a while after we get done with that."

"Well I'll be up here in the morning as soon as Daddy leaves to go cut ties because he might whip me with the brush broom for helping you if he ever finds out what we have done to Grandpa."

"Do you recon Lee and Wess will ever know what we done to him, and who are we gonna get to bury him when he dies from no hair on the brain?"

"Tell Lee and Wess what you want to do in the morning and see if they want to help us a little, maybe to get him up the stairs to the coffin or something."

"I will go tell them, but I don't think that they don't like him as much as I don't like him. He never did whip Daddy with that old leather razor strap like he whipped me for ruining his good shaving razor blade or shaving knife."

I went home and told them that Grandma had only seen one or two people scalped and she might not know all the secrets in scalping a grown man and that there is nothing meaner than a half-scalped old man. And if I didn't hold him just right, I and Grandma might both be hauled off and buried in that rat infested coffin. Daddy told me that it might be best if Grandma and I held off on the plans to murder Grandpa until some of the other relatives got real mad at him and could help me hold him down for Grandma to do the scalping.

That brought to a close our plans to do the Indian thing on Grandpa. Within a few days I sure was glad that Grandma was tired and wanted to eat her turnip greens that afternoon. If it had been morning I hate to think what we would have done to him and I might be Grandpaless that day. But time has a way curing many of our temper fits and removing hatred and quick decisions. If we had carried out our plans, Grandma might have made us move off and leave the good life that we were now living.

About that time in life, Daddy had done some farmwork for a dishonest man that promised to pay Daddy about fifty cents a day for his work, and then he wouldn't pay Daddy after Daddy had worked two weeks for him. Daddy became angry with him and called him some bad names, some of which I didn't know what they meant. He told Daddy that he would wear the ground out with him, and since it was a long dry spell, Daddy didn't want that to happen. Daddy went to the woods and found a small fallen tree with a limb growing straight up at ninety degrees to the trunk, just right to make a club-type walking stick. Daddy cut it off with his ax and brought it home and made a large hammer-headed walking stick. He bored a three quarter-inch hole through the hammerhead part of the walking stick. He then melted lead and poured the hole full of molten lead. This made the walking stick to become a lethal combat weapon in the eyes of the law and other responsible thinking people. Daddy was going to go over to this man's house and kill him with the hammerlike walking stick—it was made to kill with and not for walking. Mama was very afraid for Daddy and also for the other man. She was afraid that Daddy would kill him and might be hanged for his bad deed in killing him. She wrote a postcard to the Cleburne County mental health officer, Mrs. Verge and had Irra run over to the mailbox and mail it. The next day Mrs. Verge came over in her little shiny car to see Mama. Mama told her what had taken place. The following morning, before Daddy could get dressed to go to work, the sheriff came rolling up with the sirens going full blast and handcuffed Daddy and hauled him away and locked him in the Heflin jail. Daddy asked what the charges against him were, and they wouldn't tell him anything. The next morning Mrs. Verge came to the jail with two large men wearing white coats. Daddy asked them why they were wearing white overcoats in summer. And then they told him that Mama and Mrs. Verge had said that he was crazy and he was going with them to the veteran's hospital in Augusta, Georgia, for sometime. Daddy asked, "What will my family do while I'm in the hospital?"

"Since you are a veteran, the government will pay your wife and family about twelve dollars a month as long as you are in the mental hospital."

"I'm not crazy, who said I was?"

"Your wife said that you were going to kill a man for no good reason, and that is all they told us. That is why you are in handcuffs. Have you ever killed anyone before?"

"No. I never even had a fight in my life. I might have kinda beat this man up for not paying me the next time I caught him out somewhere. He owes me for two weeks hard work cutting trees and clearing land."

"That is reason enough for a man to want to get even with a man that won't pay his hired help. I might even do about the same thing if my check failed to come in the mail each month," one of the men said. "You don't hold it against us for coming to take you to the hospital, do you?" one of the men asked.

"No, you are doing the right thing, and I don't feel real bad about going to the hospital, but I will miss my family. They are about all I have and I won't be there to help them."

"But how much help would it be if you were in prison for the rest of your natural born days or worse still swing from the lower end of a long rope.

"Mr. Wess, I'm taking the handcuffs off you and let you enjoy the ride to Augusta because we are going to be on the road until into the night. Then you get to the hospital we will let you get some sleep and we will process you tomorrow morning. You will eat lunch in Atlanta and you can eat supper when we arrive at the hospital, for we will be starving by then ourselves and we will need some sleep by then."

"How long will it take us to get there from here?"

"These roads are pretty bad. It will take us several hours to drive that far. But if we see that it will take longer than we estimate we will stop about sundown and eat someplace. We get pretty hungry ourselves."

Daddy felt a great relief knowing that the family would be getting about twelve dollars per month. And being in the insane hospital could not be any worse than cutting cross ties and that kind of work. After arriving during the night, they let Daddy eat with the two doctors that came to Heflin for him. During that meal, Daddy was being evaluated as to his sanity. The next morning three doctors and the two that brought Daddy in had him go through interviews and several different types of tests to determine just how insane he was. The doctors determined that Daddy was about as sane as they were. On Daddy's skills and abilities he was far above the average and he scored above the average on most tests. They asked him if he had ever thought about teaching others in some of his skills. As a result of the testing and due to the fact that Daddy had never been arrested before, they all decided to let Daddy have free rein of the hospital, and they let him work in the kitchen.

In the meantime back on the farm we were all working and holding our own in the fight against poverty and starvation. We did pretty well working for Grandpa; he never let us starve. Boy, was I glad that Grandma made me wait until the next day before we scalped him and put poor old Grandpa in that rat-eaten coffin up in that dark attic. I wanted to tell him about it, but I felt that he might scalp me and put in that awful coffin to lie there and die from a good case of hairless exposure to the brain. After a few weeks, Mama got a check from the government for twelve dollars and a letter stating that she would get a check every month for that amount as long as Daddy was in the hospital.

She didn't make too much money working. There was no danger in us doing that. We made only two or three dollars per week working all the time we could find work. Now we were able to afford some things that we were never able to even think about before. However, that wouldn't last forever. After Daddy had been in the hospital for seven months, Mom got a letter from the hospital telling her that they couldn't find anything *wrong* with Daddy" and that she would not receive another check from the government. Mom was real mad! She started writing letters to the hospital telling them to let him come home, that him being there was a big mistake and that she needed him to come home. She got a letter back in a few days informing her that the county office would have to get orders from a judge to have him released. That made Mama madder than before. Since she wrote the hospital telling them to keep him locked up because he was dangerous and was a threat to society, they could not release him; neither could they send her money to live on since there was nothing wrong with Daddy's mind. The doctor that wrote the letter said he wished that he has all the different skills that Daddy had. He also informed her to spend the last check wisely since it may take months to get Daddy out.

Daddy saw the letters that Mom had written to get him in the hospital and the letters she had written to get him out. He said later that he sat back and laughed with the doctors about the way Mom had changed her mind. She took the last check and bought five large cans of Bruton snuff and six forty-eight-pound sacks of flour. Mama said if she had her snuff, some flour and a little hog lard, she could feed an army. Well, her chance was about to come up for proof. The money was cut off and Daddy would be away for another two months while the letters flew to the hospital begging for Daddy's release and telling them that Daddy never intended to harm anyone, and the lead-weighted walking stick was to kill snakes that he often found out in the road or woods where he worked. After about two months, Daddy came in carrying two large burlap sacks filled with his stuff and a beautiful reed basket that he had designed and made.

After the homecoming get-together we settled down to a normal life again. Daddy went to work again, and he also began making cotton baskets from white oak splits and selling them for about one or two dollars each. He also bottomed chairs with white oak splits for the people living within a few miles of us. They would bring him the chairs and come and later pick them up and pay him one dollar for each chair. Daddy told us that the doctors in the hospital saw his skills and advised him to go in business following these skills.

Grandfather had about six girls and four boys. They all cut cross ties, cut and sold fire and stove wood and gathered and sold kindling pine, raised and sold cotton and sometimes sold a cow or two each year. They all worked like slaves and got paid like slaves.

One day Grandpa came home from town with a new two-hundred-pound anvil on the wagon. He slid it off the wagon under a big white oak tree in the backyard. Aunt May was seeing a boyfriend from time to time. Just after Grandpa dumped off his shiny anvil Johnny came riding up on his big well groomed spotted horse and tied him up to the big white oak tree. After a little while, about an hour Aunt Lualla came into the parlor where Aunt May and Johnny were courting and said in a loud voice, "Johnny Papa is agonna kill you when he gets home. He sure is, he is going to kill you as dead as a hammer."

"Why is he going to kill me, Luella?"

"Tell me why he is goanna kill me so dead?"

"When he kills you can I have your big spotted horse, can I have him for my very own?"

"Yes I guess you can, tell me why your Papa wants to kill me?"

"He don't want to kill you yet, but when he gets home from berry picking, he is going to kill you good, because your spotted horse done went and pissed all over Papa's new shiny anvil, and he will kill you dead."

Johnny rushed out and moved his horse to another tree and got water from the mule watering trough and washed off the anvil then told Aunt Mae good by and rode of as fast as he could go. Aunt Lualla didn't get the horse and Grandpa just laughed at Luella. However, Johnny never came a-courting again. Grandpa just laughed about his wet anvil. He told us later that he bought a piss-proof anvil, for you never know what might happen on the farm.

Living on a small farm nestled in the middle of a forest has its rewards as well as its disappointments. Most of the old-timers caught and trapped will critters to kill and supply them with fresh varmint meat, that consist of rabbits, squirrel, coons, possums, beavers, ground hogs, and other things. Grandpa's brother Uncle Green lived with Grandpa and Grandma and was never married. He almost bought a beautiful Indian squaw, but the tribe wanted Uncle Green to pay too much for her. They wanted Green to give them his hunting rifle and his riding horse along with some other stuff. Uncle Green said that no Indian squaw was worth all that, at least not to him. So he never married or bought a squaw to keep him warm at night.

It was Uncle Green's job to keep game varmints in a large wire box or cage about eight feet by four feet and two feet high with a one-foot-by-one-foot-square door on the top. That was where all the live animals waiting their turn to have lunch for us on the big table. The boys enjoyed hunting coons and possums with the large hound dogs, Old Lead and Old Loud, about two or three nights a week. That gave them a time to get out with a few bottles of home brew and maybe one of Grandma's roosters that she was saving for the preacher and hunting with the dogs and have a little feast at night. Somehow the old rooster cooked in a big water bucket over a hot open fire seemed much better than eating it fried with a big fat preacher watching every bite you took. And this way you didn't even have to wash your hands. The boys and Uncle Green always had several wild animals in the box. When they would kill an animal, they would skin it and tack its skin on the back smokehouse wall to cure out and dry. The skins were sometimes sold or stored for future use or sale. We kids would sneak around on the weekends and look on the smokehouse wall to see what Grandma was going to have for dinner. Sometimes we would have a couple of possums or a big coon or two. If we saw some rabbit skins tacked up, we always seemed to appear at their house about lunchtime. We could always tell what was on the menu by going behind the old smokehouse and checking the menu or skins.

Our family usually just went out and dug up a ground hog or shot a squirrel or two each day, or jumped a rabbit and shot it. But as we grew older, it took more food and we had to harvest more wild game. At times we would borrow Old Lead and Old Loud to help us hunt the game. There was a large persimmon tree just a few hundred feet from our house in the edge of our field. At night in the fall of the year the dogs would tree from one to three possums almost every night. And so we ate possum with potatoes day after day or about forty to fifty times during the fall months. Someone said that we ate so much possum that when we heard a dog bark, we would run and climb the nearest tree.

Late one afternoon Uncle Hubert, Uncle Earnest, Uncle Roy, and a neighbor decided to go hunting for possums and coons. Grandma noticed that they were carrying a large five-quart bucket with them on the hunt. That set Grandma's thinking in high gear wondering why the bucket. Then she remembered week and months before that day.

There had been foxes coming in and taking away her chickens at times. Someone of the boys sometimes came in and told her they saw a fox catch a chicken and run up in the wooded area with it. She wondered why only the boys saw this happen. The next morning, Uncle Hubert came running in the house and told her that he saw a fox catch a chicken and run up in the woods with it. He told her to come and see the feathers that were left behind. He showed her the feathers. After the boys went to the woods to hew cross ties, Grandma went to the henhouse and discovered a board on the back of the henhouse had been loosened and put back in place without nails, and it could easily be removed without making any noise. She didn't know who all were in on stealing her chickens, but she being an Indian was going to fix the problem. She went to the smokehouse and got an old fox skin and hung it up by the hind legs and arranged it so it would fall on the head of anyone removing the loose board and begin to enter the henhouse through that hole. She had also tied some rocks up in the fox skin and punched many small nails through the skin from the inside out and then tied cords around to make it look real. Now if anyone tried to enter the chicken house by removing the board as soon as he got his head inside the fox skin would drop on his head and shoulders AND scratch him up real badly, and leave puncture wounds on his head and shoulders like a real fox attack on the person that was entering. This would teach anyone trying to steal Grandma's chickens a real lesson in life.

Well in a few days the boys decided to go on another coon hunt. As usual they carried the big bucket along together with the saw and ax, and of course the big jupe sack. As it was getting dark, Grandma watched for the lanterns to come up behind the chicken house. She didn't have to wait very long. She watched carefully as the approached the henhouse, and saw the light shimmering dimly as someone removed the board and started to enter. Then there came a loud scream. The lantern light began traveling very fast from the chicken house up into the woods and disappeared among the trees at a very rapid pace. The next morning Uncle Hubert asked Grandpa what would happen if a fox bit you on the head and shoulders. Grandpa knew all about Grandma's fox skin trap. He told Uncle Hubert that if a fox had rabies or was a mad fox that the person would probably take rabies and die in a few days.

"Is there any cure for rabies if one gets bit and takes the disease?" he asked.

"No there is no known cure for rabies. When I was a boy, we lived by a family whose only son got bitten by a rabid fox and strayed off into the woods, and after a few days the family saw a larger flock of turkey buzzards circling above a swamp about a mile away. They went over to the mountain and found their son's bony skeleton being picked clean by the buzzards. They were so afraid of rabies that they hired an old ditch digger to go into the woods, dig a grave, and roll the dead boy into it as they watched the burial from a hundred yards away. This story frightened Uncle Hubert out of his right mind. He began trembling and got up from his seat on the porch steps and ran up into the woods. Grandma and Grandpa were having a ball! They laughed so hard that Grandma almost swallowed her false teeth. Uncle Hubert always believed that he was attacked by a mad fox as he entered the chicken house.

The chicken stealing was over for good. In a few days one of the hunting boys asked Grandma if she wanted to sell him a big fat red rooster to boil out on their hunting trip that night. Of course, she was glad to sell them that rooster for fifty cents and told them that she would swap them that rooster for a big fat coon or two or three possums. She had taught them the lesson about stealing her hens to take to the woods to cook over an open fire on their hunting trips. She didn't mind them having a chicken or two, but she wanted the respect of having them ask for them or trading them for some wild critter. From that day forward she never knew of the hunters swiping her hens and roosters and inviting them to midnight snacks with their chicken-stealing friends.

Irra was about twelve years old by now. He had learned to shoot Daddy's old twelve-gauge shotgun with real accuracy. When he aimed "old Betsy" at something and pulled the trigger, the varmint usually fell.

As the children got older, we required more food in order to keep going. Irra could now take the gun out in the surrounding woods and open fields and harvest the small game like rabbits, squirrels, birds, and quails that the family needed to survive in those years of severe depression.

The last year at Grandpa's farm, Daddy bought Irra two boxes of twelve-gauge shotgun shells to help us to have game on the table. With the fifty shells Irra shot forty-eight rabbits and two large rattlesnakes; each snake had fifteen rattles and a button. It was an accepted belief that if one killed a snake and hung it belly up, it would rain within three days. Well, Irra did, and it rained in the expected time. We kids liked that, for it might mean that we didn't have to work on the farm while it was raining.

We did not have store-bought fishhooks, so we learned to make our own fishhooks from thin wire cut from our garden wire fence, sharpening them with Daddy's file. We used ravels from feed sacks for line, and an old rusty nail for the sinker. We made our floats from cork stoppers that we retrieved from old empty medicine bottles. The woods were full of suitable fishing poles just waiting to be cut down for that purpose. We always seemed to catch more fish from our homemade fishing tackle than we can with today's modern rigs. We always brought a small stringer of minnows, brim, trout, and catfish that we caught from the small creek that was behind our house.

Living on Grandpa's farm was a joy for the family. But time don't stand still for anyone. Daddy and Mammy realized that it was time to get all the children in school somewhere. Irra and Neal had been going to Corenth School, a little one-room schoolhouse three miles away. There were no buses in those days, so walking that far left Lewis and me out.

About two or three times every year Irra, Neal, Lewis, and I would go down to the creek near our house and make a dam across the small creek and then just below the dam we would take buckets and dip the water from each water hole in the creek, throwing it between our legs as our heads were facing the dam. Two would stand side beside bent over throwing the water downstream. I would usually help dip and sling water beside Irra while Neal held a six-foot-long stick to kill any snake that stuck his head above the water. He usually killed from one to three water snakes from each water hole as we went from hole to hole down the creek. Since Lewis was the youngest his job was to pick up each fish with a small cooking pan with a handle and put them in a large bucket. When the water would get only a few inches deep in each hole, Lewis would start dipping up the fish from the shallow water. We always left the real small ones from one inch up to three inches long so they could repopulate the fishing holes. This process would last from four to six hours and give from ten to twenty pounds of fresh fish. After we went down the creek for about a three-quarter mile, we would return to the dam and open up the creek again. Then we all had a fish-cleaning, fish-cooking, and fish-eating good time. But we never forgot Grandma and Grandpa. We would always give them about two pounds of fresh cleaned fish, mostly the smaller ones.

Grandpa and Uncle Green always made a few gallons of elderberry wine and stored on the back porch. After getting up each morning, they would go out on the back porch and pour a glass full of that heavenly nectar and swig it down in a hurry. One morning Uncle Green got up, and while not fully awake, he went out on the porch and poured a glass of good wine—except it was not wine. Grandpa also kept a jug of "stock dip" out there also. The stock dip was diluted with a lot of water and applied to the farm animals to kill the fleas and ticks. Uncle Green had picked up the wrong jug and poured him a glass full of the stock dip which looked the elderberry wine. He quickly drank it down. Then he tasted the difference. But it was too late. He ran into the house and told Grandma and Grandpa saying, "John, you and Irra might as well get up and get that coffin ready to bury me. I just drank a glass full of stock dip."

"Do you want us to take you to the doctor or something?" Grandpa asked as he came out of bed and grabbed his pants.

"No, I'll be dead before you can take to the doctor," Green said as he went into the kitchen and sat down at the table.

Since Uncle Green was not feeling any bad results from drinking the stock dip, they decided to wait awhile before hitching up the mules and starting to Anniston to see a doctor. Uncle Green began to feel better than he had in years. The stock dip must have cured his ulcers and killed all the worms inside his stomach. However, he took the day off from work to plan his funeral, which never occurred at that time.

The family all agreed it was time to move in or near Heflin near the grade school. Wess, our father, and our mother, Lee, borrowed Grandpa's mule and wagon and went to Heflin to find us a new home and to get Daddy a new job. The first stop they made paid off. Mr. Edd Giles rented them a fairly large three-room house that was located behind his house and beside the Heflin High School. The house was in fair condition and was only two city blocks from downtown Heflin. I'm sure many of the neighbors felt like the Beverly Hillbillies had moved in. But we really didn't care. Our chickens didn't seem to mind running with their chicken, and their cows seemed to be happy and content in the pasture with our cows. The pasture was one and one-half city block wide X three city blocks long. It separated the poor folks like us from the city folk whose houses faced the mains street and the pasture fence separated our house from them.

Mr. Giles knew Daddy's reputation as being a hard worker, so he gave Daddy a job cutting logs for him. The pay was one dollar per day. Since Mr. Giles lived only one block away, and his sawmill was located behind his house, it was very convenient for Daddy.

Daddy and Mom borrowed Grandpa's mules and wagon and loaded it with the household furniture and supplies and moved the first load. We stayed in the new home that night and returned to the farm the next day for the hog, chickens and cow, along with other items that we didn't load the first time. We got settled in rather quickly. Our outhouse actually joined the back of our house; however, we had to go outside to get to it. And the high school dumped their papers and trash in a few trash drums and burned it near our yard; we always had plenty of toilet paper. Now since we were located almost downtown, we could walk two to four city blocks to buy anything we needed. Boy, this was great! But since we didn't have any money to buy very much, it didn't help much.

The high school outside basketball court was only about thirty or forty feet in front of our house. Many of the games were played at night. We would sit by our two front windows and watch the ball games without having to pay. One night Daddy sat by the window and watched the game. The girls were wearing the basketball uniforms with their beautiful legs hanging out. Mom must have become jealous. Well he was watching them so much that he wouldn't come to supper while they were playing. The next time they played Daddy found a big thick feed sack curtain tacked over both windows. Daddy didn't seem to notice the curtains until the girls began to play a few nights later. Then he said a few well-chosen words to Lee. I don't dare print these words at this time in this story. Mom won the argument and let Daddy take out the bottom nails and raise the curtains just a little.

The school year was almost over when we moved to Heflin. Mom registered us in the grade school which was only two city blocks from our house. Irra and Neal were in Mrs. Johnson's third grade class. Lewis and I were placed in the first grade class with Mrs. Cole as our teacher. These teachers were very dedicated and had great compassion for every student in the class. These teachers were very thoughtful of us. They knew how down we were financially and also how we were taught honesty by our parents. If one of us was absent from class, they would inquire as to what was wrong and come by our house to see what was wrong. Each teacher seemed to know where we came from and wanted to help us to find ourselves and to inspire us to stay in school and to be all that we could be. Always they encouraged the class to try to come out of our poverty conditions and climb a little higher on the ladder of success. Poverty was a great giant that we must rise up against and slay. A good education was the very first and the greatest step that we must take. Every student in the school was fighting this battle; there were no rich people in Heflin, only a few students a little more fortunate than some others. We were on the bottom of the pile as to our condition. However, they wanted to see every student climb up out of desperation and utter poverty and be somebody in society. These teachers have passed on by now, but what the teaching they did is still living on.

The teachers at high school would grade the test papers and test notebooks and discard them in the large trash can that was located about thirty feet from our house. We would go to the trash cans and cut the unused pages from these notebooks for our use in school. We gave some of the less fortunate students. As we rummaged through the trash pile, Mr. Johnson, the principle of the high school, saw us and came over to see what we were doing going through the trash pile. We told him that we were cutting the pages from the notebooks to use for our schoolwork. He began smiling and told us that we were doing a good thing to save the unused pages from the notebooks.

Lewis and I went out in a slow misting rain to gather in some baby chicks that we were raising. We stayed out playing with them too long and we became wet and cold, and our shoes were filled with water from chasing them through a large mud puddle. Boy, was Mom mad! She whipped us and made us put on dry clothing. The next morning Lewis and I could barely talk, and it was very difficult to breathe. Mom gave us cough syrup and some kerosene and sugar. Nothing she gave us seemed to help. After all else had failed, she summoned Dr. Wright, who was the county health doctor, to come by and check on us. He came and pronounced that we each had a bad case of pneumonia. He gave us some flu powder and went to his office. In about two or three hours a county nurse arrived at our house to look after us for a few days. The next day she came in to check us over. She brought each a nice shiny pocket knife, and also one for Irra and Neal. She told us that her husband was as a policeman in Anniston and that he had taken the knife from men that he had arrested while on duty. We didn't care where they came from; we were just glad to get them. My knife was a small two-blader with pearl handles. The nurse came by every day to check on us and see that we were taking our new medicine that she brought us. After about two weeks we were able to get back in school. Our teacher allowed us to study hard and catch up on our schoolwork. We were very proud that we had gone from living in a tent with a tree stump and sleeping on horse feed sacks filled with grass hay and old oak leaves placed on the ground to a real three-room house with glass windows and real beds with cotton mattresses to sleep on.

We were promised a better life—and now we had arrived! Daddy had bought Mom a new cast-iron cookstove with four cooking eyes, a warming closet over the top of the stove and a six-gallon water reservoir on the right of the stove. Now she could cook, heat water, and keep the leftover food warm all at the same time. Mom would get a fire started in the firebox of the stove and set a cast-iron cooking pot down in the stove top after removing one stove eye. She would remove another eye and set a twelve-inch cast-iron skillet over it. After pouring the pot almost full of fresh tap water, she would put in about two pounds of black-eyed peas or dried Kentucky wonder bean and about a pound of sowbelly white fat meat and cover it with a cast-iron lid. Now she would slice some thick slices of ham or white side meat and place it in the hot skillet. It was now time to put on the large cat head biscuit and put them in the hot oven. After taking up sizzling ham or bacon, she would begin frying fresh eggs. She would fry about a full setting of eggs, about twelve to fifteen eggs were a setting—depending on how big the hen was and how big the eggs were. By the time the ham and eggs were on the large platter, the biscuits were cooked to a golden brown. At that time we would set the table and all sit down to a meal fit for a king. We had fresh milk and coffee to drink for each meal. If the food looked good enough, Daddy would say grace over the food. If it didn't look good enough, he would begin eating. For he said he would never say to the Lord "and bless the hands that prepared this food" if the food didn't look good. This kept Mom on her guard while cooking the meals. At times it would make Mom go in the back room and cry, but she didn't cry long, for she was afraid we would eat her portion of the meal while she was in the back room crying. However, after threatening to leave us over this action, Daddy began praising her for her good cooking. The food was so good that we had to be careful not to be stuck with someone's bent, crooked-pronged fork while trying to stab something off the platter. One day Irra asked Daddy how all the prongs on the forks got bent. Daddy told him he had bent them trying to pry the top crust of some of Mom's cathead biscuits which she cooked before she got her new stove. Mom taught us some table manners. She taught us to never try to stab some food with our fork if there were more than three stabbing at the same piece of food at the same. And she said to not cuss at the table very loud, for the Lord might not have gotten out of hearing range after the benediction or blessing the food. We all began to live by her teaching.

There was a large cemetery across the street from our house. From time to time people would come there to mourn and cry over the graves of their loved ones or friends. Since it was a large cemetery, there seemed to be something like that taking place every week. My mom would always pull a chair up to the kitchen window and sit and cry as long as the people were at the grave. At a funeral this could last for an hour or longer. Daddy spoke to Dr. Wright about Mom's reaction to this, and Dr. Wright told Daddy that he should move her out of town where she would not have to see and hear this every week. He said that since we always lived out in the country, we would be far better off to get out where we could stretch our legs and live somewhat like all the family was accustom to. After all, here in Heflin we were bottled up on every side by a high school, a pasture, and a big cemetery, and also a sawmill. There was no room for us to hunt, fish, or go walking except in downtown Heflin, and there were no fishing or swimming holes along the street, and we couldn't even take Daddy's old twelve-gauge shotgun out on the streets. Now something had to be done to protect Mom's sanity, and it had to be done rather quickly. We discussed the matter, and we all agreed that we should try to find a house about a mile or two from downtown that was joined by a large wooded area and move out. Daddy could still hold his job with Mr. Giles, and we could walk to school. But first we must find such place. Mom and Daddy wanted a place where they could have a garden and that was not possible while living in Heflin unless they plowed up the football field or the basketball court and we didn't think the hard ground would be suitable for a vegetable garden.

One Saturday morning Lee and Wess got up early with moving on their minds. Mom said, "Wess, I'm tired of wading through cow manure twice each day to milk our cow and fighting off the other people's cows. And I'm sick and tired of the rich people around us not even willing to take time to talk to us. We are no different from them, except they are rich and wear finer clothes and they take a bath more often than we do."

Wess said, "Well, Lee, where should we begin looking for a house with a garden and a pasture? It may take some time to find a place close enough to town where I can walk up here to get to work."

Lee replied, "Someone told me a few days ago that about a mile west of Heflin there was an empty house up on a little hill in front of a log house. It is close enough for you to walk up here to work for Mr. Giles, and that little bit of walking wouldn't be all that bad. And the kids could walk to school."

That morning Mom and Daddy decided to walk down there and find out who owned the house! They found the house and began seeking the owner. They stopped at a large home just past the empty house. It was where Mr. Leo Jones lived, and he owned the house. He told them to go up and look at the house and if the liked it he would rent it to them for five dollars per month. Well they looked it over real good. It was better than any house that we had ever lived in. There was a chicken house, a large fenced garden, a big barn, and a large pasture. The house had three large rooms and a large porch across the front. The house had ceiling overhead and on all the inside wall. Mom and Daddy really liked the house. It even had a real good water well out back with a well shed over it. This meant no more carrying water from someone's home in town. They went to Mr. Jones's house and rented it from him and paid him a month's rent. He even loaned them his wagon and mules to move the next week. Daddy told him that he would work for him two days for the loan of the wagon and mules, but he said that Daddy would not owe him anything. He told Daddy that he had odd jobs around the house and farm that he could do when he was not in the log woods and it would pay the rent and bring in some money too.

On Monday, Daddy got the wagon and began moving. After loading up the household things, they tied up the cow to the back of the wagon and across town, and down the road they went. After unloading, they went back to get the wash pot, washtubs chickens and hog. We had put the chickens in our chicken moving wire cages. After this load, we set up the furniture which consisted of a stove, table and four chairs, two beds, and a dresser. We were all really excited with our new home! We boys had woods on which to roam and hunt and a large creek down the pasture to fish and swim in. It was nice and clean around the house and large yard. At this time school was out, and we took advantage of all the bird hunting and pleasures available.

When we moved in Mr. Jones had began plowing and planting his crops. He mainly grew corn and cotton. He got Daddy to help with the plowing and planting and plowing the crops when Daddy was not working for Mr. Giles in the log woods. We boys helped a little if he needed us to help out. We didn't like that very much, but since he paid us some money, we gave up some of our bird-hunting and fishing time to help him. I suppose Mom's threatening us with that big dogwood brush broom helped us choose to work for Mr. Jones too.

Mr. Jones was a graduate from Auburn University, and his two oldest sons, Woodroe and Lee, were students at Auburn. They were all learning to farm in a scientific way. They knew just the right type and the right amount of fertilizer for every type crop they were growing. For cotton they used 6-8-4, and for corn they used 3-10-3. They used other types for vegetables and other things. I don't know what they used for watermelons, but whatever it was it was powerful. One could almost walk across the watermelon patch stepping only on very large melons. Since we liked watermelons so much they gave us all we wanted through the season. We offered to work and pay for them, but Mr. Jones said that since we didn't sneak in and steal them when we wanted a melon, we could just go in the patch and help ourselves. There were many hundred melons and they didn't attempt to take them to the market to sell them. Well, we got away with two or three every day till the first frost. Since frost doesn't hurt the taste of a good watermelon, we went beyond that. He let us gather a few and store them in our barn.

Mr. Jones was so grateful for us living nearby and helping him and his family on the farm. He told Daddy that we all were the hardest workers that he had ever had working for him. Daddy helped him in all his spare time and we children helped him whenever he had something for us to do, such as helping with planting, hoeing the crops, and any light work that we could do. When Mr. Jones's family was not in college or school, they would help him also. One day during the summer, Lee and Woodroe Jones came to Daddy to see if they could work for him long enough to earn fifty cents each so they could go to a baseball game in Anniston. Daddy had just contracted with Mr. Jones to plow his large cornfield for three dollars. So he let Woodroe and Lee plow the corn from about seven in the morning until about twelve o'clock for ten cents per hour each. They each hitched up a mule and began plowing. The plowing was very hard because of the old last year's cornstalks that had been cut up with the stalk cutter into short pieces and plowed under. Daddy went out into the field to check on them. As Daddy came near them, they we very disgusted and were using some bad language that I'm sure they didn't learn in college. If they could have met the man that invented the stalk-cutting piece of equipment, they would have murdered him. They described him with words that Daddy had never heard before! Daddy told them that he would give them a dime each so that they could each get a cold drink. That made them very happy. Since neither of them had a watch, they asked Daddy how they know when it was twelve o'clock. Daddy told them that when the sun got directly overhead and they were standing on their shadow, it was about twelve. Daddy went ahead and paid them each sixty cents and went about his other work. Sure enough when the sun got directly overhead, the boys hit out lickety-split for the barn with the mules. Within about fifteen minutes they had changed clothes and were out in front of their home hitching a ride to Anniston for the ballgame. They were two happy boys! Daddy wasn't feeling too bad himself, for they had done well over half of the three-dollar contract to plow the field. Mr. Jones was laughing and told Daddy that was about the hardest he had ever seen the boys work and he didn't have to give them the money for the ballgame.

The Jones children seemed to be perfect. They had a good mother and father, and all the family was just perfect in all their daily lives. We tried to live up to their standards, but you just cannot make an apple tree bear pears or peaches. We were a good honest family, but somehow we were not as perfect as the Jones family and other families living among us just out side Heflin City limits. However, there were some very lowlife families living just beyond us. Some of them were so lazy that if they were sitting on the front porch and a snake came slithering toward them, they might just raise their feet and let the snake crawl through the front door and into the house.

The Rollins boys were not always as honest as Mom and Daddy had raised us up to be. We deceived our parents at times. One day we decided to find some way to get some money to buy candy at Mr. Brown's store in Heflin. Momma had several hens setting on large nests full of eggs; each hen had about twelve to fifteen eggs in their individual nest. We boys decided to take a few eggs from each nest and take them to Heflin and trade them to Mr. Brown for large sticks of coconut candy, one egg for one stick of coconut candy. Boy, that was a good deal! We took about three or four eggs from each nest until we got a dozen eggs. We then took them to the creek and washed them with soap and creek water until all the stains were washed off each egg. We knew that no one wanted to trade candy for eggs that were about ready to hatch. After getting twelve large sticks of candy for the eggs, we decided to give Mom and Daddy one stick each, leaving us with two sticks each. After Frank returned from the store with the candy, we went out behind the barn and ate our candy—all of it. Irra took the two sticks of candy to Mom and told her to give one to Daddy when he returned home from work. Momma asked Irra where he got the candy, and he told her that Mr. Jones had given it to him to give to her and Daddy. The next day she went out behind the barn and picked up eight candy wrappers. She knew that we were lying to her. So she thought up a plan to find out the truth. Well I guess it was born in her, for she was part Indian; her mother was a pure Indian squaw, and Indians have a way of wanting the truth from the white man. Momma got Lewis to walk up the railroad to Heflin with her. After finding the candy wrappers, she knew that Lewis might tell her the whole story. She had promised Lewis some candy when she got to town. "Momma, I know you are gonna give me some candy, but where are the eggs to trade for it?"

"Is that the way you boys are getting candy? How does the trading work?"

"I guess Frank takes eggs to town and trades them for candy."

"Where did you get the eggs?"

"Well, the old setting hens are so mean we thought that they would set too hard on all them eggs and crush some of them, so Irra and Neal decided that we should take a few eggs from under each hen so they could set down easier and not break all the eggs. Mr. Brown would give us candy for the eggs before the hens broke all the eggs."

"Who thought up the idea of swapping eggs for candy?"

"We all thought of it together. Irra and Neal told Frank and me how we could do it. We would go to the hen's nest and take a few eggs and when we would get a dozen we would get a little lye soap from the soap pitcher and take the eggs to the creek down under the railroad tressel and wash them real clean and Frank would take them to town and do the trading. We knew if the police caught him you and Daddy would not let him stay in jail too long for you loved him more than you loved us."

"How do I know you are telling me the truth? You might be just making this up."

"You can ask Irra, he thought of it first. And where is my candy? You promised me some. And there is more candy wrappers up in the barn loft. Plenty more. Look under the setting hens and see just how many eggs are left. One of them only has about four and another one decided to quit her nest and leave her two eggs and find something else to do since she would have to do all that setting and stuff for only two baby chickens." Mom turned around and started back home.

"But where is my candy? You promised me some candy. You boys are going to learn not to steal, even if it is only eggs from a setting hen. Just wait 'til I get you home." Boy, Mom was madder than an old setting hen that had had her eggs stolen right from under her. She walked so fast that Lewis couldn't keep up with her as she walked hurriedly down the railroad track. She was crying as she came across the pasture and into the yard. Neal saw something was wrong and met her in the cotton patch by our house. She told him to get out of her way as she cRossierd the yard and went into the house. She grabbed a large butcher knife and almost ran out to a peach tree and began chopping long watersprout from the tree trunk that sprouted from the tree trunk just above the ground. She chopped off about eights or nine of them about five to six feet long. Then she made all of us boys sit down on the floor of the front porch and started yelling and preaching to us. It was worse than when we were attending a church revival under the preaching of Rev. Arce Haywood! He could lay it on you thick, but I think Mom had him beat with her sermon to us! And the worst part she never had an alter call so we could repent to avoid the wrath that lay in store for us. At least Brother Haywood let us repent to escape the wrath of God, but Momma had no mercy and she didn't give an altar call.

After her sermon, she grabbed Irra by his arm and grabbed two peach tree switches, and round and round they went. Irra was screaming and Mommy was just a-beating. After she finished wearing the switches down to about two feet long, she let him go and grabbed for Neal, but Neal started running around the house, however she caught him out by the barn. She dragged him by the arm and went back to the front yard and grabbed two new switches. Since Neal had run from her she gave him a double dose of peach tree sprout tea. Next it was my turn to take the medicine. I was crying and begging and everything that I could think of to get out of the whipping that I was about to receive at the hand of an angry mother. But to no avail—the die was cast—no forgiveness and definitely no mercy. The hens wouldn't have forgiven us either, for they were setting on half-empty nests and with hopes of only a half-family of baby chicks to raise up for the big fat preachers and others to eat. It seemed that more of our young roosters have died that fat preachers could live! She grabbed me with her right hand, and the peach tree limbs began to fly. It seemed that I got a little more than the others because I did all the egg trading and candy delivering to the others. Lewis was next, but she had only one scanty switch waiting for him. She gave only about half the licks that she had given us. When it was over, we looked across the cotton patch in front of our house and saw the Jones family out in the backyard, the Wheeler family, and another family from across the railroad tracks standing out watching all the commotion that was taking place. Someone told that as they listened to all the hollering and screaming they thought that a funeral was about to take place. From that day forward the old setting hens never lost an egg to the egg bandits. They were left alone to hatch their little flock of babies. At that time I didn't know anything about women preachers, and I don't know much about them now, but I believe that if Mom had been in church and had preached that sermon in a revival meeting, the altar might have been full of repenting sinners. The porch held four, and they all had repented and were sorry for their egg-stealing deeds. But if God had turned a deaf ear to their cries and begging for forgiveness as these four did and they received none of it, that would be a sad day at the Great Judgment that is to come to all.

Sam Jones had taken a liking to us four boys, and he and his brother Houstin were spending some time with us bird hunting, fishing, and just playing in the woods that joined the Jones property. The corner of the woods lay beside the Jones home and just east of our house. There were several acres of woods on the other side just beyond the farmland. Mr. and Mrs. Jones seemed happy that their children could mingle with our family, and have someone to be with without very much cursing and no dirty language. Sam and Houstin never said curse words or used vulgar, dirty language. It almost made us stop cussing and using dirty word—around them. To see us with them, one might believe we were in church or on a church picnic or something. We would save up all that dirty words, so we could use them when we were far away from them. After all the big egg-stealing ruckus and punishment was over, we were playing with Sam and Houstin in the wooded area at the back of their house when Sam looked at Irra and said, "Irra, I have been praying for you a lot for the past few weeks."

"Why have you been praying for me so much? Have I been all that bad?" Irra replied.

"When we see you getting all the whippings all the time, and knowing that you boys are not all that bad, we pray for God to stop at least some of them."

"Do you believe it would help if I learned to pray? Mom has been watching us, and we can't get away with very much since we moved to Heflin. Before moving up here we could cuss and call each other bad names, but since we moved up here they whipped us every time they hear us do it. They tell us that people in and around town don't do things like that. Sam, could you tell me how to pray for God to hold Mom back and not let her hit me so much?"

"Well, you get off by yourself and tell God how you feel and ask him to help you. We go to church and the preacher tells us to talk to god just like we are talking today and when you have finished always tell him 'amen.' The amen is sorta like putting a period at the end of a sentence, it lets the Lord know that you are through talking to him and the next talking will be to someone else. And you definitely don't want God to hear some of the things you call others and all the bad language you said you used to use."

"Well. Sam, if that is how it works and I can make God stop me from getting whippings, we might start stealing Mom's eggs and not get caught next time."

"Irra, I don't think God will let you do that. He don't want you stealing eggs, talking ugly, or shooting Mrs. Rollins's chickens with your flip. Irra, you have to be honest with God and he will be honest with you. God said, 'Thou shalt not steal' and 'Honor your father and mother' and you have not done these things. That is why God told your mother to whip you hard, for she is closer to you than he is."

"Well I wish god would stop telling her all this stuff about us so Mom would just leave us alone."

"Just try praying and stop doing the things that Mr. Rollins whips you for and see if it works."

Well, all of us boys began praying and telling God what we wanted and telling him how he could help us. Sam Jones had started a revival in our young lives, and I don't believe he ever knew it. We all started living different lifestyles, we quit cussing, well almost stopped and we began to obey our parents and stopped talking back to them when they told us to do something. Mom and Daddy saw a great change in us but we never told them why. We thought that if we told them they may make us start going to Church, and we didn't think we had that much religion at that time in our lives. Yes, Sam Jones had a great influence in us boys' lives, especially in my life. I began feeling that someday I could be a preacher and tell others what Sam had told us, and maybe some kind God-loving women would catch their prized frying-size roosters and feed me like other preachers were feed day after day. As I now look back to that day Sam spoke with all us boys, I can see how each of our lives took a great change for the better. I was always afraid of four kinds of spiders—big ones, little ones, dead ones, and live ones. After I learned how to pray, I just talked to God when I was near them. While picking cotton, there was always a large green and brown spider about the size of a silver dollar when he was spread out in the top of almost every stalk in the field. While picking cotton, I had to continue praying for God to give those spiders the lockjaw and not let them bite me. He must have heard me, for I was never bitten and the spiders seemed to run from me and hide. Maybe they saw my guardian angel standing over me with a spider swatter in both hands. Yes, this was working for me now, and much of my fears were gone! And my newfound friend—the Lord—had done a miracle in my very own life and in my brother's lives also.

While I was living there that year and a half the Lord seemed to take a great liking to our family. We had better clothes to wear, more food on the table each meal, and Mom and Dad always had plenty of Bruton snuff sitting on the mantle over the fireplace. And we could get water without carrying it from a spring or a neighbor's well; we had our very own well in our yard. We grew better gardens and had some fruit trees as well.

On one hot day in the fall of the year, we saw a huge dark cloud coming in from the northwest. It seemed to be more dense and darker than we had ever seen before. There was much thunder and lightning as the cloud passed across the narrow valley about two or three miles north of us. It seemed that it would never pass by. It seemed to just stop over the valley. As we stood by the storm pit or storm cellar, we all watched it very carefully to see if it changed its mind and started toward us. After about an hour, it began moving across in an eastward direction somewhat passing us by. It only sprinkled rain where we were. As the cloud began passing slowly away, we heard a great roaring coming from the fields in the narrow valley down behind our house. Within a few minutes, we saw a great wall of water about four to five feet deep sweeping down the valley and cornfields near our house. We ran down the little hill to see it better. Mr. Jones had several acres of corn just above our pasture fence. The corn was ready to be harvested but was still in the field. The water came above the ears of corn and soaked them real badly. What the water didn't knock down was ruined. Someone up the valley had a field full of large pumpkins that floated down the valley and got lodged in our pasture fence, which were four strands of barbed wire and a solid hedge of bushes. When the pumpkins hit the grown-up pasture fence, they could go no further. For the next two days, the whole family gathered fresh pumpkins and put them in the barn. We had two or three wagonloads of pumpkins. We didn't know how we could use all of them. We soon found out that our cow would fight you to get a cut-up pumpkin, and our two hogs liked them just as well. The corn crop was a total loss for the Jones family. Mr. Jones told Daddy that he could have all the corn if he wanted it. In a day or two after the cloud burst and flood, we began gathering the large ears of corn and carrying it to our barn in sacks. It was hard work, but we kept on working until we maybe had fifty or sixty bushels of fairly good corn. Some of it was beginning to rot in the shuck, so we shucked it and spread it out on the ground to dry. It made real good cow and hog feed, and we saved some of the undamaged corn for our cornmeal supply. The Lord must have taken a liking to us, for we thought that he might have sent that cloud burst so we could gather where we had not planted or sawn. Sometimes I wonder if Sam teaching us to pray for a better life had anything to do with God sending a great rain to wash up a huge harvest of pumpkins and corn just to help us have a better life. I do declare it was worth one's time to ponder over and think about.

We stayed on the Jones farm for the fall and winter, working, going to school, doing bad things, and getting whippings with tree limbs and dogwood brush brooms. We kids were much more well behaved since our first prayer meeting with Sam; however, it didn't cure all our sins and desires. It seemed that we were doomed to doing some upsetting things that led to a season of punishment. It seemed that our little beady eyes could see more to get into than ever before. From the first light of dawn until the sun went down and the stars came off their hiding place, Daddy and Momma were working and we kids were hunting something to get into that would make Momma and Daddy madder than an old flogging setting hen. But as they kept on a beating us, we just kept on surviving. During the winter, Daddy was working in the log woods while we boys were in Heflin grade school.

Sometime after Christmas, I believe it was in February, a house became vacant that was between our house and main road that led into Heflin. The house was only about one hundred yards from the road. Mom really wanted that house. She wanted it so badly that she went over across two cotton fields and a large pasture to Mr. Brown's house to see if they would rent it to her. Mrs. Brown was a kind, sweet woman that owned much land in that section of town and suburbs. She had a large wooded pasture just behind the house, and had a few young heifer calves in it. She told Mamma that if we would sort of look out for calves she would rent the house to her for five dollars per months, and if we couldn't pay her with money she had some work around her big house and other land that we could do to pay the rent. Boy, Momma grabbed up that deal quicker than a hungry hound dog could snap up a freshly cooked biscuit that had been bake in bacon grease! After renting the house Momma decided to let us see it before moving in. The house set on a large level lot with plenty of yard all around it. There was a large garden place on the left side that needed fencing, a barn in the back, a chicken house, and a big hog pen joining the barn. The pasture fence came up to the barn in back. There were cotton fields on each side of the house and along our drive. Two rooms of the house were built from large logs and seemed to be over a hundred years old. Joining it at one corner were two rooms, the living and dining area and large kitchen. There was a L-shaped front porch across the front of the two sections of the house. Each section had a large fireplace for the only source of heat we had.

There was a water well on the north side of the house. Momma said that the water would always be good and cold since the well was on the north side of the house. One of the best things about the house was that it had wood ceiling overhead and some of the outer walls. The floors were made of wide rough-sawed pine lumber that was worn down slick, and there were no cracks in the floor wide enough for us to see the chickens under the house. We all got busy and spent two or three days cleaning the house and yard. We would never move into a house that had been left filthy, and the floors littered with old clothing, dog manure, and other filth. We moved a lot, but this was the filthiest house that we had ever seen. The family that had just moved out had taken the barn doors off the hinges and some boards from the barn loft and burned them for firewood. Mrs. Brown had made them move because of their filth and their destructive way of living. Everywhere we lived we always left the house and outbuildings in better repair than they were when we moved in. Mrs. Brown knew that and almost gave us the house rent free. And most of all, the Jones family and the Brown family seemed to care greatly for us because we were honest, hardworking people that cared for the other persons property. Almost every place we lived we had to get hammer and nails and cow-proof the barn and pasture, hog-proof the hog pen, and chicken-proof the henhouses. But some renters that lived there before us were to lazy to cut firewood and wood for the stove.

After a few days cleaning and repairing the house and other things, we were ready for the big move. Mr. Wheeler, who lived just across the road and about half a cotton field down from us, let us rent his big dray wagon and mules to move our things. After we got through moving and drove the wagon back to his barn, Mr. Wheeler was so glad to get the other family out of the house and get us moved in he didn't take any pay for the rented mules and wagon. He told Daddy that since he had got to know our family, it was worth more than the rent for the mules and wagon just to have a good hardworking family living that close to him and his family. Mr. Wheeler hired our whole family to do some work on his farm from time to time. We plowed the fields, planted cotton and corn, and cultivated the crops. Mr. Wheeler had a son, Charles and a daughter, Mary Alice. They were about seven and eight years old, and very bright and lovable children. Mr. Wheeler must have been a road commissioner or something, for he hauled creek gravel on his big dray wagon and scattered it on the roads around Heflin, and he did a good job on the roads.

Mr. and Mrs. Wheeler decided to build a new home about a half mile closer to Heflin, almost in the thickly settled residential district. They bought the land and bought a large pile of different framing lumber after letting it dry and cure out for several weeks they began building. Daddy was the first one he hired to help him begin building. I never knew that Daddy was also a carpenter, however he was and a good one at that. They worked on the new home for several weeks, only as their other work aloud them to take time off to build. When the house was almost finished Mr. Wheeler began thinking about his water supply. In those days even some of the people living downtown had to draw water from a well on their porch or in their backyard. Mr. Wheeler was wondering who he could get to dig his well. Daddy told him that he had dug a few wells in his younger life and had cleaned out many existing wells. Mr. Wheeler bargained with Daddy to dig his well. He wanted it dug in one certain spot where he could build a porch around it. Daddy told him that he would have to first find out where a good vein of water lay deep beneath his yard. Then Daddy cut a forked branch from a hickory bush near the house. He then cut off a part of the branched, leaving only about eighteen inches of each branch. He was asked what he was going to do with that forked stick. Daddy replied: "I am going to locate a vein of water so I can dig straight down to it."

Mr. Wheeler asked, "Do you really think that will work?"

Daddy said, I've dug many wells using the "water witch" and I always find a good vein of lasting water."

Daddy took this device in his hands, one branch in each hand with his palms turned up and began to walk all around the back of the house. He walked over where the Wheelers wanted the well, but the water witch refused to move. After walking around for a few minutes in the side and backyard, the water witch began to point down. Daddy walked around and across that point in the yard and it always pointed down at the same spot, and he could not hold it tight enough to stop it from turning and pointing straight down. After approaching that spot from many different angles, he drove a stick down into the ground. He turned to Mr. Wheeler and informed him that if he found water anywhere near his house, this was the only place. The Wheelers were very disappointed that it wouldn't be on their back porch. However, they told him to build a large well digger's windlass from a large tree log about ten inches thick and about eight feet long. As he built the frame, Mr. Wheeler went to town and bought fifty feet of one-inch grass rope and a large five-gallon wooden bucket, Daddy sawed off a pick handle and a shovel handle to about twenty inches long. One just can't use long handles in a thirty-six-inch water well. After building the rig and digging the rest of the day, Daddy was down about eight or nine feet. As he dug, he dug out little holes in the wall on two sides to use as steps to climb out if he needed to, and the other two workers went to sleep at the windlass. Mr. Wheeler had hired a man whom he called Buck to work one end of the windlass and a young black man called Slim to work the other end of the windlass. Daddy would not let just one man wind up the large bucket full of dirt over his head. He wanted two so if one forgot about the danger, the other man would hold on the windlass and not drop a hundred-pound bucket of dirt several feet on his head. He said that a relative of his was killed when a wasp stung the windlass man and he released the windlass and the bucket hit the well digger so hard that it drove his shoes six inches into the soft dirt in the bottom of the well. He said that the ninety-pound bucket of dirt fell forty feet before hitting him and breaking his neck.

Well digging is a dangerous job. One of our country friends was digging a well for one of our neighbors when he hit a vein or pocket of natural gas, and before he knew it he went unconscious and could not call for help and died in the well. Without knowing of the gas, another worker slid down the rope to help him and was suffocated also. Now there were two dead men at the bottom of the well. Afterward they found out that pouring a lot of water in the well would make the gas dissipate and seem to go away. After pouring about a hundred gallons of water, they were able to send a brave boy down there and tie a rope around each man as more water was being poured down the well and the two men were windlassed to the surface—one at a time. That is why Daddy wanted a man on each end of the windlass. He was always afraid that he could hit a pocket of gas with the next stroke of the pick. Down at the bottom of a three-and-a-half-foot-diameter well, one doesn't have much working room for himself, the bucket, and the tools. Since Daddy was six foot two inches tall, he had to dig with his butt against one side and his head against the other side and really folded up to do the digging and filling the bucket. However, he managed with the short-handle pick, shovel, and mattock. The handles of the tools were only a few inches long, and the tools that he was not using seemed to always to be in his way, but he had learned to keep them back between his number ten work boots and just keep on shoveling up dirt, filling the large bucket and sending it on its way to the top where it would be emptied on the large dirt pile about ten to fifteen feet from the well itself. The first day, the well digging crew went down about ten feet. The next day they decided to get an early start before the sun was up. The only light Daddy would have down there as he dug deeper was from a large mirror that has been removed from the dresser and held by someone on top, held at an angle so as to reflect sunlight down the well, giving the effect of a large light. The mirror was secured with a small rope and tied to the windlass frame to prevent it falling down the well and hitting on Daddy's head. Since they got an early start, they went down about ten feet deeper, totaling about twenty feet. The dirt was beginning to get more moist as if water was near. At the end of the day, Mr. Wheeler asked, "Mr. Wess, do you think you are near water down there?"

"Yes, we are only about five or six feet from water according to what I see in the muddy dirt. Tomorrow night you will have at least five or six feet of lasting water," he replied. The next day Daddy came prepared. He was wearing his high rubber boots that came up almost to his knees and his ragged overalls. The deeper he dug, the muddier the dirt became. After going about four feet deeper than the day before, Daddy put down the shovel into the ground, and some water started gushing out. He yelled up to the windlass crew, "I've hit a gusher, we have to work fast for another five or six feet." Daddy kept digging as the water kept pouring in on him. They drew out water and dirt until about sundown. At that time Daddy cleaned out all the loose mud and dirt and water the best that he could. The vein of water was coming in about chest high from the bottom; he knew the Wheelers would have lasting water since it was coming in as fast as the windlass crew could draw it out. Daddy then sent out the tools and he came up last. Since it was late and everyone was dog tired, they didn't cover the well or remove the windlass frame from over the well; that could be done the next day.

Early the next morning the Wheelers were very excited about the new well and went out side to look things over. They let their baby daughter down to play for a few minutes while they were looking at something about the house. The baby was just old enough to stand up and walk pretty well. Somehow her little curiosity led her over to the well, and she fell in. When Mr. and Mrs. Wheeler came from around the house, they could not find the baby. Mrs. Wheeler screamed, "O my God, she must have fallen in the well." They ran over to the well and heard laughter from down below, and they could hear a little splashing of water. Mr. Wheeler grabbed up the mirror that was left on the dirt pile and held it to reflect sunlight down the well. Sure enough the baby was paddling herself around in the cold water and laughing and just having a good time. Charles, their son, was sent across the field to get Daddy to go down there and retrieve the baby. He ran up to the well as fast as he could, and holding the mirror, he could see Little Ann down there having the time of her life floating around, splashing water, laughing, giggling, and having fun. Daddy slowly let the bucket down until it hit the water beside the baby. He then took hold of the rope and slid down the rope, being very careful not to hit Little Ann. As he tried to let his feet touch the bottom, he told them to bring the bucket up a little; then pouring the water from the bucket, he placed the baby in the bucket and had them toss a small rope down the well so he could tie the baby so she could climb out of the large bucket. And after making her securely latched in the bucket he told them to haul her to the top while he stayed below. After briefly examining the baby and finding nothing wrong with her, they let the bucket down for Daddy. He had dug out little steps in two opposite sides of the well so he could hold the rope and climb out. He said that he would never dig a well and not have a way of escape just in case his workers got drunk, went to supper, or left him down there for the night. Somehow he never really trusted any of the top crew that he had ever had. He always played it safe. After dressing Little Ann, her mother took her outside again and let her down on the ground again. She started laughing and walking as fast as she could toddle toward the well. She wanted another swim at the bottom of the well! Mrs. Wheeler then took a washtub and about a gallon of water in it and sat Little Ann in the tub. Immediately she began splashing and laughing. Then they knew she was all right. Daddy and Mr. Wheeler built a well curb and placed it over the well with a well windlass, rope, and bucket. Now the Wheelers would have about seven feet of good, clear, cold water to draw from the well and use. And now the well was no more a threat to Little Ann.

One night as we were about to retire for the night we heard a loud knock at the front door. Daddy went to the door. Standing there was a cowboy-looking man and a fairly well-dressed woman. His boots were well worn and looked as if they were about ready for the trash pile, and the woman's shoes were low-heeled, well-scuffed gold-colored walking shoes that had seen better days.

Daddy asked, "Can we help you?"

"We need something to eat. We have been walking down the railroad since yesterday and we have not eaten since yesterday morning about nine o'clock."

"Come in and set down at the table" Daddy replied.

Mom got up from her chair and started to the kitchen and said, "Frank, will you help me get the food from the kitchen?" as she went into the kitchen with me following closely behind. After they went in the kitchen, she opened the kitchen door that went out on the porch, closing the door behind her, and told me to run up to Mr. Wheeler's house and get him to go to the city hall in Heflin and tell Mr. Adams, who was the chief of police, to come quickly and check the people out. Then she began setting the leftover food on the table, setting the table for the two people. Then she got them two large glasses full of buttermilk. Mom kept the two talking as they ate. The conversation was low toned and was meant to keep them there long enough for the police to arrive. And arrived they did within minutes. Chief Adams and Mr. Jones, the night-shift policeman, opened the door and commanded the two strangers to stand up and step away from the table. Chief Adams asked them to put their hands over their heads and began searching them. Chief Adams retrieved a long-barrel .38 pistol from the man. And Mr. Jones began searching the woman. She requested that she be taken into the kitchen to continue the search where all eyes would not be on her as she was strip-searched. Mr. Jones retrieved a small-caliber pistol from her underwear and about six hundred dollars from her panties. After the search was over, the policemen let the two sit down and finish their meal. I thought that was rather humane of the policemen. Then they were handcuffed and hauled away to the Cleburnee County jail. Before leaving, Chief Adams told Mom and Daddy that the two were being sought by the Atlanta police for robbery. It seemed that they had robbed an Atlanta bank three or four days before showing up in the Heflin area, where they were finally arrested and in the hands of the Heflin police. We got a letter of thanks from the Atlanta police force for helping bring the two to justice. From that day forward we were respected by the police and the merchants of Heflin, for they had heard the news of our help. Helping the Heflin police force to catch the two bank robbers always held our family in their highest esteem. After this event when we went to town, the people of the town would treat us like family and not like poor trash that we seemed to be.

The two and one-half years that we lived on the Jones and Brown property were the best and happiest years of our lives up to that point. We were all in good health and we all worked as much as we could to have a decent lifestyle. But we just didn't have enough religion to go to church, just enough to keep us from cussing very loudly in public, and especially in school. Daddy worked very hard to provide us with a decent living, and Mom did the housework and did most of the gardening. However, if it had been a crime to pull up weeds and chop grass out of the garden, I reckon we would have been locked up in jail because the weeds and grass seemed to gang up on us at night and required much of our time the next day. We always had a table loaded down with good stuff from the garden to eat for dinner and supper and meat, eggs, chicken, gravy, hot biscuits, butter, and syrup for breakfast. Now in my later years I wish we could return to that simple type life!

During the years of our lives we always seemed to have plenty to eat and a good roof over heads at night. Daddy always said that if a man had a good wife, good children, a good bed to sleep in, and plenty to eat, there was not much reason to ever stray away from home. And I suppose he was right, for my father never mentioned leaving the family, although life was very hard on him at times, almost all the time. The whole family pitched in and did our share of work to make life easier for the whole family. We all pitched in on the farm as a sharecropper for Mr. Jones, working from just after daybreak until it got so dark that we couldn't tell the crop from the weed and grass. And it really paid off! Mr. Jones told us that we were the hardest and most conscientious (whatever that big word meant) workers that he ever had on the farm. Daddy was very proud of what he said about us being hard workers, but that other big word Daddy didn't understand and to him it might be an ugly or bad word. So one day Daddy asked Mr. Jones what it meant. Mr. Jones told him that "Conscious meant that you know what is going on" and "enctious" means "just let her rip." So from that time on we tried to be conscious of what we were doing and we "just let it rip."

During the summertime after the crops were "laid by" (after all the plowing and hoeing was done), we would go to the mountains nearby and pick huckleberries to carry to Mr. Brown's and Mr. Owens' store and sell them for cash or trade them for merchandise.

On a good Sunday we would go to the woods together and pick up to eight to twelve gallons of berries. We would bring them home, clean them and put them in quart-sized wooden cups to take them to the market where we would sell them for eight to ten cents per quart. By doing this, we could always have food, buy school clothes, and pay some on our doctor bills. And sometimes Mom could buy her some store-bought clothes and shoes.

After the berry season was over, we boys would go into the woods with Daddy and help him cut down white oak trees, split it up, and carry out on our shoulders to be used to weave cotton baskets and to be used in putting bottoms in chairs. After getting the wood home, Daddy would split the wood into "bolts" or smaller sections and further split it into smaller splits to weave chair bottoms and cotton baskets. While Daddy used a wooden mall and primitive gadget called a "frow" to make the bolts into splits, we boys would dress the splits down with a "draw-knife" and any type of knife we could get to make them slick, smooth, and shiny. Other men made and sold cotton baskets, but Daddy was the only one in Heflin that knew that word "coucous-enough" that made and sold baskets. So Daddy was conscious of what he was doing and he let her rip! Our baskets sold much faster than other men's because they were woven tighter and were woven with smooth shiny splits all even in size. Many times Daddy could sell his for a dollar and a half where some others could not sell theirs for one dollar. Daddy always said, "Even with buying a cotton basket, you get just what you pay for." The family would set up late at night to help Daddy make at least three baskets each week to carry to Heflin on Saturday and sell. Many times he would take orders for baskets for future delivery. By applying that big fancy word that Mr. Jones taught him, he was well aware of what he was doing and he was letting it rip.

45

During the two to three years there, we boys got acquainted with three families of boys. There were the Taylor family, the Holt family, and a black family, the O'hara family. These families lived a mile or two down the railroad track from us. Sometimes we went to school with the Taylor and Holt boys when they went to school, but they didn't seem to care about school since their parents couldn't read or write; they couldn't even count money.

The O'hara family was black. Many times we would go swimming with the O'Harrow boys and usually walked up the railroad tracks to school which was about a mile away. The O'Harrow boys had to walk about a half mile further down the tracks to a run-down one-room schoolhouse. We were too young to know why the blacks and the whites went to separate schools, and in our school each grade had a room with a teacher for that grade and for them all grades were crowded into one room with poor lighting and one teacher. We boys talked to our parents about why they could not go to our school. About all that they would tell us that it had always been that way and they thought that it would always remain the same. However, that just didn't cut it with us boys. We all talked the same and looked the same except the color of our skin.

All of us boys would go down to the creek running under the railroad tressel and go skinny dipping each day during the summertime. There was only one black girl that would go in with all the boys; she was a sister of the black boys that went in swimming with the crowd. She looked to be about fourteen or fifteen and had all the necessary body parts to be a beautiful girl. Her mother would make her wear a little something to keep her from looking as if she was just "one of the boys"; however, we could all tell the difference. The swimming hole was well hidden from public view by a field of tall corn on both of the creek. The passenger train seemed to slow down for the Heflin stop, so the passengers could wave and yell to us as we would line up buck naked the creek bank as the train slowly passed us by. At our age we should have known better, but we were too young to really care. We were all old enough to know better but not yet old enough to know why.

It seemed that about everywhere we moved we wound up close to real cemeteries. This last move was no different. It was somewhat different, for this time the cemetery was just across the road from our house. Several years ago, there had been a small church by a small graveyard, the church had burned, leaving the grave sites to be grown over by grass, weed, bushes, and trees for several years. If there was anything that bothered our family, it was having to live with only a narrow road between us and the spooky graveyard. For years, as our pastime we would sit around and exchange scary ghost stories, sometimes until the late hours at night. Many times we children would be afraid to go to bed after the ghost stories had ended. Most all the graves had only unmarked stones as grave markers. Anyone could see that someone was buried there, but with no names on the markers no one could tell who. It gave all of us the creeps every time we looked over there.

One morning about seven o'clock we saw three men come to the graveyard and cleaned a spot about eight by ten feet square and start digging what appeared to be a grave. They kept on digging and putting all the dirt on only one side of the grave. We kept watching them and after a while Mommy started to cry. When we asked her what was she crying about, she told us that grave digging and coffins and dead people made her very sad, and if they kept burying dead people over there like that, she was about ready to move as far away from there as she could get and stay within walking distance of downtown Heflin. About three o'clock we saw an old rusty Model A pickup truck drive up to the graveyard and stop near the grave. Some people were sitting in the cab and others on the truck bed. They unloaded two straight back chairs and set them facing each other, and then taking what appeared to be a wooden box made from plain unfinished lumber, the kind that were used to build barns. They rested the box on the chairs. Within a few minutes, a few people had gathered around. At that time we realized that wooden handmade box was a small coffin. It must be a dead baby. The people were dressed in plain work clothes and most were barefoot. Mom decided that we all could go over and see the corps and join in with the small crowd of about eighteen people. She put on her best dress and shoes and made us put on our other pair of clean overalls and clean shirt. We went over across the road to the funeral. One man with clean pants and shirt took a claw hammer from his back pocket and pulled the nails from the lid of the small casket. The people began to walk up and view the body. We went over also. It was the body of a very small baby girl. She seemed to be about five or six months old, and she was very beautiful. She had a lot of blond curly hair. The casket was lined with a new-looking baby blanket that was tacked in the casket with shoe tacks and a few small shingle nails. However, the lid was one rough pine board that had no lining. A part of the baby's face was missing, as if something had eaten it away. The chief of police and a doctor from the CCC camp drove up in a police car. The doctor examined the baby from head to toe. He then asked the parents what caused the death and what happened to the baby's face.

The father told them that the baby had fallen off the back porch and died within a few minutes. "How high was the back porch?" Mr. Adams asked. "It is about head high or about seven feet. And there is some big rocks on the ground where the baby fell," the father replied.

"What happened to the baby's face?" the doctor asked.

"Well we had a big tomcat that came in the house while we were sleeping and got up on the bed where the dead baby was and ate off one ear and part of the baby's face before we noticed *what was going on*. When we saw what had happened, I got my gun and started chasing the cat. After a short spell one of the boys caught him, and I got my double-bladed ax and took the cat to the chopping block and chopped off the cat's head. You can check the cat's guts for baby parts if you want to," the father replied.

"Why didn't you notify my office before today?" the chief asked as he covered the baby's body with the blanket in the casket.

"Well, we didn't think anyone cared what happened to us down there in the woods." the father replied.

The chief and the doctor walked out to the car so the two could talk privately. After about five minutes, they returned to the coffin and told the family to go ahead with the funeral. At that time the mother informed the chief that there was no funeral arrangement made and that they planed to just bury the baby. The kind doctor told the crowd to take their hats off and bow their heads for prayer. Then he asked what the baby's name was. The mother weepingly told him that her name was Mary. He offered up a word of prayer and said a few words of comfort to the family and helped the father place the lid on the coffin, which was gently nailed down by one of the men. We all went home weeping for the unfortunate baby and her family. After this, we all had a greater respect for life and a greater dread for death. Daddy told us that death was so final and it was an appointment that we did not make but one that we all would have to keep. That didn't set too well with us boys; we seemed to think that we could live a carefree life and not worry about anything, but this funeral, though simple as it was, had all of us thinking. We began thinking and talking about going to church the coming Sunday; however, by Sunday that feeling had somewhat vanished and worn off. That Sunday Daddy went on with his work as usual and the rest of us went to the mountains to pick berries. But we all talked about the event from time to time and kept mentioning getting into church. But the churches uptown were too high-class for poor folk as we were to attend, and the nearest country church was several miles away—that left us out of the churchgoing business.

Daddy had been offered a good job with a local lumber man to cut logs for one of his mills. He would pay Daddy about two to three dollars per day to supply the logs for his mill. Daddy grabbed that offer immediately without even asking Mom. When he told her, she stormed out a few curse words at him and then came over and hugged his neck and told him that she was proud of him for taking the job before someone had gotten it. He would need someone to help him cut the timber, and after asking around, someone told him about Old Buck. Now buck was not the most brilliant man on this planet, but he could count to ten slowly, and could make a *B* for his name; however, he was a very hard worker. Even though he wasn't the sharpest knife in the drawer, he was a good man—I think. Buck lived about three miles from us, so Daddy agreed to let him board with us and pay him fifty cents per day. He didn't smoke but, he chewed tobacco and cussed a little now and then. They went to work the following Monday. After a few days came payday. Buck was paid two one dollar bills and two quarters, and he left for home; it was Friday about dark. We had a hard time living without him and his wild tales that weekend. Then came Monday. Buck came in at daylight while Mom was cooking breakfast. He said, "Wess, I got a real good deal from Mr. Jack, our landlord. He took that old paper dollar bills and gave some real money for them. He gave me two quarters for them, and I took the quarters and gave one to Maggy so she would go in the barn loft with me and have a good time. And she borrowed the other quarter to buy us some snuff."

Daddy asked, "Buck, do you think that was wise? Now what do you have to show for your weeks work?"

Buck said, "Well we had a good time in the barn lift. But don't tell her daddy, for he told her if she went up in the barn loft, a snake might bite her or something worse. And I think I still have the other quarters if she didn't get them from me while we were doing stuff in the hay loft."

One Sunday afternoon Buck came in just about dark and told us a wild story that was true and kind of funny. He said that old Jack, his landlord, came over to their house on Saturday late in the afternoon to see his sister Mary. Buck and his family lived just across the little dirt road from Jack's house and only a few yards from Old Jack's large barn. The old farmhouse they lived in was very much run-down and needed much repair. Jack came in and struck up a lively conversation with Buck's sister Mary. "Mary, will you go up in the barn loft with me and have a little fun?" Jack asked Mary as he sat beside her on an old wooden bench.

Mary replied, "What will you give me this time?" Old Jack looked at as if he was disgusted. Then he replied, "I'll give you a dime if you will go, and you know that I always make you smile."

"I don't need your old dime. What else could you give me?" Mary said as she moved in a little closer to him on the bench.

"I'll give you a nickel box of Scott Red Rooster snuff if you will go," Jack was pleading with her for her love.

I'll go with you if you won't tell anyone else. And only if you stop seeing my sister Lue. She tells everyone that you love hers more than mine, and I don't like that at all. You told me that I struck your fancy more than she did. When you have a box of sweet snuff, I'll climb that ladder with you and roll in the hay till the rooster crows if'n he crows pretty quick, for I'm afraid that the bugger man will get me for doing this with you. And I think he comes out at night."

Old Jack was a little man about sixty years old and had a little handlebar mustache that turned up on the end and a little small chin goatee that hung down about an inch that he kept blackened with shoe polish. He weighed about one hundred twenty pounds when he is wet, and he always had sheepy grin on his face as if he was trying to hide something from everyone. At that time the two started for the barn. There was a ladder built in the barn hallway that went straight up into the barn loft. Mary started up first. Her big flaring dress tail made Jack look up as he followed her. Her big white legs were in Old Jack's sight all the way up to her waistline as he followed on her heels up the ladder. When Mary got to the top, she put one knee on the ceiling floor as she put her hands on the floor to get up in the loft. Old Jack had seen about all that he wanted. He turned loose of the ladder and got him a handful of what he came up to get! As he grabbed her in her private parts, he forgot about the ladder, slipped, and fell eight feet to the dirt and cow manure floor, which was hard dry clay dirt and fresh cow patties. He began to cuss and moan and groan in pain. Jack had broken an ankle, sprained his wrist, and fractured a rib or two when he landed from the eight-foot fall to the floor. Mary climb back down and helped him up and cleaned some of the cow manure from his clothes and helped him across the road and on to his porch, and since he lived alone, she helped him into the house and in to his chair. Mary demanded her snuff and a dime extra for helping him to his house. She then warned him to keep his hands off the "things" until she got paid first, her snuff first and his pleasure next and to not grab for things before getting himself out of danger from falling off the ladder.

Old Jack was a dirty old man that had tried to get with all the women he could contact around Heflin and on the road that went from his house to Heflin which was about two and a half miles from where he lived. One day as he came up the road in his buggy to get his mail from the post office, he saw Mammy out in the yard doing some flower gardening. He stopped the buggy in front of our house and then drove the horse and buggy up into our front yard and turned around. Mom went over to the buggy and asked him what he wanted. Being a dirty old Jack, he began to tell her as he wiggled the horse reins across the horse's back so the horse would pull the buggy away from the house a few feet at a time. Mom would follow beside the buggy as Jack would lean way over the side of the buggy to talk to her in a low voice so we children could not hear. He leaned over and touched Mom on the shoulder. Irra saw him and decided it was about time for Old Jack to be moving on. Irra was a real good shot with a slingshot or flip as we country boys called it. He had a real strong flip made from old automobile inner-tube rubber strips and an old leather shoe tongue for the pocket. We would break up old cast-iron stove parts to hunt birds with. Irra hid behind the tall cotton plants growing on the other side of our driveway and got up even with the horse, and while Jack was leaning way over to whisper something to Mom, Irra put a large cast-iron slug into the pocket of his slingshot or flip, rose up, and shot the horse right on his ding-dong with the iron slug. The horse jumped up in the air and started running down the driveway, leaving the driveway and across the cotton field, jumped a three-foot-deep ditch and into the road heading home. Jack was hanging over the side of the buggy when this all started and was still trying to get back into the buggy seat, trying to reach the leather reins as he went out of our sight yelling and cussing the horse.

Old Jack never knew what went wrong that day. Buck came in the following weekend and told us that Jack's horse went wild and ran the buggy into the hall of the barn, stripped the new buggy top off, and completely demolished the buggy. It hurt Jack pretty bad. About three days later, Daddy saw Jack in Heflin on one crutch and with his left arm in a sling. It appeared that Old Jack had gotten the worst of the deal that day. He traded that horse off for a smaller horse and bought him a new buggy. Before this incident Jack had been taking the shortcut road by our house, but never went to Heflin that way again as long as we lived there. That day we received fun and laughter to do us for a long time. When we finally told Mom and Daddy about what happened, Mom said, "You little devils sure know how to break up a dirty old man's romance before it even starts."

A few years later we learned that Old Jack was courting a married woman above Heflin. One day he came calling on her while her husband was working, but he came in early that day. As he was walking up the driveway, Jack saw him coming. As the husband came through the front door, Jack jumped out the window, leaving his pants on the floor by the bed. Jack jumped in the buggy and headed south on the Highway 78. He had the horse in full gear and doing top speed when he heard a gunshot behind him. As he entered Highway 78 the horse never slowed down at all. A large rig trailer struck the buggy, killing old Jack, the horse and making splinter out of the buggy. As Daddy told us the story, we were all saddened for about five minutes, and then we all had a good laugh about what we did to him a few months earlier. Old Jack was quite a guy in his adult life; it seemed that all who knew him loved him except the ones that he had tried to put the make on or their wives. Buck told us later that his sister Mary had grieved very much over the death of Old Jack, and at one time she said that they were talking and planning to sneak away to Georgia and get married. He said that she had lost a lot of her weight since his death. However, when one dies, some are gladdened and some were saddened. Old Jack was loved by some and disliked by others. But that won't bother Jack anymore, for he is long gone to meet Saint Peter in the great beyond, perhaps to take his journey in the opposite direction. You know, that one leaves on his journey to eternity and not even his closest friends know in which direction he went.

The two and half years we lived on the Jones farm were the best years that we had ever had. We had plenty to eat, a good place to live, plenty to wear and all that good way of life. It came with a price tag. We worked hard and took advantage of every money making opportunity that was laid before us. We didn't want to wind up like the boys family that we ran around with. Rather, we took after the Jones family. Being around a well-educated, well-mannered, and kindhearted family seemed to wear off on us. The more time we spent with the Jones family, the less we time we wanted to be around the carefree, nonworking families that lived beyond us. They will never know the influence their family had on us. Daddy and Mom had always taught us that we would become like the people that we kept associating with, and now I'm totally convinced that they were right. While living there, we all did odd jobs to earn extra money for the family.

All was not work; we boys had time for goofing off and having fun, fishing, bird hunting, swimming, and just walking around. At times we would walk up and down the railroad looking for railroad workers' torpedoes, the explosive device that was placed on the train tracks to set off a very loud bang when hit by the train wheels of the train engine. This would warn the train engineer that there were track repairs being made about a mile away and to slow down or to stop if three went off in succession. These devices were a ball of explosive held on the railroad track by a strip of lead about one-half inch wide and a quarter inch thick, wrapped down around the track to hold the explosive on the top of the rail. Some of us boys, no one seemed to know which, would remove the explosive devices from the track to get the lead strips to form into fishing-line sinkers. It wasn't good for the railroad crews, but it made fishing a little easier, and it was better than an old rusty nail tied to the line. One day one of us plucked off three torpedoes that had been placed about fifteen feet apart on the track. These explosive devices were to signal the train to come to a complete stop quick. Well, since they were removed, they didn't, and the train kept going until it hit the spot where the railroad workers had removed some cross ties and a section of rail; then it stopped suddenly and the engine completely ran off the track and several boxcars were crisscRossierd between two high dirt banks on either side. Luckily, no one was hurt or killed in the accident. However it was the only wreck that had ever been in this part of the south for many years. The sound of the train wreck and the box cars crashing side by side and the steam locomotive engine was nearby people running through the fields, pastures, and woods area for miles around. Many people knew that something had happened to the train and they came running to see what it was. There was a large crowd gathered to see if anyone was hurt or killed. It took several days to clear the track again and put the railroad in operation. Sometimes I wonder how much it cost the railroad for us to have a few fishhook sinkers. There were railroad detectives running everywhere trying to find the missing torpedoes that caused the railroad disaster. After a few weeks all the big investigation was over without them ever finding out who removed the signal torpedoes from the railroad tracks, and we just kept on fishing with their lead sinkers. However, those lead sinkers cost the railroad people enough money to have bought several box cars full of lead. Sometimes when I go fishing and put on a new sinker I think of the old-fashion railroad lead kind. It was more fun back then to make our own sinkers out of torpedo-strap lead strips.

For most young children out in the country, it was sometimes hard for us to find enough things to entertain our wondering minds. We just had to be doing something to occupy our time and mind and to keep us busy. One day as we boys were walking down the railroad track, we wondered if we might design us a sled rail track to glide down the steep hillside in Mrs. Brown's pasture which was just out behind our house. Well, we put our minds together and dreamed up a design for our plan for the project. We began work on the track. Daddy had a large stack of firewood logs cut and split out in the woodpile. We borrowed some of his firewood logs to use for cross ties for the track. The sawmill right behind and near our house had a large pile of wood strips that had been from the edge of the large boards that they were cutting, and it was all free for anyone that wanted to clear it away. From that pile we gathered some of the larger strips for the rails, which we nailed to the split firewood cross ties—leaving a thirty-inch space between the rails, making sure the top side of the rails were smooth and even so the sled would ride smoothly over the joints in the rails. The track was about seventy-five yards long and ended about twelve to fifteen feet from the wooded area where the grade level became much steeper than where the track was located. The track was designed so that when the sled reached the end of the track, it would hit the dirt and stop within about eight to ten feet from the end of the track. The dirt acted as a braking system for the sled, bringing it to a slowing stop. After finishing the track, we had the task of making a sled to slice down the wooden rails. Well, since we had a barn with two cow stalls and only had one muley-headed cow, we decided to take one stall door off its hinges and use it for a sled. It worked almost perfectly after we tore it to pieces and nailed two stabilizing runners to its underside. However, it was heavy. Now it was time for the test run. We put it on the track at the top of the rails and loaded ourselves on to the sled and tried to get it going. It just barely moved a few feet. After all this work and it wouldn't go! It made us mad enough to start cussing again. Then we came up with a brilliant idea. We got two of Mom's cow feed buckets and headed over to the railroad track and picked up two buckets full of large chunks of grease that had fallen of the train axles on to the cross ties and slag along each steel rail. After applying a coat of grease to each of our wooden rails, we decided to give her another trial run. All four of us got on the barn door sled and shoved off. Down the track we went like a streak of greased lightning! When the sled hit the dirt, the sled stopped a few feet before we stopped. We boys just kept on going for about eight to ten feet further on our faces and bellies. We decided to do it again; however, the sled got faster each time we took her down the track. The grease had filled the pores in the wood on the track and smoothed out so as to make the sled go faster each time we rode it down the track, and further we slid on our bellies on the dirty at the end of the ride. It seemed that we began to like this better than fishing, swimming, or hunting birds with our slingshots.

Some of our friends living further down the track that we had been swimming with had watched us having fun with our sled track. While we were out working picking cotton for Mr. Jones, they would invite themselves over to enjoy our sled while we were not there. This kind of made us mad. Where were these boys while we engineered, designed, and built the track? Now they wanted to enjoy the fruit of our labor. That made us mad. We decided to get even with them. Irra got some heavy wire and nailed it to the top end of the sled to use like a bucket bail to pull the sled up with. As the sled would go down the track, the handle of wire bail would hit the cross ties as the sled went down the track. Irra drove three large nails in the top of the last cross tie at the bottom of the track, letting the nails stick up about one and a half inches in the middle of tie. Now when the sled went down, the bale handle would catch on the nails and the sled would come too a sudden stop—letting the riders plow up the dirt as they rolled down the steep hill. We got a big bucket of fresh cow manure from our cow stall and poured it out about four feet below the track in the path of the riders and then another bucket full three feet below the other pile. This was good fresh squishy kind. We lightly covered the soft manure with straw and dead leaves. We took the sled up the hill to the top of the track. Now we waited for our friends to come and take a sled ride as we watched through the cracks in the barn hay loft. After a half hour had passed, we saw the boys coming up the railroad track going to town. When they got about even with our house, they cut a beeline across the pasture to our sled track. We were about a hundred yards from the sled track. Then all three got on board, kicked her in forward motion and headed down the track. Then the bail handle caught on the nails! All three boys went facedown in the fresh cow manure and dirt sliding several feet further down the dirt part of the stopping area. As they got up, we could see the manure on their "going to town" clothes. As they got up, they were saying all their choice curse words as they headed toward the creek that runs under the railroad tressel. We were rolling in the hay and laughing so hard that we couldn't talk for several minutes. We were laughing so much. We made sure to take Daddy's shovel and remove the cow manure before we used our sled again. This operation seemed to cure some other people's desire to take a sled ride while on their way to town. Irra removed the nails that stopped the sled, and now we could ride to the bottom of the track and not slide on our bellies to completely stop.

After Mr. Wheeler moved into his new home, he sold his old house and some land to Mr. Jones. The Jones family decided to tear down the Wheeler house and build a new modern home for the family. The home the Jones family was the most modern home in the neighborhood, but it wasn't quiet as large as the family needed. They needed more bedroom space; now the new home would have all the space they needed. Mr. Jones saw some of Daddy's carpentry work on the Wheeler home, and he hired Daddy to help build his new home. Daddy felt very proud to have someone like Mr. Jones let him lead out with most of the building of his new home. And it kind of made all of very proud to see Daddy come from a log cutter to be a carpenter, and a good one at that. When the home was completed, all our family joined in and helped move the family in. It was something new for us. We were used to moving our stuff into a new place but we didn't have near this much stuff and things to move all at one time. However, all the furniture and things fit right in and with one empty bedroom left empty for new furniture.

Boy, now the Rollins family was proud. We now lived just across the road from a high-class, well-known, and well-respected family—the Jones family. Now all of us boys definitely had to be on our good behavior because we now lived just across the road from one of the most respected families in the Heflin area. While we lived there Mama and Daddy almost made us quit cussing and saying dirty words and calling each other dirty names loud enough for the Jones family to hear us. It was almost like the preacher was living with us. Sometimes we had to go over the hill in the cow pasture do to our real serious cussing and stuff. Mama and Daddy were trying to wean us of cussing and dirty language; however, the boys that we sometimes went swimming with and played with cussed and talked dirty all the time. We were trying, but sometimes when we got mad we would let her fly; it just seemed to fit in in certain situations. One day we were all out in the garden putting up a new section of garden fence. Daddy told Frank to go get him some cold water to drink. Well, Frank had heard one of the Taylor boys call his father a dirty name. Frank blurted out the same name, "You long-legged, gray-haired SOB go get it yourself." We had never seen Daddy run very much, and we thought that a middle-aged man couldn't run very fast, but we were mistaken! Daddy jumped up from what he was doing and made a lunge toward Frank. Frank took off running out across the cotton field with Daddy about twenty feet behind him, both jumping cotton plants and cotton rows like horses at the Kentucky Derby. They cut across the cotton field and disappeared out behind the edge of a small wooded area. A few seconds later, all the neighborhood could tell the old man that couldn't run so fast had won the race. One never heard so much screaming and hollering as Frank was letting out! Frank learned the most valuable lesson of his early life—don't use the same language as some lowlife boys that you get acquainted with and sometimes associate with. If the boy that Frank heard say those well-chosen words had got the same beating that Frank got, his vocabulary would have changed. Somehow, we all seem to take up some of the habits of the people we run around with and mingle with. If you want to smell like a skunk, just play with one. The smell will always rub off on you. After a long lecture from our parents, we never played with the Taylor boy very much again.

We began to seek out new friends in our surrounding neighborhood that were of a better quality than some of the ones that lived a mile or so down the track. We started playing marbles with the Lambert boys who lived on a little hill across the track from us. These boys were in a good, well-mannered family. Mr. Lambert was a Postman and had a mail route way out in the country. We never knew the name of his oldest son, everyone just called him Churn or Churn Jar. He got this name because he had a six-gallon milk churn jar full of beautiful glass marbles that he had won at school playing marbles for "keeps." It seemed that every day at school he would play marbles for keeps and take a pocket full of marbles home and put them in the churn jar. That is how he got his name "Churn Jar" Lambert. Everyone seemed to like Churn Jar Lambert even though he had won a lot of their marbles and put them in the large churn jar. He was so good that there wasn't anyone in school who wanted to play for keeps with him; if they did, he would win their marbles and deposit them in his marble bank—the old six-gallon churn. After school we would go over to his house and practice playing marbles with Churn Jar. He would give each of us ten marbles and let us play with him until he won them back, and as usual that didn't take very long. We all learned a lot of marble-playing skills from him.

About halfway between where we lived and Heflin lived the Reid family. As well as I can remember, Mrs. Reid was a widow living alone with one son about our age named Russel. We liked him as a friend. Mrs. Read's old cow had a little bull calf. Russel fed him until he was about two months old and got tired of all the feeding and looking after the calf. Russel's mother told him that they didn't have time to see after the calf and to see if he could find someone that would take the calf off their hands. Russel asked around to find someone that would take the calf for free. After a few days trying, he saw us going to town and offered us the calf. We jumped at the idea, a free calf that was about old enough to graze in the pasture or be tied out in the grass up behind our garden. We tied a rope around his neck and tried to lead him down the road home, but he wouldn't get in gear and move out of his tracks. Mrs. Reid saw us, and she bursted out laughing and said, "Maybe he is out of gas—try pushing him."

We tried to push, to pull, and to beg him to go but to no avail. After a few minutes, Russel's mother came out with a two-gallon bucket with about a quart of milk in it and told us to let him drink a few swallows of fresh milk and he would follow us to the moon as long as we went in front of him with the bucket of milk. Lewis ran in front of the calf with the bucket, and the calf ran down the road all the way to our house where we tied him up the porch post for Mom and Dad to see our prized possession. Mom and Daddy were proud of us for getting a bull calf to get started in the cattle business. The Thrower family, the Bennett family, and the Atkins family all had cattle and land, so why shouldn't we? After all, they had to get started some way—maybe with only one bull calf. Mama told us that we could get him started on a little of her cow's milk, and she would spare some of her bought cow feed for him.

After a few days, the little bull calf was eating her cow feed and started eating fresh tender grass where we had him tied up around the garden and house. As the calf grew up, we boys each had a fond interest in him. We soon learned that if one of us needed a little money, we could sell our 25 percent share of the calf to one of the others. At first we would sell our share for about a quarter to one of the others. After a few weeks the value shot up to fifty cents. Then seventy-five cents. And finally a dollar bought a quarter intrence or one's share in the little bull. When one of us would sell our share to another, we then work hard to raise enough money to buy it back. This selling and trading went on for weeks as Little John, the new name that we gave the calf, grew bigger and more beautiful every day. All of us boys had bought back and sold our quarter share of Little John many times. Neal seemed to take a liking to Little John more than he let us know. Irra sold Neal his share for one dollar. Before Irra had time to raise the money to buy his share back, Neal told Lewis that if he needed some money, he would buy his share for a dollar and a quarter, the highest price that we had ever sold for. Lewis grabbed up the deal and collected his money. Neal was smart. He had been working a little and had saved up some money that we didn't realize he had. Now he would try to buy Frank's part of Little John. But Frank loved Little John too, and refused to sell to Neal. Neal had an old air rifle that he had traded for somewhere. We all liked the air rifle too. Then Neal said that he would give Frank the air rifle and a dollar for his part. But Frank wouldn't give in. Neal decided that he would give Frank the rifle and two dollars. Now that got Frank's attention. Now Neal was the sole owner of Little John. He set a price of any 25 percent share would cost five dollars. This made the other three of us angry; Irra and Neal almost got into a fistfight over Neal's plans to keep the little bull for himself. Little John was not so little by now, and we had broken him to ride. We would take turns to ride him in the pasture and up and down the driveway. Daddy had been watching our trading and knew what the going price was; however he kept quiet. Now it was time for Old Dad to call us in to the living room for a friendly chat; well it was more like a court of law than a friendly chat. Daddy asked Neal, "Neal, do you own all of the calf yourself?"

"Yes, I paid each one for their part of Little John. He is mine, and if they want their part back they will have to pay me five dollars," Neal replied.

Daddy then asked Neal, "Did you ever tell anyone of them that you would sell their part back for the same price that you bought it for?"

Daddy then turned to Irra. "Irra, did Neal promise to sell your share back to you for the same price that you sold you part for?"

Irra replied, "We had been selling our part of Little John back and forty any time we wanted to and Neal is the only one that bought our part and won't sell back for the same price."

"Frank, how about you? Did you ever sell your part to Neal and tried to buy it back?"

Frank said, "We always sold our part and bought it back for about what we had sold it for. But now Neal wants to keep him for his own bull, and that ain't fair."

Daddy asked Lewis, "Lewis, what about you? How do you feel about the final trading that has been going on this last go around?"

"Well, I guess since Neal has Little John, we won't have to feed him anymore. But is Neal going to let us ride him anymore?" Lewis replied.

Daddy said, "He belongs to Neal now, and whatever Neal says or agrees on is his business. Neal has the complete right to sell a share to anyone of you for whatever price he wants to; however, you don't have to buy that share back if it is too high. But I think that Neal should let each of you ride the bull like you did before."

"I'll let each of you have riding right for fifty cents each month. You can't keep riding Little John without paying me first," said Neal.

Frank replied, "What if one of us gets mad about all this and decides to go out there and shoot the bull?"

Daddy said, "I think that is what we have been doing for the last hour, I think we have been shooting bull all the time that we have been sitting here. If any of you want to be back in the cattle business, you will have to pay Neal for your part to get it back, and it is up to Neal to sell your part back at the price he decides you will have to pay him." From that time on Neal never sold any of the ownership of little John to any of us. Little John soon grew up to be a large bull and remained as gentle as a kitten.

Early one morning a neighbor, Mr. Hanvy, came to our house and told Mama that Mrs. Jones died during the night giving birth to a baby. The baby was born dead and the mother bled to death in just a few minutes. She had the baby at home with only a neighbor attending. There was no doctor available to attend her before the baby was born, and there was no time to get her to Anniston to the hospital. The Heflin school let out early so some of the students could attend the funeral. This was one of the saddest funerals that we ever attended. The mother and baby were buried in the same casket, the baby in the mother's arms. There were more flowers there than any funeral that we had ever attended before. The Jones family was well known and had many friends in all parts of the county. The Heflin schools let out at lunchtime so everyone that wanted to could attend the funeral. Daddy and Mama dressed up in their best clothes, Daddy in his blue serge suit, Mama in her store-bought light blue flowered dress, and we boys in our newest overalls and clean long-sleeve blue shirt and attended the funeral. We all looked splendid, whatever that means for a sharecropping, log-cutting family. When people looked at us, they might have thought that we were living a few city blocks to the heart of Heflin. Mama and Daddy looked much younger than they really were, and we boys looked as if we had never stole all them eggs and had never smoked rabbit tobacco and cussed like that we had been doing all these years in the past.

We wanted to take a picture of our family all dressed up, but Daddy's old Kodak camera was out of film, and we would have to change clothing before one of us could have gone to Heflin to get more film.

Sometimes it takes only one thing like dressing up for the funeral to put a family to thinking about what they are and what they could be if they all put their mind into the thinking mode and make the proper decisions for their future. Neal had learned the value of a bull calf and it almost made him a cattleman; Daddy had dressed like a real uptown preacher; and Mama had seen how beautiful she could be when she really took pride and dressed up. All us boys began to wear cleaner clothes and even started combing our hair when we went out in public. The death of Mrs. Jones had brought a great change in our appearance when we went out in public. This would last as long as we lived near downtown Heflin but soon began to wear off when we moved out of this area.

Our family lived at this same place for several months longer, Daddy working for the logging industry and doing a lot of side jobs to help us along. The rest of us hoed cotton and worked in the fields for our neighbors around us, picking berries, picking cotton, and doing anything that we could do to make a little extra money to afford new clothes and stuff so we could literally "keep up with the Joneses." Mama began to get more into the social life with some of our more-well-to-do neighbors. She was amazed at how quick that she found that she could accepted in the circle of some of the landowners and businesspeople. She even showed some of the younger ladies how to sew quilt tops, how to take flour sacks for quilt linings, and how to quilt in their living rooms. Mom was an artist when it came to sewing and quilting. She always made and sold several quilts each year. She could frame in one quilt in a day with one of us boys helping her wind the frame when she quilted. All four of us boys would help her stretch the quilt lining between the quilting frame and secure it onto the quilting frame, stretching it tight like a trampoline or banjo head. Next we would cover the lining with a layer of cotton, carefully keeping the cotton in an even layer the same thickness over the entire lining so there was no thick or thin spots in the cotton. After sewing the top to the lining all around, she would take a piece of chalk tied with a string and make quarter circles about one inch apart getting smaller on each circle, then sewing the lining and top together with the cotton in between. It would take one day to finish the quilt if she got an early start and if she could get us boys to help her get started. However, this was the easy part. Sewing the small pieces of cloth that she had bought in a "scrap bundle" that had come from a sewing plant and she had bought from Mr. Brown's dry goods store was a very hard job. She had to cut the pieces of scrap cloth into the design that she had chosen for that particular quilt. That is why so many families slept in the cold from not having enough quilts to keep them warm in a cold, unheated bedroom at night.

One fall after all the crops were gathered in, all cotton was picked and the corn was in the crib, Daddy took a job working for one of Mom's relatives. He has a fairly nice house down on a little sloping hill near the river. The house was ceiled overhead and most of the walls. The old house had been used for a barn to store sargum seed and corn in. It was badly infested with mice and large rats, some as big as squirrels. These large rats created a real problem. After we cleaned out the house, the rats were hungry. After moving in we had to stop up several holes to keep the rats and mice out. We straightened out old tin turpentine or rosin catching cups and nailed them over the holes. Daddy borrowed Mr. Prater's large dray-type wagon and his large mules to move us to the river home. This time we would have to make two large loads to move all our stuff. Neal and Daddy had taken Neal's big bull over to Grandpaw's pasture to stay awhile; Grandpa's cows needed a boyfriend to father their calves and Neal's bull was becoming courting age. There was just no way to make a young adult bull happier than to put him in the pasture with half dozen young courting-aged heifers. After delivering the bull and introducing him to the lot full of ready-to-get-acquainted heifers, Daddy and Neal went over to the Prater farm and got the wagon and mules and headed to the house to load up and move the first load of furniture and stuff. It took the rest of the day to load up and get the first load. It was almost midnight when the wagon was unloaded by lamp lights. We set up two beds and the stove so we could eat and get a little sleep. The first night there was almost like camping out. It was something different, big rats running around the house with little fear of being evicted or harmed in any way. But this would be their last night to take over the house.

The next day after the other was moved, we stopped up the entrances to our house. From that day forward we used our slingshots to get rid of a lot of rats; to us boys it was fun. It was more fun than shooting Mama's chickens or even birds. At daybreak we all pitched in and hitched up the mules to the wagon while Mom cooked about a setten and half of fresh eggs a large pan of biscuits, some thickened gravy, and hot black coffee. After feasting on the good food we all loaded ourselves in the big wagon and went to get our final load of stuff. With each load of the furniture and other things, people would gather along the roadside to watch us going by with Daddy and Mama sitting high on top of the load and hog and chicken coop crates hanging over the wagon bed. Daddy made an art of loading the stuff on the wagon. Our cow had been delivered with the first load, so now we four boys got to ride high on the wagon with Mom and Dad. We must have resembled the Beverly Hillbillies! People were laughing as we went by, but we didn't care; we just threw up our hands and laughed with them. Besides we were getting a new place to live and they were not. And this time we were getting a bigger and better house than we had ever had before. The new home had two large rooms on the front with an eight-foot-wide hall running from front to back with one room on either side of the hall. You entered the house through a large single door in the front of the hallway. The large living room was on the right, and the large bedroom was on the left, with large windows facing the road which was about fifty yards from the front of the house. The kitchen and dining room were directly behind and joining the living room, with a double fireplace between the two rooms and with a door on the left of the partition wall that divided the two rooms. We also had a large L-shaped back porch that we could step out of the hallway and kitchen on to the porch. The water well was located on the back porch so we could draw water from the well without leaving the porch. There was a large wide beautiful front porch all the way across the front of the house with wide rock steps built with real cement joint in the middle of the porch and a swing on the porch hanging by chains from the rafters.

This was a dream come true! The biggest and the best house that we ever lived in. Sometimes some of us wondered if the mansion of heaven would be more beautiful and much better than this, without the rats, of course. About seventy-five yards behind the house was a large barn with a tin roof and with a large hallway with two stables on each side of the hallway. We were also blessed with a large pasture behind and joining the barn. Down about a hundred yards a small creek ran through the pasture. About three or four hundred yards the creek ran into the Tallapoosa River. Between our house and the river were large fields on each side of the road, the fields running within about thirty feet from the riverbank, with only a thin row of trees separating the fields from the riverbanks. Just about the bridge was a large swimming and fishing hole where the water was about ten feet deep in the middle. Our parents wouldn't let us swim in the river, but they let us dam up the small creek running through our pasture and use it for our swimming hole. And dam up the creek we did! We built a four-foot-high dam at a narrow place in the creek where there was a wide place in the creek with the water about two feet deep. Now we had about five-foot-deep water in the center of our swimming hole. This was the best swimming hole that we had ever had, and it was close in. This was where we spent much of our time that summer, swimming and fishing.

We boys had been told to not go down near the river unless Daddy was with us. He had taken us to the river fishing a time or two and we liked it very much. We began catching a few catfish, something that we had been catching while fishing with hooks at the other places where we lived. This created a real desire for us. Now our table would be blessed with more than the three to five minnows that we had been catching. Daddy hardly ever had time to take us to the river except on Sundays or maybe an hour late in the afternoon after he got home from cutting logs all day. And he wasn't as carried away with fishing as much as we boys were. However, he bought us some fishhooks when he went up to Heflin to buy groceries and stuff. He even bought us a roll of kite string to use for fishing, but no sinkers. We always made our sinkers from old rusty nails that we picked up from the ashes where old rotten lumber had been burned around the wash pot. A burned rusty nail always makes a good fishing sinker, and if your line got caught out in the water on a rock or sunken tree or something and your line is broken, you don't lose a good store-bought lead sinker; you only lose a good hook and a rusty nail and maybe some kite string. And when one begins fishing on the big waters of the forty-foot-wide Tallapoosa River, one must be careful not to damage his fishing equipment because it is hard to replace. We found a large patch of wild bamboo growing in a neighbor's pasture about a quarter mile down the river from us. We cut about thirty bamboo fishing poles about fifteen feet long for our fishing poles. These bamboo poles worked real well while fishing on the river, but we had to shorten some of them to about ten foot to fish in the little creek that ran through our pasture. It was difficult to stand on the creek bank and fish with a fifteen-foot pole and be able to look at the fish eyeball to eyeball and get the worm and hook just in front of him so he will see the worm while fishing in a six-foot-wide creek. You sometimes have to let them see you with one eye and look at the bait with the other eye. However, we became pretty good at outsmarting the smaller fish. But if there were some larger ones in the small creek, they must be smarter than us for we seldom caught any of them. The smaller one seemed to think that we had come to hand-feed or something, for they seemed always falling for our clever tricks and getting caught while looking at us eyeball to eyeball.

Sometimes we would catch Mama working, and while Daddy was in the forest cutting logs we would sneak down to the little creek to where it ran into the river. Sometimes we would fish maybe a foot or so out in the river but we reasoned that it was still creek water and not directly out in the river; well that would still be fishing in the creek's water, and since it had not mingled with the old muddy river's water, we felt that would be all right. We began to catch some two-to-four-pound catfish in that fishing spot. But since we had been warned not to ever go alone, we made up a good story as to where we caught the mud cats that we were taking home. After we caught one we would take the fish up in the clear water in the small creek and wash all the yellow mud from the fish with soap using a rough feed sack, making sure we cleaned all the mud and color off that we could. Well, we got away with this until Irra and Neal slipped off the muddy riverbank after a quick summer rain and fell in the river. When we went home for them to change into some dry overalls and shirt and Mama began to wring the muddy water out of the wet clothes, our secret wasn't a secret anymore. Now we knew what was coming as soon as Daddy got home from work. We went out to the peach trees and cut some small tree branches from the bottom of the trees, one for each of us, and took them to Mama for to beat us with. But she refused and said that our daddy would deal with us when he got home from cutting logs. Boy, we sure hoped that he would be too tired to beat us very much and the switches would be so small that they wouldn't last long. He came just a little after dark, too dark to go out, and cut larger peach tree switches, and he was too tired to use them. He told us that he would settle with us the next morning. And settle with us he did! The next morning at daylight it was time for our punishment. We had not slept any that night. It was kind of like a prisoner on death row waiting his execution by hanging or by being rocked to sleep in the arms of "Yellow Mama," the electric chair down at Folsom Prison. At daybreak Daddy had to get us up. We would normally be up eating breakfast of eggs, gravy, hot biscuits, syrup and butter, and hot coffee. Now we could see why the condemned prisoner is offered his last meal the night before his execution; they lose their appetite just minutes before their time. Daddy wasn't eating either. Mama had all the good stuff and things cooked and on the table, but no one seemed very hungry. After getting up and dressing for the occasion, we boys had on two shirts and two pairs of overalls. We needed extra padding to suit the occasion. Daddy had his long wide leather belt hanging over the back of his chair. Now we knew the small peach tree switches just wouldn't go over with him. All four of us boys and Mama were crying. He then had us sit down at the table. He began to lecture us about the danger of the river. He had never given us a long lecture before a whipping before; boy, we were sure going to get it this time! Then he asked, "How long have you boys been crying? Your faces are red and your eyes are red and swollen. It looks like you have been crying all night."

Irra replied, "We talked and cried all night. We know how easy for anyone of us to fall in the river and if it has been raining and the water is high we could be drowned, and we don't want that to happen. Daddy, would you let Mama whip us? We don't want a whipping with that big old black belt. Can you let her whip us this time?"

"Lee, don't you think that since they have been crying all night and more crying may make their eyeballs swell up, maybe they would go blind or something?"

"Well I kinda believe that since they are well prepared with extra clothing, just a few licks won't hurt them so bad. And if they get away with it this time, the neighbors may be called in to hunt their bodies next time," she replied.

Then Daddy let each of us tell our side of the story to him. As Neal was confessing to his part in the off-limits fishing trip, he went further than he should have. Neal told him where all those catfish came from that we had been catching. Daddy's face turned red and his now-thinning hair seemed to stand up like that of a porcupine or a wild boar that had been cornered by a pack of hog-hunting hounds as he grabbed for that leather belt. At that time Mom yelled, "Wess, since they have told us everything, couldn't we just forgive them this one time?"

"I don't think a prison warden would forgive a prisoner just as he is standing on the platform with the noose around his neck," he said as he pushed his chair back from the table, saying as he grabbed Irra by the hand and giving him five lashes with the heavy belt, "I can forgive you for going down there and falling in the river, but I can't forgive you boys for not telling me where you caught them big mud cats. If you had told me where you were catching them, we could have been living like a king on catfish and corn-bread hushpuppies. We might have taken one of Lee's kinfolks' fish basket trap and put it down in the muddy water where they couldn't find it and we could have been catching a lot of fish. For if you can catch them there with a hook, you can catch them in the basket."

Then he threw the belt down to the floor and turned Irra loose. As Irra start to run out of the house, Mom blocked the door. She then turned around and said, "Wess, I think these boys have learned a lesson and at least we have found where we can put the fish basket that they are going to 'borrow' from one of my kinfolks. I think we should let them go back down there where they caught the big fish and get a stringer full for our supper; don't that make more sense than stopping our only fish supply?"

"Well that does sound like a good idea, but I'm not doing it to save this food until tonight," he said as he went to the stove, took up the big coffee pot, and poured us all a cup of hot black coffee. After that we immediately "borrowed" two fish basket traps from someone a little further up the river. We had been taught not to steal but to borrow, so we took the old fish basket and patched a few holes in them, which isn't like robbing a bank or something like that. However, in a week or two we cut some wire from our garden fence, replacing it with good slabs from the sawmill, and used the wire to make our own fish baskets. They worked better than the ones we had borrowed, so we returned the stolen ones to where we had "borrowed" them.

From then on as long as we lived on the river, we had a pretty good supply of fresh catfish. However, we never told our fish stories to our neighbors or even bragged at all about our secret fishing—the mouth of the creek where it joined the river.

As soon as we moved in the river farmhouse, Daddy began working for Mom's sister's husband and his brothers' cutting loss in a large stand of large pine timber—about three hundred acres. It was the best timber that Daddy had to cut in a very long time. Daddy really liked his job there because he got paid in cash at the end of the workweek, and they run their truck by our house to and from work and he had free transportation to and from work. He was getting good pay for his work, and he liked working for these men very much. Although they drank a little, they didn't bother him any, so they kept right on a drinking and he kept right on working.

When springtime came the Prater family began plowing the river bottom land that lay between our house and the river and a much larger field just across the road from our house. This was good fertile land and was getting ready for planting. They hired us to help with carrying the fertilizer and seed to the planters as they planted the corn and cotton crop. They were also letting us do other odd jobs around the farm, and they paid us well for our work.

One morning, Mom told Daddy that was about time for him to go call Dr. Caffey for it was time. We were out in the yard pitching horseshoes as usual early on a Saturday morning. Daddy came out and told us that Lee was sick with the flu and that we could fix us a little picnic lunch and that we could go down and fish in the mouth of the creek where it ran into the river but to be extra careful and not fall in and don't come back until he came for us. Irra asked him why we could not come back from fishing until he came for us. Daddy told us that Mom had caught a new type of flu and that it was very catching and the doctor would see if it was safe to come back until he had treated Mama. He left with Ramon Prater to drive him over to the nearest telephone to call Dr. Caffey. After we had been fishing, eating, and trying to stay warm by a small fire that he told us we may build if we got cold during the day, Daddy returned about three o'clock and told us that we could come home and see what Mom had. Well, we were tired from fishing and pretty cold for it was the middle of January, and they didn't wear two pairs of clothes that day. As we entered the room we quickly felt bad for Mama, for she looked bad and we thought she might have more than the flu. Then she said, "Come over here and see what I have." Then she and Daddy started grinning.

Frank said, "You just want to give us the flu or something so we will have to take some plain old bad-tasting flu powders or something worse. I'm getting out of here before you give me the flu so I can't go to school on Monday. The teacher will paddle me if I get the flu and don't take her my homework.'

However, we all went over to the bed and stood beside her. She began smiling and pulled up a baby blanket and said, "Meet your baby sister."

Neal looked disgusted and said, "Is that the kind of flu you had? Did that lame old doctor leave that old girl here for us to have to look after? Daddy, go call that lame old doctor back and swap her for a little bigger baby boy. We ain't needin' no lame girls fishing, bird hunting, or nuthin'. Daddy, you should know not to bring anything like that for us boys to play with and run around with. And when Mama has the flu again, maybe he won't start trying to bring us any more babies, and besides baby girls don't sleep with boys and the beds are not big enough for two on one bed and three on the other. And someone said it was real bad luck for boys and girls to sleep in the same bed for the boys talk about bird hunting and fishing and girls want to talk about other stuff like washing and cooking after they go to bed; she will just have to sleep out in the storage room or maybe in the empty cow stall in the barn. I hope that doctor will come back and get her before it gets dark."

Then Mama wrapped the baby in a soft blanket that she had been saving go such an emergency and handed her to Neal and said to him, "Neal meet your little sister Margret."

Neal reached out his arms, took Margret, and started grinning and said to Mama, "I guess if you have already named her, the doctor probably won't take her back, and I reckon she can sleep with me and Irra if she don't cry and keep us awake so we can't do our schoolwork."

"She won't keep you from studying, for you don't even open your books or even take them out of your book satchel and that is why you probably won't pass again this year," Irra said as Neal passed little Margret over to Irra.

All of us began to laugh and smile as she was passed from one to the other. This process went on for several minutes. Each of us boys wanted to hold her longer each time. Lewis finally said, "Since you all won't let us have a dog, we might as well keep her and teach her to hunt with us and maybe she can learn to jump rabbits for us to shoot at with our flips, but how much will she eat and what can we feed her?"

From that brief introduction we all accepted Margret into our family; however, we sure hoped that Mom never got that kind of flu again—not anyway soon. The family found more joy having a baby around than we would have had for a pack of rabbit hounds.

The rest of the winter was pretty hard on us because of the cold weather that we were having. This house was the warmest house that we ever lived in during the winter because we had three fireplaces, one for the kitchen, one for the living room where Mom and Daddy slept, and even one for our bedroom which was across the hallway from the other part of the house. Daddy had Tom Prater, his brother-in-law, to bring him a load of slabs from the sawmill that they all worked at. We sawed them up for firewood to burn during the wintertime and to also use for stove wood. As Daddy loaded the logging truck with slabs, he picked out the biggest oak slabs that he could find in the slab pile for the oak wood makes a much hotter fire than the pine and the oak will burn if it is not dried out after you get it started burning. It burns so hot that it dries the wood out ahead of the actual fire, so it is burning dry wood. Green pinewood will set there and smolder and smoke while one freezes stiff waiting for it to get in a hurry and burn, which it never does.

Everywhere we ever lived we had a big garden. Here we had a real large well fenced garden with a six foot good, one inch wire mesh, the type we cut from the back side of the fence and made fish baskets to catch the large catfish that we wintered on. But we had replaced the wire that we "borrowed" with pine slabs. Daddy borrowed Uncle Tom's big old brown horse and his plow to fix our garden. The garden was good soil, the loose sandy kind. He plowed it up real good and plowed furrows for the rows and made some raised beds for the onions and a few other things. We boys got cow manure from the cow stalls in the barn and strewed it in the rows before planting all the things and stuff that we were planting that year. Mama really liked beets raw, cooked and pickled. It took us about two days to fix and plant the garden and put out about a bushel of onion sets and two rows of cabbage plants. It was in early April and we didn't put out Mom's tomato plants at that time. She had planted tomato seed in an old bread baking pan that she had filled with good rich soil with a lot of manure, sowed the tomato plants, watered real good, and had been setting out to sun in the daytime if it was a little warm and bringing them in and putting them under her bed at night. The plants were about five to six inches tall and were ready for a good setting out in the garden. But if they were set out too early, the frost might kill them and she wouldn't much like that, so we waited another three weeks to put them in the tomato row in the garden. By that time it was time to plant the squash, beans, okra, corn, and other summer crops. In a few days we had a good stand of everything that we had planted. We wound up with about fifteen different vegetables in our new garden, and they were all growing very fast. If there was one thing that Mom and Daddy could do, it was to have a good-looking garden filled with all kinds of good eating stuff. That year as usual the garden kept us going, along with a few rabbits that we killed and with the fish we caught and a few loggerhead turtles that we got out of the creek near the river. The way we caught the turtles was easy. When we killed a chicken, we would take the chicken guts and head and hang them in the creek water about five hundred feet from the river. The turtles would smell that chicken stuff down in the river and come up to get it. Sometimes we would find as many as three large turtles in the clear water trying to eat the chicken parts through a jupe or burlap sack. They were for the taking—so we took them for supper. Many turtles have died that we might live! And wild turtle meat is good eating too, even if it was difficult to hold his legs up and dig it out with a long pronged fork. Most of the time we even cooked it in the hull.

Our barn was covered with corrugated galvanized roofing tin. It was nailed down with lead-headed roofing nails. The lead heads were just the right size to make a lead fishhook sinker. So Irra saw all the lead sinkers up there on top of all them nails. So since we had not had any lead sinkers that caused the train derailment just south of Heflin, Irra decided to do the only goodly thing and deroof the barn and let our cow sleep in the cold and rain and get them lead roofing nail heads, but how? He finally got the answer, since the lead heads were soft he got a long wood strip from our woodpile and went down there and began punching the strip against each nail head until it would come off and slide down the roof to him—each one a new fishing-line sinker. Well, after he had knocked all the lead heads off on one side of the barn, he started on the other side of the roof. Then came along the big man that we were renting the place from. The smoke hit the fan. I didn't think that a fat man could cuss that loud, but he did. He even said bad words that would make the Taylor boys blush and hang their heads in embarrassment and shame. He yelled and cussed for about a half hour, until Daddy came home from work and went down to the barn to see what he could do about all the yelling and cursing. The big fat man told him what he caught Irra doing. Fat boy told Daddy to get up there and pull the headless lead nails and to replace every one of them with new lead-headed nails or we could find us another place to move into. Daddy agreed to do it the next day and looking up toward the house he saw Mama standing on the back porch with old Betsy, Daddy's twelve-gauge long-barrel shotgun kind of halfway pointing directly at him. He began begging Daddy to please not let her shoot him, and he told Daddy that if he could put the nails in the roof that we could stay there as long as we wanted to.

The next day Daddy left about five o'clock going to Howel and Turner's country store about four miles away. There he bought five pounds of roofing nails and two pounds of big framing nails to build a ladder so he could climb up on the roof. When he arrived at home about nine, he began to build the ladder from some carefully selected slabs from our slab woodpile, using some large strips for the rungs that he had taken his ax and crudely cut. The ladder looked like something from the stone age, but it was just for a one-time use and it worked well; he didn't fall of it very many times as he went up on tin roof, taking Irra with him to help him pull the old nails and drive in the new ones. Pulling out the old nails was the hardest job. Daddy's old claw hammer had only broken claws to fit over the nail heads to pull them out, and it just didn't want to cooperate with Irra and the rusty nails. A little while after lunchtime, the job was completed. We all waited for the job to be done before we went in to eat. We were all there except little Margret; she was breast-feeding, and there wasn't need for her to have to wait because of Irra getting a pocket full of lead roofing nail heads for his fishing-hook sinkers. We don't believe the owner ever came back to see if we were done with the barn roof.

When we all went in for lunch that day, Daddy and Mama gave us a long lecture about other people's property. We were pretty good at times; sometimes we were bad for the railroads and barn roofs, and that not all. One day Irra wanted to make him what we called a "match-head" gun. It required a short piece of quarter-inch tubing about six inches long, and we had nowhere to get it. Well, the gas line on Uncle Jim's old Model A Ford had just what he needed running from the gas tank to the carburetor. He filled it with the corner of Daddy's big ax-sharpening file enough so he could break it off. The gas started pouring out of the tank where he had removed the gas line. He held his thumb over the open gas line until Neal could trim a small stick and drive it into the small gas-line opening to stop the flow of gas. The next week when Uncle Jim got in the car and tried starting it, it wouldn't hit a lick. He kept trying until he ran the battery down and went in the house. In a few days he decided to take the battery to town and get it charged at a garage. After he got it charged, he decided to check to see if the car was out of gas. After raising the hood, he immediately saw that his gas line was gone. Even though Uncle Jim attended church pretty regularly, he lost all his religion for about an hour while he stomped, walked around, and cussed. He never found out who took his gas line, but if he had ever found, out I believe there may have been a shooting or a hanging on a limb of a big oak tree next to the barn where he kept his car. Irra made his match-head pistol or zip gun and shot a rat or two with it, along with a few of Mom's baby chicks. In case you are wondering why I don't describe how we made our zip guns, it is because we don't want to tell the secrets of our very own design to others who might make a larger gun and use it for more things than shooting rats or their mom's baby chickens. They may get into shooting their Mom's full-grown chickens and stuff like that.

One day while we were playing and bird hunting out in the wooded area a little ways north of our house, we looked through the woods in an old logging road we saw something like a brown cone shape hanging down from a low limb over the road about four feet above the ground. As we got nearer, we saw something flying around it like bees, and as we got a little closer to it, we could see that it was a swarm of bees, perhaps coming from a farmer about a mile away who also raised honeybees in the woods near his house. When we got closer we could see that these honeybees were of the same home-grown type because they didn't try to sting us as we got within ten or twelve feet from the swarm. They probably decided to leave their present home and go out and make a new home and make it on their own giving their mother Old Queeny to start her another brood or surplus swarm with their very own queen. We hurried home and told Mom; she told us that when Daddy got home about six, he could help us get them and bring them home to have for our very own.

When Daddy got home we told him about the bees. He had us take a nail keg that we had been using for a seat at the table, and we went over to the bee swarm and try to get them into the nail keg to be their new beehive. The bees didn't seem to like the idea at all. Then Daddy told us that his father used to scrub green peach tree leaves in side the hive to make them like their new home. Irra ran back home and brought back a big peach tree limb covered with green leaves. After stripping off some leaves, he rubbed them on the inside of the keg until parts turned green. He easily placed a large flat rock under the bee swarm very slowly. Placing the keg on the rock, he moved back and gently shook the limb above the keg. The air became brown with flying honeybees. They began lighting on the keg until was completely covered with bees. They slowly went down the keg and began going inside. We stood back and watched as the whole swarm slowly crawled down under the bottom and disappeared from our sight. However, there were a lot of the swarm still swarming around us and the new hive which was becoming their new home. The nail keg sure was a better home for them than a dirty old hole in a hollow oak tree somewhere out in the big woods. In a few days, Daddy decided to bring them home. We waited until it was good and dark on night and went for the beehive. We had already prepared a good place for them by placing a large flat rock up against the trunk of a large peach tree.

As we arrived at the beehive, Daddy had us be very quiet as he raised up the keg and gently set it down on a burlap sack, then raising the sack and tying it around the keg with a small rope. He then took up the keg and carried it to the prepared new location. Sitting it down on the rock, he untied the rope and let the sack fall, leaving access for the bees to come and go as they desired, and some mad bees desired. We ran with the lantern a few yards, leaving Daddy there to get stung all by himself. However, it didn't take him very long to join us with a few bees trying to find him in the dark and sting the daylights out of him. As we went in the house, making sure there we no bees following us, one of us said, "Now we are cattle men with one cow and Neal's bull calf up in Grandpa's pasture an we are beekeepers with our new beehive. Mama and Daddy laughed a little as we all washed up for supper. The Rollins family was forging forward in this unfriendly world; they were advance, very fast. Each time they moved, they had at least one more item added to their wealth, a bull calf and now a hive of bees. Now all we had to do was keep moving and accumulating object and things, at least one at each place we lived and in about a hundred years we would have a lot of items. That is if some of them didn't tie, rust out, or were not lost or stolen. But at least we were not moving backward—it was always moving forward and getting ahead one thing at a time.

One day while Daddy was at work, Mama decided to visit her sister May who lived about a half mile away. We all put on some clean seated overalls and took our journey up the pretty steep hill to where she lived. Aunt Mae and Uncle Tom lived with his mother and father and Tom's two brothers, Raymond and Jack, and another man who boarded with them and worked for them in the sawmilling and lumber business. When we arrived, there was no one home except Aunt Mae. All the men were at the mill working except her father-in-law, Jim. He was down at the river checking his fish baskets or traps. In about half an hour, Jim came walking up the road from the river carrying a large catfish weighing about fifteen pounds. We helped Jim clean his fish and get it ready for frying. We were waiting for an invite for lunch, and after Mom made several comments about how good the raw fresh fish looked, Mrs. Prater told Mom if she would help her fix dinner so we could eat some fish. Now, we were used to cleaning, cooking, and eating catfish, but they were not this big. It sure was some good eating. We saw them take about one-third of the fried fish and put it back for the working menfolk. That afternoon we boys went down to the spring to bring up a bucket of fresh cold water. The spring had been modernized. The Praters had taken a big icebox like one puts in the kitchen and took the bottom out and set it down the spring. It had a large door and metal latch, and the water came up to just under the door. The ice department sunk down in the water about one foot. They would open the door and set gallon jars of milk in the water in the bottom of the box to keep it cool. Just below the spring the little stream branch had been cleaned out for about ten feet and was about three feet wide; the bottom was covered with thin gray mud. It looked real nice. Lewis decided to step off in the muddy bottom, and when he did, he stepped on the top of some drink bottles that had been buried in the soft mud and covered with soft thin mud. We pulled up several of the bottles and examined them very carefully after washing the mud off the bottles. They were all filled with a kind of murky, muddy-looking water and capped off with drink bottle caps.

Irra opened one of the bottles with his bottle opener on his knife and smelled the contents. It smelled somewhat pleasant; then putting his finger down in the bottle until it was wet, he put his finger in his mouth and tasted it. It tasted some what like Mr. Dempsey's wine, but it wasn't nearly as sweet and good. We did not ever know why, but we dug out about forty or fifty bottles of that stuff and opened some of them and bursted the rest all around the muddy hiding place. About the time we were through destroying the stuff, we decided to taste some more of the heavenly nectar. It smelled pleasant and tasted even better. We each drank about a bottle each and started back up to the house. I was less drunk than they were becoming, so they let me take the water to the porch and yelled that we were going home through the woods. Mama and little Margret could get home the best way they could, for we didn't feel much like assisting an old woman and baby back to the house. As we went through the woods, we got very sick and began vomiting along the way.

When we all got so sick, we just knew that we were poisoned for sure. We were afraid to tell Mama what we had done and what we had drunk. She came home with Margret just about time for Daddy to come in. After he came in and saw us lying around about as sick as a poisoned dog, he asked what we had been eating. We told him about the fish dinner that we had. Mom told him to run up to the Praters and see if the fish had made any of them sick. Jack and Ramon had gotten in and went down to the spring for a bottle of cold "home brew." To their surprise it had all been broken and poured out. The smell of the heavenly nectar was so strong that one could smell it up to the yard. They were fighting mad! They ran all the way up the hill to the house and asked if they had seen anyone going to the spring that day. Mrs. Prater told them that the Rollins boys had brought up a bucket of water. Daddy was going across the yard as they were coming out of the house madder than an old setting hen after someone stole her eggs to buy coconut candy from Mr. Brown's store in Heflin. They knew who had destroyed all their home brew, and Daddy was going to catch the blunt of it. They cursed him and called us boys all the bad names that they could think of, and I think they must have been running with the Taylor boys because of the downright filthy language that they were spouting at poor old Daddy, and at that time he didn't even know what it was all about. They made him go down to the spring along with the other menfolk of the family and showed him what had happened. The boys wanted to fight Daddy, and Mr. Jim wouldn't let them hit him. Daddy later told us that if he had his gun, he would have shot at least one of them, and if he had had his lead-filled walking stick, he would have knocked on some heads. They had him come up in their yard and fired him from his log-cutting job and told him to move within a week.

Daddy was out of work, out of money with no transportation—one might say that he was up the creek without a paddle. He did not know which way to turn or which way to go. After Mama and Daddy had a long powwow about the entire situation, Daddy decided to go to Heflin and talk to the Cleburne County sheriff and tell him everything. It was a crime to make homebrew and sell it to another person, but to make it for your own use seemed to be all right so long as you didn't get so drunk that you bothered other people.

The next morning Daddy left for Heflin about daylight. We always got up about daybreak or a little earlier, for the Lord made daylight so we could see what we were doing, and it was a great sin in his sight for people to throw it away and not use it—so we used it every day even if it was Sunday, raining or whatever. We came out of that bed and ate a good breakfast and started doing something even though it might be setting around fussing with each other and talking about and cursing our best neighbors. And we sure did do a lot of that at times. To us we never had a real good neighbor, most of them even wanted us to pay back or bring back what we had borrowed from them earlier.

After walking for about three hours Daddy arrived in Heflin and went directly to the county sheriff's office. Mr. Johnson was now sheriff, and he had just arrived at his office to begin his long day of listening to other's complaints, laying aside his own feelings and desires, I'm sure he had rather be fishing or hunting with that long barrel pistol he was carrying strapped on his left hip with but of the gun pointing out front because he was left-handed. He knew Daddy from somewhere but Daddy couldn't remember from where since we had never had a run in with the law, maybe he had earlier worked around where Daddy worked. As Daddy stepped into his not so well kept office the sheriff said, "Mr. Wess how can I help you today?"

"Do you know the Prater family living down near the river just this side of Beason's Mill and Cedar Grove Church?"

"Yes, I believe I do. They are a fine family and they have never given me any trouble here in my office and if anyone has not been arrested for something I always believe they are good honest folk, for God knows we have plenty of the bad kind. Just last night my deputy and I stayed up almost all night trying to catch a man that beat up his wife and kids while he was wild from drinking some home brew that he bought from a neighbor. He got away so far, but John was still out there chasing him in the woods. I have got to go over to my house and get two bloodhounds, and then he will soon be caught. We had the man locked up that sold him that stuff," Sheriff Johnson replied.

Then Daddy unloaded on him all about what had took about the Prater family and what had happened as a result of it. Daddy was beginning to cry because he had never been fired from a job before, had never been evicted before, and had never been in this situation having no job, no money and having to move within a week.

Mr. Johnson said, "Mr. Wess, I know you are an honest and good man, for you have never been arrested for anything, and I know about the man and woman that you turned in for the Atlanta bank heist, for we jailed then and got a little reward money so we could put new bars on our jail windows and doors and get a lot of good new things that the jail needed. The reward should have been yours, but due to some foul-up in the paperwork, they sent us a thousand and two hundred dollars. That soft chair you are sitting in should be yours, but it is ours now and I want to thank you and your family for the brave work you all did and the way it has helped our jail, and most of all for getting these people off the streets and off the railroad. Now as soon as we round up our men today, we will go out there and talk with the Prater family and get something worked out."

"What should I do while this is taking place?" Daddy asked as he got up from the chair. Mr. Johnson had him set down again and told him to go over to the Red Cross and welfare office and tell them that you need some help, and that you are a hard worker but you are out of work and really need some help now. I've got to get the bloodhound and get over and find John and then get my running wifebeater and child abuser."

Daddy went over to the welfare office which was only a block away. (If one goes two blocks in any direction you are out of the main business part of town.) He went in and got in line; there was only one person ahead of him, and he waited his turn for the welfare worker to call him over to her desk. After a few minutes she called him over to her desk and had him sit down and asked what she could do for him. She knew him because we had lived next door to her when we lived in Heflin. Then Daddy poured out his soul to her, explaining in full detail all that had taken place the day before. She looked at him; he was beginning to cry, and she said in a gentle voice, "Mr. Rollins, since I know you are a hard worker we sure will help your family—that is why this office is here, and don't you even think about moving yet. I will turn a report to Sheriff Johnson, and if anyone moves it will be the family that has caused this trouble, and if Sheriff Johnson finds out that they have sold just one bottle of that stuff, someone will be locked up. We are a federal government organization, and we can't let good people like your family be put out in the road with nowhere to go while others sit around drinking their home brew and watching you suffer. Does your wife have a sewing machine, and can she sew garments like children's clothing?"

"She can sew real well, but since we don't have a machine she has to walk about eight miles to her mothers to use her machine, she makes all our kids' clothing except the bigger boy's overalls," Daddy replied as he began looking much more perked up and relieved.

"Go up to Owens's store and buy you a new sewing machine on credit and this office will give you two dollars to pay down on the machine and make sure you get a lot of different-colored threads—a spool of each color and get at least ten or twelve colors, he knows what you need. I'm calling him now and telling him to let you have this and you can pay him two dollars each month until it is paid for. He will deliver the machine for you and take this big box of precut children's garments and the sewing machine home and let Mrs. Rollins sew the garments, and we will pick up the cloth in about a week. We will bring her a check for four dollars and a new box of precut garments. If she sews pretty fast, it will take her about three or four days to do this and her housework too. And while you are here in town when Mr. Owens's truck come by for the box of cloth I'll fix up of groceries for your family and all this stuff is free—you don't have to keep working for that family and you don't have to move either. You and your family are under federal protection, and the sheriff will let them people know it," Mrs. Gilrd said as she handed him two one-dollar bills and got up from her chair and went over to another desk and picked up the phone to call Mr. Owens. Daddy left the office with mixed emotions; he wanted to cry because of all the good things our family would receive, and he was having the last laugh in the matter that made him have to come to town that day. This was one of the better things that were to happen to this year. Mr. Owens was waiting for Daddy at the front door of his big store. He greeted Daddy and took him over to the sewing machine department and let him pick out the one wanted. Daddy took the best one with the prettiest cabinet. It would cost Daddy only thirty-seven dollars and fifty cents, and he didn't have to pay any tax or delivery charges.

The machine and thread and instruction papers were loaded on Owens's delivery truck; the driver was a young black man full of fun and laughs. They picked up the stuff down the street at welfare office and off they went laughing and joking and telling wild stories along the road as Daddy was coming home, a much happier man than he was when he left. When they arrived it was a little after lunchtime and Mama had a large lunch on the table for the family covered with a nice cloth table cloth. After we unloaded the machine and canned food and other jupe sack full of other things, flour, cornmeal, sugar, salt, lard butter, dried bean, dried peas, and a lot of other things, we went in to sit down to have lunch; but Joe, the truck driver, didn't want to come in and sit at the table with us. He said for him to never sit at the table with white folk because he was black and also because he might not have good table manners. After one of the boys took his plate over to the stove wood box and made Joe some room at our table, Mom and Dad finally got him to sit down; maybe the smell of hot biscuits, hot gravy, and fried chicken helped a little. Joe was bashful at first, but in a minute or so he was laughing and putting the food down like the others. This was something we all needed; we needed to get acquainted with some black folk and associate with them and them associate with us so we could understand more about each other's race. Mama was so proud of Daddy that she put her arms around him and cried. Here he had gone to town and done something that would make life easier for the family, and she could do the sewing and look after little Margret at the same time. She had always wanted a sewing machine, and now she had one—brand-new that no one had ever sewed on before. Now we didn't have to move anywhere, and we had more store-bought food than we had ever had at any one time, and we could get that much free each week and Mama could make four dollars a week for sewing on her new machine with all that pretty colored no. 50 sewing threads. She even had a pack of twelve machine needles in case she broke one while sewing. As Mama and Daddy sat and talked about how the Lord had blessed them, they wondered why. Irra was pretty smart since Sam Jones told him how to pray, so he told them that it may be because the Lord sent us down to the spring three days before and broke the bottles and poured out the devil's home brew. We were very happy and well pleased with the way all had turned out.

Since Daddy did not have a regular job he could start making cotton baskets again, bottom a few chairs for neighbors and make some baby beds and playpens for babies to sleep and play in. Now he could do the garden work, fish a little and do odd jobs for other people so long as the welfare people never found out. They had given him about six months to find steady work. He knew that he could find a good job at any time, for everyone who hired him liked the way he worked and the perfectionist way he did everything that he did. Even if he went to milk the cow and could not "bad luck" his way out of it, he would first take a bow to the cow and apologize to her for taking the life-sustaining milk from her, and thank her when he was done. We never knew whether the old cow knew what he was saying or if she even appreciated his thanks, but she kept right on letting him pull he long tits and giving him her milk. Daddy was making about as much working like this, and maybe a little more than when he was cutting logs. And Mama was getting her sewing done within two days and rest the rest of the week, until she got her check and another box of garment parts to sew together.

The welfare lady really liked Mom's sewing, for she would add a little something extra to some garments, such as pleats and lace to the little girl's dresses and belt loops to the older boys' pants. Mom sewed every garment with pride, and she could do six days' sewing in about two days. The way that she managed that was that she cooked breakfast and lunch together and put on a pot of beans for supper and baked some corn bread after the biscuits we done. We might have to eat cold food for two meals if we didn't want to fire up the old stove and warm it up. However, we never complained, for she was making us money to live on and she wasn't out there in the garden bossing us around. Daddy was and he let us goof off more than she did. He hardly ever threatened to whip us "within an inch of our lives" like she often did if we left a few weeds or very tall grass in among the collards or taters or other green stuff that we were growing in our garden. Now about all Mama had to do was to cook three meals a day, wash iron, sew, keep house, take care of our little sister, bawl us out a few times a day, rejoice when we were not underfoot in the house. Sometimes she was downright mean to us—she would make us go in our room and study our schoolbooks especially when it was raining, snowing or something. Daddy was much easier on us boys; he only made us do some little things and stuff like going out in the woods and cutting down white oak trees, and sometimes hickory trees and lug them on our shoulders to manufacture wood splits and parts for him to use in his basket making, chair bottoming, baby beds, hickory ax, hammer, pick and shovel handles, and a lot of other things and stuff. Since he was not working in the log woods, he was good to us, but he was sometimes the most gosh awful Daddy that we ever had.

One morning Mama woke Daddy up before getting-up time; it must have been way before daylight. Our little sister Margret had become sick during the night, and she had a real bad case of diarrhea, vomiting, and high fever. And Mama wanted him to go to Heflin and get her some medicine from the county health office. Well, Daddy got dressed real fast and up the road; he went walking as fast as he could. It was still real dark and he was carrying a torch made from kindling pine splinters about a foot long to light his way on the road. When he got to the health office, they were just opening up. He explained about the baby's condition, and the head nurse thought that it very important that someone check the baby over real good, so she agreed to send the other to our house in the county health department's car and take some medicine with her for Margret.

When she arrived at the Rollins home, she got all the information from Mom that she could get and examined her over from head to toe. The nurse watched the baby for a while, while she looked up some things in her large medical book about babies and what they should and what they should never eat. She then told Mama that the diet for Margret had to be changed. She should be getting more solid food such as meat and grain cereal and to boil all the water and even the milk that she gave her. There was something wrong with what she was eating and drinking, and most of her diet had to be changed. After the nurse gave Mama some type of baby food to be mixed with warm water, she left for her office. Mama fixed some of the baby formula and fed it to Margret. She was still sick, and the food just wouldn't stay down. Mama didn't trust that old nurse anyway, so she decided to take matters in her own hands and do what some old black lady told her to do a little while back. Irra was called in and told that she wanted him to go in the woods and find a small red oak tree about as big around as a half-gallon fruit jar. Then with the sharpest blade of Daddy's double-blade ax, he scraped the outer bark of the tree, making strokes only to his left and never to his right. When this was done and the inner part was smooth and slick, he was to step backward seven steps and look toward the son, close his eyes, and walk forward to the tree with his eyes closed; and when and only when he felt the tree again without looking could he open his eyes. After touching the tree, he must open his eyes and then take the ax and cut seven chips of the soft bark with only upward strokes of the ax. Irra began to do what she had told him to do, but there was a yellow jacket nest about a foot from the tree. As soon as he started scraping away the outer rough bark of the tree, the little fellows came to greet him with a not so warm welcome. There is just one good thing about yellow jackets when they attack you; they attack you on the low part of you first, this is the feet and legs. I reckon this is to attack the running part of a person first so the feet and legs will crank up, get in high gear, and you begin running to get away and leave their nest alone. This sure worked with Irra; he ran off and left Daddy's sharp double-blade ax under the tree by their nesting ground. The yellow jackets settled down quickly, and Irra, after counting the seven stings on his feet and lower legs, walked back very slowly and ran up the hill a few yards away and proceeded with his witch-doctoring adventure. Irra returned with the bark and seven yellow jacket stings on his feet and lower legs. Mom boiled up the brew while putting turpentine and kerosene on his seven stings. As Mama was boiling the red oak tea to give to her only girl baby, she was crying all the while. Daddy and all four of us boys gathered in to see what she was crying about, and she told us. She said that all the time that she was having boys that she wanted a baby girl. Now that she had little Margret she thought that God was going to take her away from her for some reason.

Somehow when we get into trouble or were about to lose something so precious to us, as a beautiful baby girl, we then began to search our soul to find out why. Was it because that we never went to church? she wondered. Well, is it because we boys destroyed all that old devilish home brew? Or maybe it might be because of our cursing at certain times when we got disturbed or something? Or maybe God needed Margret to come up there and live with him because we boys didn't want Mama to have a baby girl? Somehow we will never know the real answer to this question for after Margret got the medicine and a few drops of the old ladies remedy of red oak tea she got better about as fast as she got sick. While she was real sick we were all praying for God to make her well again for we all loved her, and maybe we might have promised to walk down the road about one and a half miles to Cedar Creek Church. But now that she had recovered we could see no need in bothering God with the matter any moor and just let the good people go to church. It was a country church and we had good enough cloths to wear to a country church but we just could not get up enough religion to make ourselves go, and besides the catfish needed their Sunday ration of big red worms that we had dug up behind the stables at the barn. Now Mama had another home remedy to store up in her home remedy bank of her mind, and she had quiet a few of them stored up. She told us not to write any of them down for if we did it was bad luck of the worse kind, for if we wrote them down they might kill the patient and not cure them.

We stayed in the house on the river for several months after Daddy was fired from his regular job cutting logs. We had done real good with Mamas garment making and Daddy's baskets, baby beds and handles to fit anything from a small hammer to a nine foot handle for a briar blade. Mom's sewing machine was paid for earlier than she had to pay for it. She had made enough garments it seemed to cloth half the children on the welfare relief program in Cleburnee County. One day when the welfare office brought her the sewing package for the week she told Mom and Dad that in six weeks they were going to have to give up helping them with the rent, food and the sewing. She liked Mama's sewing skill so well that she offered to pay half the money Daddy had paid for the machine, so Mama let the worker pay her a check for eighteen dollars and Mama had eighteen dollars to get her some cloth and make her some dresses and things for her self. But Mama never left Daddy or us out, she bought him two pairs of overalls and us one pair each and she even bought Daddy two new shirts. We were all so happy of all that had taken place, even Daddy getting fired and us almost getting run off from our home. Daddy said one day, "I sorta think the Good Lord has done went and taken a liking to us after all. "However, we just couldn't make ourselves go to church, but I'm sure that all of us prayed secretly from time to time as we felt the need to.

At this point in time in this writing the author would like to explain who I really am. The name given me at birth was James Franklin Rollins. That is what is on my birth certificate down in Montgomery, Alabama. It now appears that Mama named me after Daddy's foreman where he worked at the foundry ramming or molding cast-iron sewer pipe. To some relatives, which have departed this walk in life and have gone to the Great Beyond, Daddy's boss may have been named James Franklin. It has been thought by some that while Daddy was in the foundry, he may have been given a new family member by his boss—me. After my birth on January, 23, 1926, Mom named me James Franklin, his boss's name. He made Mama change my name to John Frank Rollins, but it was never changed on my birth certificate. That makes me not to be the one that I always thought I was until a few years ago when my I got the birth certificate that I requested in order to get a passport to travel outside the USA. If that be the case, I might be the son of my dad's boss at the pipe foundry where Daddy worked. If this be true, then my daddy's boss was bossing my daddy around. Now no would like their son's father bossing them around. Perhaps that is why he quit his job making seven to ten dollars per day and moved to Cleburnee County and started cutting logs for about seventy-five cents per day. He surely didn't change jobs to get better pay.

Sometimes a husband or wife by their action can ruin a good life, and like our life can never be the same, for it is said that "One's life is like a diary in which he means to write one story but always writes another." At the beginning of this true story of my life, I mentioned how I was about to end my life; but one night at midnight I was awakened by a mockingbird singing, and I got out of bed and fell on my knees, and God and I had a quiet time of reality and fellowship together. And after falling asleep again, the Lord let me remember my past life from birth until that night. This is a true story as best as I can recall it in my mind. Some names have been changed, and there has been a little "puffing of the goods" as many do in advertising and storytelling; however, the story is basically true. If you don't believe me, ask my mother and father when you get inside the pearly gates of heaven and they will back me up; you will see. It had been said that one can tell 10 percent truth that one can see to back up the story and 90 percent lie, and well over half the people that hear or read it will believe every word of it.

It seemed that Mom and Dad were somewhat religious and seemed to want to go to church, but we only went a few times now and then. If it had been a crime to be a Christian and go to church and we had ever been brought in court for it, we could never be convicted. While we were moving from house to house, Daddy had an old "camelback" trunk that he kept his blue serge wool suit and all his papers in. It held several songbooks and other cherished items. As a boy, he attended a singing school for ten full days at a church. The teacher was really good, and Daddy learned how to sing and read music by note. He could sing sacred harp notes and could lead singing and the "so fa la mi re do" and stuff tike that. He would take his songbooks out and sit by the fire in wintertime and sing to us from time to time, and that was about all the entertaining that we ever were accustomed to.

Well, we had used up about all the time the welfare people were able to help us, so it was time to take on the task that we were now faced with. Daddy had to find a job, and we had to move from our home near the river to maybe some run-down shack away out beyond God's country and begin life in a different place, with different neighbors and friends. This was nothing to look forward to, but time was short and it must be done.

Daddy got up about five and set out on his journey into the land of needed opportunities. That morning he went to Heflin and began to talk to some landowners about renting a house. He met and talked with a Mr. Thrower who ran a grocery store, and who had farms to rent out as sharecroppers. He offered Daddy a house and small farm in Goose Neck Valley, about five miles from where we now lived. Mr. Thrower would let Daddy live there free, and we could raise all the corn and cotton that we could cultivate with one mule. We would give him half of everything we grew, and we would take the other half. Man, this was something different for us. We had a cow, a bull, and a nail keg full of honeybees, and we had land rented almost like we owned it. Boy, the good Lord must have really taken a liking to us—and Mama and Daddy were still dipping filthy snuff and Daddy even chewed old unsweet tobacco. We even used bad language and cussed a little sometimes when we got mad enough.

The next day Mom and Dad decided to go look at the house and scout out the farmland. They walked about five miles and finally arrived at what they thought was the house. They went over to a neighbor and asked if that was the Thrower place, and they told them to go on past that house, cross a creek, take the first little road to the right and it would be the first house on the right with a little barn to the left. When they arrived, they were both was disappointed; this was only a small shack of a house. It was only about twenty feet off the road. It was built with boards and buttons, and most of the buttons had been torn away and burned as firewood by the last sorry, lazy family that had lived there. And it was very filthy; the small side room had been used for a toilet with human dung piled in the back side, and it smelled to high heavens, and the rest of the house been on the relief program for there was about a one horse wagonload of empty cans piled up in the corner of the kitchen and dining room, the same type of canned goods that we were getting. The fireplace was full of wood ashes with the nails that had come from the baton and ceiling boards from the kitchen. However, they had moved out without tearing the ceiling down in the living room; there was one wide board torn down, and it was so wide they had tried to chop it up into firewood in the living-room floor, but their ax was too dull to chop it and just splintered it up a little. Daddy and Irra later put it back up so the living room would be completely sealed overhead. But the kitchen and side room had no ceiling at all. One could see a lot of daylight shining through the cracks where the roof joined the wall and through the cracks between the boards of the walls. The wind would sift out like cornmeal in a sifter before cooking. The whole house was well ventilated for summer and well ventilated for winter too. It would take a lot of fixing up, but we would clean it up and move in as soon as we could. Mama and Daddy looked around the garden and small barn that was built across the road where the cow and maybe Neal's bull could be sheltered. The little barn had one cow stall and one corn crib with a small hayloft and nothing else; however, it didn't seem to have leaks in the tin roof. As they looked around they saw some good farmland down in the creek bottom land and a large field of oats and vetch growing just beyond the pasture. It was summertime and the oats and vetch were beautiful; the oats were just in full bloom and the vetch was like a giant purple blanket waving in the breeze as the wind blew against it. One could smell the wonderful smell of the vetch blossoms coming from across the field and pasture, and it was a much more pleasant odor than was coming from the side room of the house. The house set at the foot of a pretty steep hill covered with medium-sized pine trees about six to ten inches in diameter and about twenty feet tall. However, this would change beginning as soon as we moved in. That hillside was designed by the Lord for growing cotton and not for growing pine trees.

After looking the place over Mama and Daddy decided to rush back home and bring us boys back with a shovel, a broom a pitchfork, a large bucket, and a hammer and some nails. As we walked down the road to our new home to be, other people living along the road stood and stared at us and probably wondered where that mob is going walking so fast. We were walking along the road in a line like dairy cows walking in a straight line across the pasture headed to the milking barn to be milked late in the afternoon. However, we were walking much faster than the cows usually walk, Daddy leading the line with Irra next carrying little Margret in his arms and Mama trailing the procession. It must have been quite a sight as we hurried along, each one carrying a tool or something. Neal was carrying a sack half full of foodstuff for us to eat about lunchtime, Daddy carrying his double-bladed Bluegrass hickory handled chopping ax, Irra carrying Margret on his hip, Neal carrying a sack of food, Frank carrying a shovel, Lewis carrying a hoe, and Mama carrying two buckets—one for fresh drinking water and one to carry out the human manure left in the side room of the house. Someone in the line was also carrying a broom to sweep up the place. When we arrived at our new home, we were all saddened and disgusted with the house—had we left paradise where we lived to come to this godforsaken place? Well we had, and it was because we found that blasted home brew at the Praters' spring and decided to waste and destroy it. All the joy of living in paradise was gone for good, the fishing down on the river was gone, and it seemed that we boys had destroyed our joy of living for good. Irra started crying and asked, "Did that lame old home brew cause all this?" By that time Mom was crying, and Daddy and the rest of the family were crying.

"Yes, son, you kids really messed things up for us. Things can never be the same. We have reached the point of no return. Lee and I made a bad mistake when we left Anniston for no good reason at all. I left a good job to move out of town because Lee thought that Frank had little dark beady eyes of an outlaw, and because of that move we have been slaving and paying for that mistake ever since. And it seems that there will never be a time to return to a normal life again. If I had stayed at the foundry I would have made foreman by the end of the year. Later a fellow worker said that two months late a top man died and all the foremen were promoted to higher positions, and that I would have been given Mr. Franklin's job." Daddy was crying by now; we all were. We all saw what bad decisions can do for a person, or in this case a whole family.

Then Mama spoke up and said, "My mother was an Indian, she was brought up in the ways of the Indian tribe that she belonged to, and her grandfather was once the chief of the tribe. However, he had let her father attend the white man's school for a while, and he was smart; he could read real well and had studied some old law books that he had found in a trash pile somewhere. And he had come up with a good formula for man to live by. He summed it up like this, she told me, and I will never forget it as long as I live; and if I and Wess had followed it, we wouldn't be moving in this run-down shack."

Daddy asked her, "Lee, do you still remember that saying?"

She replied, "Yes, I can tell you some of it and maybe all of it."

Then she started by talking about *need* or *desire*.

No. 1.   One has a need or a desire.
No. 2.   One now has a *plan* to fulfill that need or desire.
No. 3.   *Take action* to fulfill the plan.
No. 4.   The *results* of that action.
No. 5.   The *delayed results* of that action.
No. 6.   The *ultimate results* of that action.
No. 7.   The *reward or punishment of that action.*

"The Indian people are wise and work this formula in most of their daily lives. You boys never tried to keep this wise saying, and now we are receiving the longtime results of your action; we have already seen the quick results of your action by us having to move and Wess losing his job. Now we are going to see the delayed results of your action by having to move here and having to live in this awful place for God only knows when. The ultimate results of Wess and me moving out hear will be haunting us for the rest of our lives and you children are suffering from that move, and will be with you for the rest of your lives, You boys are about one-sixteenth Indian yourselves. And don't you ever forget your heritage. You will have the full right to wear a feather headpiece two days each month, but that don't give any of you the right to skelp anyone you want to just because you are mad at them or something. Now let's get on with our delayed punishment for you boys doing away with all that home brew—at least you could have slipped me and Wess a few bottles to drink for our stomachs' sake.

"Boys, what's done is done, and you can't recall that day and start over again. I suppose that a lot of people who shot someone dead and tried to run away from their crime and were finally caught and sentenced to hanging really wish that they could recall that day of the shooting and could put that bullet back in the gun and not do any shooting. But it is too late to repent after you have been caught and brought to the ultimate results of the crime. The ultimate result of you boy's crime we'll all feel the rest of our lives, now get on the punishment by shoveling up that mess in the side room, and take it across the road and down in the pasture or away out in the pine thicket and dump it out. While you boys do the cleaning, Lee and me will go out to the next house and get some fresh water from the spring just across the road from our house. That is where we will get all of our cooking and drinking water from; we have a well out in back, but we won't use the water except to wash with and scrub our floors with, and I think they need it right now. We will do the scrubbing maybe tomorrow while we get ready to move," Daddy said as he wiped tears from his eyeballs.

Daddy and Mama walked out the small graveled road to the other house to get some fresh springwater. They took the opportunity to meet the family that lived in the big mansion-type house about two hundred yards from our shanty. As they arrived, they saw the most beautiful house that they had ever seen out that far in the country. It was sitting on nice level land about fifty feet on the left side of the road—our house was on the right overlooking this house and another big farmhouse about a quarter mile down at the end of the road, and on a little hill stood a big farmhouse with a large level yard and a big barn. The family that lived there was named Burke. The family that lived in the big mansion-type house was named Rossier, John, Molly, and their twelve-year-old-daughter Sarah Jane. They called her Jane, and she was very beautiful but a little overweight, and with long sandy-colored hair a little curly near the end. She was the most beautiful girl that we boys had ever seen; we even argued about who was going to win her hand in marriage. We might have been crazy, but we were learning the facts of life, and we wanted to see which one of us could teach her. Mom and Daddy were just swept off their feet with the size of the new house. They met the family and found that Mr. Thrower owned their house and they were renting just like we were. Right then Mama and Daddy decided to get them out of that house and move in instantly. The family would have four large rooms with a hallway running from the large front porch with two rooms on each side. There was a large kitchen and dining room and living room joined together with a double fireplace to heat both rooms. On the other side of the hall were two large bedrooms heated with a double fireplace also. The large house had beautiful double windows with stained glass down halfway and beautiful stained wood below. The back hall door had only one wide glass-paneled door painted white. All the walls and ceiling were sealed with beaded tounged and groove sealing and was painted off-white. The front porch was sealed also. This must have been the home of a plantation owner or the home of some Arbechooca gold miner. There were mining shafts within five hundred feet of the house up in the woods across the road from the house. It took someone well-off to build an expensive home like that, but no one over around there could tell us who built it.

Daddy and Mama went back to the "little shack by the side of the road" and helped us boys clean it up. We didn't talk very much the rest of the afternoon. The house was pretty well cleaned out and cleaned up the best that we could without scrubbing the floors with a homemade corn shuck mop. Some of us boys would bring a well rope and bucket for the well in the backyard and bring the corn shuck mop to clean the floors and get it ready to move in. Daddy rented a wagon and two strong mules to move us in. He paid the owner of the mule team and big wagon two dollars for the use of them for one day. We boys went over there the next day and got the well windlass working with the rope and bucket and began to scrub the floors in all the house real good where the people who lived there before had used the little side room floor for their bathroom. Frank went down to the small creek in the pasture and got a lard bucket full of fine sand and scattered it on all the floors, and we scrubbed them again to make the old pine lumber shine pretty again, and they really looked clean when we finished with them. Since there were small cracks between the boards in the floor, we didn't have to worry about getting rid of the mop water; we only had to worry about having it stay on the floor long enough to scrub it, and when we had finished scrubbing it, we tried to mop it dry the best that we could and let the wind blow through the doors, windows, and cracks and do the rest.

The next day Daddy got up early and went to get the wagon and team of mules. It was about five o'clock, for he always wanted to tackle a big job early. He used to tell us "if a job is worth doing, it is worth getting an early start." Mama and Daddy had got some big cardboard boxes that they were saving to pack things and stuff in for to move, and they packed up most everything that needed packing, being careful not to pack it so things would get broken or damaged. This was easy for they had gotten a lot of experience in packing, unpacking, and packing again to move somewhere else. While he were gone to get the wagon, we boys started disassembling the stove, the beds, removing the mirror from the dresser, tearing the bedstead or frames down, and taking all the stuff out to the porch where Daddy could put the mules and wagon in low-speed reverse and back the wagon up against the floor, being careful not to damage the floor or knock the porch down but really not caring whether he did or not, for he would never walk on that porch again once we moved out. As we loaded the furniture and stuff on the wagon, we had moved so many times that we all knew where everything went but a few items that we had accumulated since our last move. These items would have to go on the wagon the best that we could place them. We had boxed up about twenty chickens the night before, and Daddy had built a hog-shipping crate the day before while we cleaned the floors of our new house. All these things would have to go on the last load. Since we were moving a short distance this time, we piled the stuff way up high on the wagon and let a lot of it hang way over the top bed of the wagon.

Because we started very early, we arrived at the new house about nine thirty and began unloading. It was hard to set up the things in a much smaller house, so some of them went on the front porch and a storage building just above the house. As we started loading the second load, Mama told us to gather everything from the garden that we could. All of us boys gathered beans, cucumbers, tomatoes green corn, squash, lettuce, beets, turnips, and a lot of other stuff. We arranged places for all these things the best we could on the last load. The wagon was filled to the top and piled high. This load was more or less unloaded in the yard quickly so Daddy could return the wagon to the owner. Irra and Neal moved the stove in place and hooked up the stovepipe into the stove flue that was directly above the stove while Mom, Frank, and Lewis started setting up the beds.

We all worked like a perfectly run machine, and most of the furnishings were in place quickly. The kitchen cabinet was set up quickly, for the stove, cabinet, and dining table had to be set up so Mama could cook some supper. But we forgot to get about a hundred fruit jars full of good things from the cellar. We had to rent the wagon and get a load of canned vegetables and a few little things that we had overlooked the day before. Daddy took Frank and Lewis the next day to really finish moving. We loaded all the canned stuff, some stove wood, our toy wagons that we had made, and a lot more vegetables from the garden and loaded the wagon down.

Then we went out in the garden and cut everything down with Daddy's briar blade and a large butcher knife. We were not about to leave anything for certain people to gather for themselves. We even pulled up all the onions and garlic in the garden. We pulled up all Mom's pretty flowers and threw them out in the yard. We went to the barn and got two big buckets full of fresh cow manure and, after we peed on it, threw it in the water well. Daddy told Lewis and me that it would sweeten and purify the well water for the next renter. After dropping about five or six slabs from the sawmill into the well and a few cornstalks into the well, we hightailed it toward Goose Neck Valley to our new home. We unloaded it quickly, and Daddy took the mules and wagon over where had rented them, and the man didn't charge him for the second day. This third load was unloaded in the yard just above the house and on the front porch. There was a cellar under the house with a door opening outside with a sloped shutter over it. All the canned goods were taken and stored in the cellar. All the other things were coming in place while Mama was fixing us some good food to eat. It was late in the afternoon, and the sun was sinking behind the hill just west of us, and we were all very tired and worn out. As we all sat around the table, however, Mom's good cooking was very lifting to us. At first as we looked around the somewhat small kitchen no one was saying very much. Daddy decided to break the silence and said, "Well, we will all get used to this little house quickly, and we will all join in and start nailing and doing the little things that will make the house look pretty good. It won't ever take the place of the other house, but we'll make do with what the Good Lord has provided us with, and we'll soon be living in that big house that John Rossir and his family lives in."

"But the Rossir family is living there and when are they going to move?" Irra asked as the others at the table perked up.

Mama said, "We are going to bad-luck them and cast a spell on them and they will be getting out of that house in a hurry to save their own hides. Wess and me will cast spell on the family until they can't stand it any longer. But if anyone of you tells anyone outside this family, the spells won't work. Wess and I know a few spells and how to work them, and we will get more if these don't work. I'm going to get your Indian grandma to tell me how that black mancast spells on the old man that stole Papa's horse. You boys will have to help us when we are ready." After we talked a little, the food tasted better, and we were all getting revived and our spirits we getting much higher. A shack of a house was no stranger to us. We had lived in a house that was this bad before when we lived on Grandpa's farm and his little house, but since we had lived in much better, it was very hard and disgusting for us to have to step down to this—this was the pits! How could we ever get used to such a horrible place? It would take a lot of getting used to, but wait we would, and bad luck and horrible spell the Rossir family clean out of the valley, and we were about to start that very day.

Our family had just decided to use all the witchcrafts and cunning devices that we could come up with to get the Rossir family out of the big white house near us. We knew that it might take a long spell of magic tricks to get the job done, but we were willing to do whatever it took to get the house empty for us to move in, and since both houses were owned by the same man, we felt that we could just move in and tell him later. But first we had to get the big house vacant of the present renters.

The next day Mama sat down at the table and began writing down all the things that she could remember from what she had been taught as a little girl while she was growing up with an Indian mother and something else as a father. In the olden days and nights, folk would sit around the big fireplace in winter and usually out on the porch in hot weather and talk of witchcraft and casting spells on other people to punish them or to get rid of them so as to get to obtain their belongings or property. As a small boy I listened in on some of these conversations at my grandparents' house and others' homes. In those days with no radios and no television and with only the new fashions pictured in the Sears, Roebuck catalog there was not too many things to talk about. In those days people would use witchcraft and stuff like that to get a man to leave his wife or a wife to leave her husband so the person casting the spell could gather in the spoil and maybe get the person left behind. However today in our modern times we are more merciful toward our victim, now we have mercy on the poor victim and just poison them or shoot or stab them to death and dispose of their bodies in any one of several different ways. A poor widow woman living about three miles from Grandpa's farm was pretty well known for her witchcraft spells. She would cast a spell on a person that she didn't even know for a few bushels of corn or a few gallons of sorghum syrup. Some said that she would "spell" them into the grave for a good cow, a fairly good horse, or a good brood sow or two. I heard some say the graveyards were filled with her artwork and tricks.

We wanted the Rossir family to leave the big house, but we would not call on this woman until all else had failed. There were a lot of things for us to do before we would go that route. Besides, we were just beginning our planning stage of the "getting rid of the Rossir family" game. Getting them out might be done very quickly or it may take a few months, but they were going if we had anything to do with it. I would lie awake at night and wonder if someone would come along meaner than us and wanted us to move out of the big house. Mom and Daddy always taught us children that we would reap what we sowed. With that being the case, we began to wonder about what we were setting out to do to the Rossir family. However, the big fat mama and the little dried-up man really didn't matter very much, but their beautiful blond daughter was a different story. She was just what each of us boy was looking for to spend our adult life with. When you are witching a family out of the house of your dream one must forget the welfare of the bewitched and think of only self and your own family. It is dog eat dog and do what you have to with no regrets afterward. Although we knew the journey that we were about to begin may wind up with the very thing we were about to do might be used against us if that family ever found out the truth. But we were about to embark on the treacherous journey of witchcrafting the family out of that beautiful home. But where would they go? Well, that was far from Mom's mind at this time; the desire for that big house had destroyed our conscience and ability to reason. That house had to become vacant and that was that. However, Mom wanted to go out there and get to know the Rossir family better and to look our new house over before we were to go out and claim it. The following day was Sunday and was a good time for Mom and Daddy to get more acquainted with the family.

Leaving us kids behind, they walked out to their house. They invited Mom and Daddy in to their home and gave them the grand tour of the house, showing them all the rooms and furniture, especially the kitchen and dining room. Mom eyeballed all the furniture in each room and remarked how nice it must be to live in a big house with all the nice furnishings like the Rossiers had. After the visit was over, as Mom and Daddy were on their way home, Mom was laughing and telling Daddy how nice it would be when the people were out and our family could move into that mansion among the big shade trees and a little brook running through the yard, and with the barn and stables and milking shed only a few feet from the west side of the big side porch running across the west side of the house. Of course, it would be real close and handy, but the smell would be horrible at times, especially during a long rainy spell, with all that wet manure so close to the house. And the large hog pen was close enough for one to throw the table scraps out the kitchen window and into the hog feeding trough below the window. Boy, that would be real handy—but what about the smell? Daddy told her that he would move the hog pen back a few yards as soon as they got moved in and settled down. Mom was so sure that she with the help of others could conquer and bewitch them out of that house that she even ordered some material from Sears, Roebuck and Company to make five pairs of curtains for the large windows in the front part of the house. She said that we could take gunny sacks and make curtains for the rest of that house. The following day she went out with her cloth tape measure and measured each window to make sure the new curtains would be just right for each window while the Rossir family was gone to Heflin. While measuring for the curtains, she saw a big white mean-looking bulldog chained to a tree out by the hog pen. The dog tried to break the chain and get to her, and she got away from that side of the house as soon as possible. As she walked home, she thought of the very first conjuring spell to put on the Rossier family—the old dog tail hair spell. The dog's tail hair spell went like this: you clip some hair from the end of the dog's tail and bury it under the doorsteps that would be used to move the furniture, and after the next full moon the family would get a sudden desire to move and take their dog with them. But if it rained the night of the first full moon, they would put off moving until the next full moon. Well, this was worth a try.

That night after we all settled down at the supper table, Mom laid out her plan before us. Daddy said that he wanted no part of it, for he was real afraid of dogs biting him for it

83

may have rabies. We boys had seen the big bulldog while fetching water from the spring just above the Rossirs' house and we were not overjoyed at having to cut hair from that dog's tail. But Mom said if we wanted to live and fine home, we must carry out this task at once. We all began to try to come up with a safe way to get the hair from the tip of the dog's tail without getting eaten alive, for this was a huge dog. We talked about giving him sleeping pills so he would sleep through the whole clipping process, but we didn't have any sleeping pills and it was too far from Heflin to walk up there and buy some. So we had to think of some other plan fast. Irra put his thinking to work. He said if we would get too small tree trunks about ten feet long and about four inches in diameter and nail an old bed quilt to the poles, we could throw the quilt over the dog and one stand on each pole while one of us would clip the hair off the dog's tail. We all agreed on that plan. Irra and Neal would hold the poles and slam the quilt over the dog and then stand on the poles while one of us would do the haircut. Since I was left-handed, we decided to let Lewis give old Rover the tail clip.

The next morning, Irra and Neal went down on the creek bank and cut two poplar poles about ten feet long to hold the quilt. Returning to the back porch, they proceeded with nailing the old quilt to the polls. Now we had to just wait for the Rossier family to take their next trip. The Rossir family usually went to Heflin every Saturday if it wasn't raining, for the old Model T Ford that they owned didn't have a top to keep out the rain. Saturday morning came, and at about seven o'clock Johnny, Jane, and Hollie loaded up and left for Heflin. As soon as they left, we headed for the job of clipping the hair from the tail of that big gosh-awful bulldog. Irra carried the poles with the quilt and we ran down the road to the house. We all stopped and looked at the bulldog and then looked at the house. We decided then and there that it would be worth the effort to go through with the hair clipping. The dog was barking and trying to get to us as Irra and Neal each took a pole and ran up and threw the quilt over the dog and stood on each pole, while Frank lay on the back of the dog to hold him down while Lewis clipped a wad of hair from the tip of the dog's short stubby tail. Irra and Neal retrieved the quilt and poles, and then they buried the dog hair under a big flat rock doorstep at the front entrance of the house and hurried back home before someone saw them doing what they were doing. As soon as we got home, Mom circled the next full moon on the calendar that she kept hanging on the kitchen wall. Now it was just a matter of time to wait.

The house that we were waiting for was a big four-room house with a large eight-foot-wide hall with two large rooms on each side of the hall and a fireplace in the living room and also in the kitchen and dining room. There was a long front porch on the front of the house and a long back porch on the back. It had a gabled roof and large windows and a front door at the front of the hall and a large back door going out on the back porch. The white paint was beginning to peel and spots of bare wood showed in places; however, it was still the best, the biggest, and best well-kept home in Goose Neck Valley. There was a water spring just across the narrow road in front of the house with the spring branch running through the side yard. There were small minnow in the little shallow holes of water as the stream ran through the yard and into the pasture near the back of the house.

The house had a grooved ceiling all through the house and hallway; this was paradise. We had never lived in a house like this, and to inherit this one would be a dream come true—and it surely was only a few days to wait. We would keep looking up at the moon after dark to try and see just how long we would have to wait for our dream to come true and we could begin moving in the new house. We waited and the full moon came and went, but the Rossiers were not moving. We waited for the next new moon to come and came it did but no moving out. Had we done something wrong? Had Lewis cut the hair from too far up on the dog's tail or something like that?

After a few weeks had passed, we decided to hold a special family meeting and maybe try something else more powerful than the hair from a dog's tail to make them move out and vacate the big house; after all, we believed that the big house was the answer to our prayers and that the Lord was going to just give it to us, just as soon as we could cast a spell on the Rossier family and made them volunteer and move out of their own free will. By now it seemed that the dog hair spell must be out of date or something had gone wrong. Could they have caught on to what we were doing and somehow "outspelled" us? We decided to walk up to our grandpa's house and try to get some new spells to make them move.

The following Sunday morning we all put on our cleanest clothes and started on our way just after daylight. The journey was several miles and it would take about three hours to walk it. By about ten o'clock we had arrived. After all the greeting, hugging, and kissing, Grandma and Mom started to fix dinner. Uncle Green went out to the possum box and got two large possums from the box, skinned them and game, them to Grandma to cut up and cook. Grandma and Mom cut them up and fried them along with a lot of other fixings and stuff. There was a large pan of Granny's large cathead biscuit and a big bowl of gravy. Boy, we had a feast! After dinner, we boys rode mules and played out in the woods while the older folk talked of witchcraft and spell-casting for the rest of the day. About four o'clock we started for home with some new knowledge of what to do next. Mom's and Daddy's spirits were high. They had gathered enough knowledge of spells and witchcraft to move half of Cleburnee County—so they thought. It was surely enough to get the Rossier family on the move and get the big house for our family. We decided not to do any of the cruel things that day, for it might be bad luck to do witchcraft on Sunday because after all we claimed to be Christians even if we didn't go to church. And we didn't want any more bad luck.

About five o'clock the next morning, which was Monday, it was time to get the game started. Mom kept a list of most of the things that we were doing to do to rid the big house of the Rossier family.

1.) First we caught the Rossiers' big yellow cat and we boys killed it, skinned it all except the nose, ears, and tail, and hung it up on their back porch while the family was about a half mile away in their cotton field completely out of sight of their home. When they came home that afternoon, they were fighting mad. Mr. and Mrs. Rossier came running out to our house and asked us if we had seen anyone around the house. Mom told them that she had seen a tall slim man with a nice hat riding out that way on a large spotted horse, and that she could see some kind of feathers in his hat. This was a big lie. Mom was describing one of Grandma's Indian relatives that Grandma had told Mom and Daddy could cast spells strong enough to make families completely die, or lose all their possessions. So far as we knew, Three Feathers Joe was out in Texas where Grandma was from. We were told that he had ridden this way from Texas on a big spotted horse with two lawmen close on his trail about two months earlier. The Rossiers believed Mom's story and looked all around the house for other signs of stuff done to them. Just to find their prized yellow cat hanging upside down over their back door was about to drive them insane. John Rossier ran back home and grabbed his old-ten gauge shotgun and started looking for the Indian rider all around the fields, and got in his Model T Ford and drove several miles up and down the roads. The next day John went up to Heflin and tried to get the sheriff to come and see the cat, but the sheriff refused, telling John that a dead cat would cost too much of the county's money for him to go out to Goose Neck Valley to investigate, and that he had to get out on the other side of the county to check on a murder where a man had been shot and a cow and calf was missing. Boy, was John Rossier madder than an old mother hen when you steal her baby chicks from under her spread wings! He let that sheriff know that his freshly skinned tomcat was far more important than a murdered man and a stolen cow and calf. The Rossier family couldn't work for a few days. They just went from house to house asking questions to get some information about the tall man and the spotted horse, but no one knew anything about it. We thought the dead cat would make the family move out of the big house real quick, but after about two weeks, we had to try another spell or trick.

2.) Mom's mother, who was dang near full blood Indian, passed down a story to us about an old Indian man who could cast spells on people and livestock and make the livestock die. He had done such a deed for Grandpa and Grandma many years before. But the old man had passed on to the happy hunting ground in the sky many years ago, leaving no answer to his witchcraft powers. However, Grandma told us that he had gathered a large bundle of willow branches from the south side of a large willow tree that was growing down on the south creek bank, wading out in the cold water to cut only the limbs that were touching the water. After gathering the branches, he sat down on a large flat dock and kindled a rather large fire from some dry pieces of wood that he went into the woods and brought out to the large rock and sat in silence for a few minutes as he waved his hands over the fire. After a few minutes, he bowed three times toward the fire and began burning the willow branches in the nice glowing flames and chanting some unknown language as he burned the willow branches. Four times as he sat there before the fire, he leaned back and gave out a loud bloodcurdling scream as if he was dying. Grandma said that she went out to see what was wrong and he only said, "Leave quickly lest you die with your neighbor's cattle." The following day their neighbor hauled off four cows to the bone yard that lay deep in the woods about a mile from Grandma's house, driving the wagon up her drive and almost through her yard. The old man slept on the porch that night wrapped in a heavy Indian blanket. The next day as the cows were being hauled by the house, he was thinking, "My family will eat good for a while." As night fell, he got on his large black horse and rode off in the direction of the bone yard. The bone yard is a place in the deep woods where people haul of their dead horses and cows to be eaten by the buzzard and other wild animals.

Mom and Daddy decided that we kids could try to cast a witchcraft spell and kill the Rossier family or set them to moving and vacating the big house, for after all, now it belonged to us as soon as we could get it empty. Mom carefully instructed us how to get the willow branches and do the witchcraft. We boys set out to get the willow limbs. There were no willow trees growing on the south creek bank anywhere in Goose Neck Valley. But we knew if we wanted to live in that big white mansion among the big oak trees, we had better not come back empty-handed. As it was we walked down the creek for about four miles to where it ran into the river below Howell and Turners Store. There was an old iron bridge crossing the river just below the store. There was a dam across the river about two hundred yards above the bridge. Just below the dam was a large sandy shore where people came to fish for large mud cats and brim. Lo and behold, there was a large willow tree standing on the south bank with a lot of willow limbs dangling in the water because the water had washed some of the dirt from under its roots. This was just what we were looking for. As we gathered the slender branches from the tree, a man fishing nearby asked why we were gathering the branches. Irra told him that we used them to weave mule muzzles to put on our mules to keep them from eating our green corn while we were plowing the corn. He said that he had seen wire muzzles but never willow limb muzzles. We told him that the smell of the willow muzzles delighted the mules and that they walked a little faster and never seemed to get tired. As we were leaving, the man laid down his bamboo fishing pole and began gathering willow limbs. A few weeks later as we cRossierd the river bridge, we saw no low-hanging branches on the willow tree; however, we saw mules plowing along the road wearing willow limb muzzles.

When we arrived home with the willow branches, they were about four to five feet long, Mom showed us a big rock out by the woodpile, where we sawed and chopped wood for the cookstove. She had us go out in the woods and gather a lot of dead limbs under the standing trees to burn the limbs. She told Neal to start the fire about five feet from the large rock and sit on the rock and bow three times toward the Rossier house and begin burning willow limbs. Since she didn't know what the old Indian was saying, or what it meant, she told Neal to start chanting in a low voice. "Rossiers, Rossiers leave the big house." Each time he would say it, he would wave his left hand over the fire as he held the small willow twigs in his other hand, slowly burning them in the hot fire. After sitting there for what seemed to be forever, maybe about an hour, he jumped up and started yelling. Mom was watching him from the small living-room window, and when she saw the action, she ran out to see if maybe an evil spirit had revealed something to Neal. "Did the spirit world give you a good answer yet?" she asked.

"Hell no, but these damned mad yellow jackets living under this rock sure as hell did. About four or five went up my britches leg and stung the piss out of me. The lame Rossiers can keep that house, or maybe we could kill them or something. If you want to talk to the evil spirits, you set on this rock and argue with them. If this is their answer, I don't want to argue with them anymore," Neal replied as he quickly got out of his overalls and began slapping yellow jackets.

Maybe we can move to another rock and start over; it is still about two hours until dark," she said as she began to swat a mad yellow jacket.

"Let Irra or Frank do this stuff. If the evil spirits is mad at us for wanting that house, it may be a big rattlesnake next time, We may have bit off more than we can eat on this one, and are you sure that you know how to do this? If Grandma left out anything, we might wind up dead and in the bone yard. Them yellow jackets may be sent from the spirit world and they may have the souls of them cows that Indian killed. Them was the meanest yellow jackets that ever stung me," Neal said as he walked toward the house trying to put on his overalls again and hoping that there were no more yellow jackets up his britches legs. At that point in time we decided to stop our witchcraft efforts for the time being and wait for the spirits to take over and make John Rossier and his family move from the valley. However, we were not giving up completely; one might say that we had just begun to fight using the evil spirit world against the Rossier family.

Irra had ordered a book of magic tricks and witchcraft from some publishing company that he read about in a magazine he found in a trash dump near our house while we lived in Heflin. The book promised all sort of powers through the use of witchcraft. It told how to make a portion from a dead green frog that by putting it in any lock it was supposed to make it open. The book told him how to make girls want to get real close to him by soaking his body in the bathwater laced with honeysuckle blooms and a little honey. The book had a long list of "bad luck" things that if one did, they were sure to have bad luck. Daddy and Mom already knew dozens of the bad luck tricks or things that they sometimes used to keep from doing things that they didn't want to do. Molly Rossier was very superstitious about almost everything that she had any dealing with. A few of the things were:

"If you measure a baby, you are measuring it for its coffin."

"If you let a baby see itself in a mirror it will die quickly."

"Don't take ashes from a fireplace, heater, or stove on Saturday, or your house may burn down."

"If you set out a small cedar tree as soon as it is large enough to shadow your grave, you will die."

There were so many "bad luck" sayings that they cannot be listed at this time. Mom and Molly Rossier sat for several hours and told each other the scariest ghost stories. Mom was trying to scare her into moving out of that big haunted house and I think maybe Molly was trying to talk Mom into moving out too. They told so many stories that we boys was afraid to go to bed at night or to even go to the fields to work. Molly was just as afraid to go to bed at night. After a day or two of telling ghost stories, we decided to turn the heat up another notch or two. Mom told us to think up some real scary stuff to do to the Rossier family. The first thing we boys decided to do was to go to the creek that ran through our pasture and catch a few water snakes and put them in the water spring where we all got our water. We dammed up the creek with rocks and mud, and then dipping the water from the small fishing holes, we caught about a dozen water snakes and put them in one of our cotton-picking sacks and tied it to a pole with a rope and brought it home. We also caught about ten or twelve pounds of fish, brim, catfish, and other makes. After the Rossiers went to bed that night, we went to the spring and dipped up three big buckets of water and emptied the sake of snakes in the spring. The next morning we watched for the Rossiers to go to the spring for some fresh water and Irra and Neal grabbed a bucket and went to the spring too. Molly was crying and shouting as loud as she could, cursing the snakes and wondering how come so many came and jumped in the spring. Irra was pretty quick thinking and said to her, "Somebody told us one time that when a lot of snakes come to your house on spring, someone in your house was agonna die quickly, for them snakes sometimes like to eat dead people."

"Did you ever hear of a snake eating a dead person?" Molly asked.

Irra replied, "Yes, when one of my uncles died something came in the front room and got up in the coffin and bit all over his face, neck, and hands and even got in his shirt and bit him on his stomach. Both ears were eaten off and part of his nose. They found a large seven-foot shedded snakeskin draped across the coffin and reaching to the floor. They said that the next time someone dies and the carcass is left in the house, that will stand guard over them with a loaded shotgun to keep the snakes away." Of course none of the story was true, but Molly believed every word of it. She ran out to tell Mom about it, and Mom confirmed the story although it was a big lie. Now Molly thought the snakes had come to do an evil thing. They were about ready to move, but still they were not fully ready to start moving, but they couldn't find a house in the valley that they liked, so they stayed on. And as they stayed on, we kept on trying to scare them away. Ghost stories and scary tales flew between the two families like real bullets in a gun battle. Each family was trying to get the other family to pack up and move clean out of the valley so the remaining family could settle down and have some rest.

Daddy was afraid that Mom would go completely nuts worrying over that big house if we didn't move away very soon. Mom would sit by the window and cry for hours as she looked across our yard and down the road at the house of her dreams. We boys overheard her trying to talk Daddy into slipping in the house at night and killing the whole Rossier family and letting someone else find the bodies a few days later. However, he would do nothing of the kind. He would go along with the witchcraft and ghost tales and all the bad luck things—but no killing of the people, maybe killing their hogs, cow, mule, and a few chickens, but not the whole family, maybe just John and Molly but not the girl, Sarah Jane. Daddy told Mom that the whole mess was over and that he had better never heard anything about the big house or the Rossier family again. Mom cried for about two weeks as she sat at the window and longed for the Rossier home, but now it was paradise lost for her.

All the planning and witch stuff came to a sudden halt. We began to get on with our life, farming and normal living again. We even talked about going to Cedar Creek Church. However, the religious feeling soon wore off. We decided that a couple of his half-grown pigs would sure taste good on our table, and maybe we should have them because he wouldn't move out and let us have the big house. So while they were off in the far cotton field, the two big pigs were collected by us, butchered, and salted down in our cellar, and we nailed the cellar door shut. The only way to get into the cellar was to move Irra's bed and take up two floorboards and drop down into the cellar to get to our new meat supply. The Rossiers' chickens would fly over the chicken fence and go up the hill through our cotton patch and go all the way up the hill to our corn and pea field on the level top of the hill. This corn and pea field was about a quarter mile from the chicken fence. When the chickens had eaten all our peas that they wanted, they would spread their wings and fly back to their pen and land inside the pen. We became tired of his game chickens eating our peas and decided that fried chicken was better to eat than pea soup and corn bread. During the summer and fall, we had many a Rossier chicken for dinner. All we had to do was to go up the hill and shoot one or two chickens and circle around the hill and come home with the chickens in a feed sack walking between the cotton rows so no one could see what was happening. We were always very careful to let no one see us dressing the chickens. At times when we were sure the Rossiers could see us, we would kill one of our own chickens and put on a great display as we dressed it in plain view of our neighbors. At one time, after dressing two of the Rossier chickens, Mom invited the Rossiers over for Sunday dinner. They accepted the invitation and came over and enjoyed two of their prize roosters thinking that they were eating two of our Rhode Island reds.

We learned to get along with our neighbors, even the Rossiers. We could endure them as long as the two pigs lasted and as long as the chickens kept coming to our pea patch. Just down the road from the Rossier family lived a large family, the Durke family. They lived about a half mile from us, and their house was the last house on the road. Their home was a large house up on a little hill and in plain view of our house. We could see about everything that went on in the front yard, front porch, barn, and the garden. As we watched, looking across our pasture and cornfield, we could even recognize every member of the family: Bob Durke, his wife Betty, their three daughters Bell, Sue, and Bobbie, and two sons, Troy and Jim. All three girls were very beautiful. Bell was nineteen, Sue was seventeen, and Bobbie was twelve. Troy was sixteen and Jim was thirteen. The family was closely connected and didn't reveal information about each other. The girls dressed very nicely and wore bright colors, especially their underwear. We boys saw the under things hanging on the garden fence and we wanted to see more. As we would pass their home going to work in our cotton field a few hundred yards beyond their house, we saw the girls as they would come out of the house and line up along the road in front of the house. Boy, this made our male hormones kick in full force. The girls sat on a bench on the bank of the road and displayed the beautiful underwear they were wearing. Their brother Troy walked with us to the field and told us that the girls would go with us out in the wooded area between our field and their house and give us anything we wanted if we would give them fifty cents each. Irra asked him how he knew that Sue, the most beautiful one of the three, and the one wearing the red panties, would let him have sex with her for fifty cents. Troy said, "She lets me and Jim do it for nothing, or maybe we do some of her work for her and she goes out to the barn and spreads out her chubby legs for us."

With a big grin on his face, Irra asked, "Do you mean that if I give her fifty cents, she will let me have it?"

"Yes, if you give me fifty cents and wait here I will get her for you," Troy said as Irra reached in his pocket and gave him two quarters. Troy ran back to the yard and talked with the girls for a minute or two while Irra waited after sending the other three boys to the field to hoe cotton. Troy sent Sue out in the wooded area to meet Irra. Sue was smiling and seemed very happy.

"Do you want to do it here or get a little further up in the woods so no one can see us?" Sue asked as she pulled he dress up a little above her knees. They agreed to go a little further up in the wooded area under a big pine tree. There Sue pulled up her dress and took off her red panties and exposed to Irra the most beautiful sight that he had ever seen. She saw that Irra was bashful or afraid to go on. Sue assured him that it was all right.

Irra had never seen something so beautiful. He had often had daydreams of being with a beautiful girl and being able to do all the sweet things that boys can do to girls, but now he was about to wake up to reality and get it on with one. Her white body and legs and other things were staring up at him and seeming to say, "Come on, it is yours." He sat down beside her and began stroking her beautiful body and legs with his left hand as his right hand began touching and rubbing her most sensitive parts between her slightly chubby legs. And he was getting all this for a half dollar, and the best part was yet to come. After a few minutes, he lowered his overalls and climbed into the right position and got the show on the road. After a few minutes, they both were completely satisfied with the action, and Irra got up and got his clothing back in their proper position. Sue said as she began to get he panties on and her dress arranged properly, "Irra, I'll give you all you want if you won't tell anyone. Just walk by the house and I will meet you here in a few minutes." She very gently put her arms around him and kissed him; it was the first time a beautiful girl had ever done that. He wanted to stay there and talk and hug more, but he had to go on to the field before the other boys came to find him and see what was keeping him from hoeing cotton. Neal asked him what he had been doing, but Irra only grinned and said he was talking to Troy. It was many months before he ever told anyone about his adventure. During the next months, he met Sue in the woods and got his share of her body for free. He finally got afraid that she would want to marry him and he wasn't old enough or ready for that; however, he often dreamed of going to bed with her and waking up in the morning with all the love he wanted in a soft warm bed with him. However, he finally realized that life was more than girls and that "stuff" that he was gettin' a limited supply of for free. And it was getting on over in the year and he had to think about his future and going back to school.

From where we lived we could see the Durke house and yard very well. We could see their fields and a small spring branch where they got their water. From time to time the Durke family would have a dance and party till after midnight, this happened about twice a month. Mom would sit in our living room looking out the window or out on our front porch and watch the family plan the weekend parties. About five o'clock in the afternoon she could see Bob Durke walk out of the woods with a five-gallon jug of moonshine whisky on his shoulder and hide it in the bushes on the branch bank just below their house. As he cRossierd the cotton field with the jug, we knew that there was a party about to take place that night. About dark on the day he brought the whisky out, the crowd would begin to gather; it was made up of farmers, sawmillers, and men of all kinds. Some ladies would also come, but it was mostly young and middle-aged men. As the dancing and partying got under way, we would sit on our front porch and watch the men go down where the whisky jug was hidden in the bushes. We would also watch the girls and men couple go up and holding a lighted lantern walk up in the field above their house. The family had an old pump organ that furnished the dance music for the party. We would sit and listen to the organ blasting out religious tunes as the couples danced out in the front yard, on the porch, and in the big living room. Hearing the music going on, one might think a church-type revival was going on. However, it was far from that; it was a wild drinking; sex party was going on. This would last 'til midnight or sometimes an hour or two later. Since we didn't go to church, we would circle around through our cotton field early on Sunday morning and cross their cotton patch.

We would usually find an old cotton mattress out in the middle of their field. There were always a lot of shoe scuffle marks around the mattress and a few balloon-type things lying on the ground too. Daddy told us not to touch those things for they were evil and full of disease and evil stuff. We boys played very dumb about these things; however, we had learned all about them from the Taylor boys who were picking them up on lovers' lane near Heflin, washing them and selling them to high schoolboys in Heflin. After seeing the results of the partying, we decided that it was definitely not a church revival. After seeing what was going on, Mom and Daddy could see how the Durke family could dress so nicely with very little work going on. One night after the organ started playing and it was fully dark, Daddy and Irra decided to slip up the creek bank and see what was going on at the whisky jug. As they sat quietly about fifty feet away and well hidden in the tall cotton, they watched Bob bring the men down to the jug one or two at a time. He would pour out a small cup of the evil spirits for each one, and in return each one gave him some money; it seemed to us a dollar bill. Troy had told us boys that each of the girls was paid about a dollar every time they took a man up in the cotton patch to the makeshift bed. However, we dared not tell Mom and Daddy about the girls getting paid that much for their services because they might find out about Irra and Sue and what they were doing. Somehow during this time perhaps some of the other boys got acquainted with Sue and Bobbie. Their brothers were getting all they wanted from them and trade the berries to the girls for their services. Mom would get mad when we came in with almost empty buckets, so we would make up a wild story about going swimming or fishing. I don't think she believed us. Since we didn't bring in many berries, there were not many quart jars filled for the winter. That meant very few blackberry pies for us when we would come in from school. But as they always say, "You can't have your cake and eat it too." So we had our prize cake before, so there was no need to expect to get more reward now.

As the weeks past the Durke family took a liking to Mom and Daddy. The girls had already taken a liking to us boys and boys were also very friendly. So to keep us from knowing what was really going on at their parties, they decided to get a young preacher that had been coming to the parties to come and have a prayer meeting and preaching service one Saturday night. We were invited to the services, and so were the Rossier family. Our family put on our best clothes and walked out the road to their house. They had an old wagon seat with springs on the porch and chairs and a bench set up in the front yard. They also made extra seating by laying down large sticks of firewood and laying wide wood boards on the wood sticks to form more seating. Other neighbors were invited and some of the party gang too. The Durke family wanted to make a doubleheader out of the service. All the people were seated, with the three girls seated on the wagon seat up on the porch. The other guest we seated in the front yard. The porch was about four feet higher than the yard, and there were a few large rosebushes down in front of the porch. The rosebushes had been cut down to about one foot above the floor of the porch. About all that was left of the bushes were large trunk stems covered with a lot of large thorns. There were four lanterns and two kerosene lamps set up on apple-crate boxes on the porch, and it was well lighted. As the girls sat on the wagon seat, they sort of opened up their legs a little and pulled up their beautiful flowered dresses well above their knees so one could see the pretty underwear they had on. Sue was wearing red panties; Bell was wearing black, and the younger, Bobbie, was wearing pink.

Betty went to the organ and played the same songs that they had been dancing to the week before while the preacher led a few songs. Since there were no songbooks, the song service were not the same that one would hear at the First Baptist Church of Heflin or Cedar Creek. As the people sang, the three girls put their "merchandise" on public display. Some of the men began to squirm on their seats; we boys kind of did the same thing. There were about thirty-five people there that night. Some of the men got up during the service and went down to the spring, not for water but for a snort of the white lighting. The girls would get up one at a time and go inside while some of the men were milling around as the long song service went on. After about forty-five minutes, and after the preacher had made a few visits into the house for a drink of water or something stronger, it was time for the preaching. The preacher, we will call him Mr. Clark, got up from a wooden chair where he had sat down only a minute or two before. He was pretty well lit on the white lightning and was staggering about on the porch. He read a verse or two from the Bible and laid it in the chair and began his sermon. As he preached, he would take a step or two forward and then stagger backward. After a few minutes, we could tell that he was going under the influence fast. He started from the back of the porch grabbed on to a porch post with his right hand while making a gesture with his left hand. As he staggered into the post, the bottom of the rotting away post gave way, and Rev. Clark fell headfirst into a large rosebush. His feet were almost straight up and his head and body was down among the large rose thorns.

93

He began screaming, "The devil has done got me. Get me out of here quick!" Some of us could not stop laughing long enough to help him out of his pain and misery. Those large rosebush branches were all around his body and head. Mr. Durke grabbed an ax from the woodpile out behind the house and began chopping the rosebush just above the ground, holding each branch away from Mr. Clark's head and body the best he could while others held the rosebush away from Clark's body and head the best they could. When Rev. Clark was retrieved from "the devil" and the rosebush, his face and head was bleeding a lot. His shirt was torn and was getting pretty well soaked in blood. He was pretty well drunk by now and kept begging the devil to let him go. After being retrieved from "hell" or the thorny rosebush, John and Betty Durke removed his torn shirt and began cleaning up his scratched-up head, face, and body. Betty yelled for one of the girls to get some warm water from the reservoir of the stove to wash him off, but the girls couldn't hear her, for they had each paired of with a young man and headed for the barn and cotton field. We Rollins boys felt very bad about what was happening, not because of the preacher falling into that old "hell" rosebush, but because their girlfriends had gone out in the night with other lovers. One of the girls told us the next day that the other men didn't mean anything to them; that was just a way to get the family some money to make life a little easier for them. Somehow this eased our heartbreak a little and made each of us realize what was involved with the girls and to realize that life is not a bed of roses even for a young boy. We were used to the preacher taking up an offering before preaching, but it didn't happen this time. He must not be a Baptist preacher; they believe in the world-famous verse, "Where three or four are gathered, there shall be an offering taken." So we Rollins boys held on to our nickels and dimes that Daddy had given us to put in the offering plate or hat so we could pay the girls so that life would be a little better for them. But if Mom and Daddy should ever find out what was going on between us and the Durke girls, life for us would not be a little easier. The church part of the service broke up, and we all felt sorry for that scratched-up, skinned-up, and bruised-up preacher.

He just kept on saying, "Mr. Bob, don't let the old devil drag me into that rosebush again." His shirt was torn badly in several places, and his tough hide was just as torn up. He just kept on bleeding, and Betty and Bob kept on washing him up, and the girls kept on their trips to the cotton patch and barn hayloft. The men kept on visiting the big jug that Bob hid down below the water spring. After about most of an hour Betty started peddling the old organ again, but this time it was party time and the dancing started up. After a few minutes of watching drunk men and pretty girls dancing together, Daddy rounded us up and set out down the road for home. We all know that someone else's misfortune is no laughing matter, but pardon me and let me laugh a little even now as the incident comes to my mind. Out in the country one don't find very much to laugh about; however, this incident will keep some of us laughing for a long time. We never saw that fine young minister again. He probably doesn't like roses till this day. He is probably saying, "Give me my roses after I'm dead and not while I'm alive."

Our family kept on working very hard on the farm and trying to make all the money we could working for others in our spare time. Daddy was mostly cutting logs for sawmillers and weaving cotton baskets to sell in Heflin to other farmers. We boys would go to the big woods about two miles away on Sunday and help Daddy cut down white oak trees to work into splits to weave the biscuit. He could weave three nice large baskets each week to help our income. However, this year we didn't go to the woods to pick huckleberries very much. Mom was getting big and fat. Her stomach was so big that she could hardly walk, and she stayed inside the hot house almost all the time. Some days she would sit out on the porch to keep cool.

Early one Sunday morning Mom told Daddy to go call the doctor for she was hurting real bad. Irra asked her what was wrong and she told him that she must have caught the flu bug over at the Durke's preaching service. After Daddy went over to the Wintam home to call Dr. Caffey, he told us to go off in the woods and hunt birds with our flips or slingshots and stay away from the house until after the doctor left. Neal asked him why we couldn't come back to the house until the doctor left and he said, "Lee is very sick with the flu bug, and if you all catch the flu, you will all probably die because the doctor may not have enough medicine for the whole family." Daddy had cooked a big pan of biscuit-type bread; it was about two inches thick. We cut off a large piece for each of us and put some thick sliced ham that we sliced from the Rossiers' stolen hog in the bread. We headed for the wooded section up and over the hill north of our house. About an hour later we saw a car coming toward our house. We could see the road about a mile away, but we couldn't see our house from where we were hunting bird, snakes, and anything that could fly, run, or crawl. We boys ran through the woods and stopped up in the cornfield that was on top of the hill behind our house. As we approached the field we saw three of Rossiers' chickens eating our peas that we were growing there. Well we circled the chickens so they couldn't just up and fly away. Now we were very good with our flips or slingshots, as some preferred to call them; we decided to eat some fresh chicken. All four of us declared war on the flock. Within three or four minutes, we had won the battle and had three dead chickens for our victory. There on top of the hill we cleaned, skinned, and prepared the dead birds for a cooking over an open fire. Irra kindled up a pretty big fire, and we cut and ran hickory sticks about five feet long through the chickens and hung them over the open fire to cook. As we were waiting for Dr. Caffey to leave, which took about two and a half to three house to decide to go, we finished cooking the hens and had ourselves a real feast of partially cooked chicken, with no bread and no salt. However, we really did enjoy most of it. We had quite a bit to take home when we were really filled up.

We waited and watched for Dr. Caffey to get in the car and leave so we could come off that hill with our half-cooked chicken. Finally he came out of the house with his black bag in his hand and a box or something in his other hand, got in his little gray car, and drove away. Boy, were we glad. It seemed that he was there forever, but it had only been about three hours. When we arrived at the house, Daddy met us out in the yard and invited us in to see his new prize. He led us into the room where Mom was and said, "Come over here and see your new baby brother." He was grinning from ear to ear as he pulled back the new blanket to show off the new baby boy.

"Is he really a boy?" Neal asked as he looked at the baby. We were all looking to see if the doctor had brought Mom a boy or maybe another lame girl. Our sister Margret was now just one of us, but another girl would have been too much. Irra said, "If you ever have the flu again and the doctor leaves another baby, we will have to just kill the Rossiers and take over that big house. We just about don't have any place to sleep."

"No, Irra, Lee, and I have decided to get us a bigger house if all the stuff fails to make the Rossiers move. After Christmas we can probably rent a larger house, I'm starting lookin' around as soon as we have all the crop gathered in," Daddy replied. Daddy always made sense when he spoke, and we believed him.

We put the scrap chicken on the table and told Daddy and Mom that we were going to fry it for a spell, after washing some of the ashes and other things off the chicken. Mom looked awful hungry after a case of the flu like she was recovering from. "Is there something we can take to stop us from having the flu so that that lame old doctor keeps on coming over here and dumping off a bunch of secondhand babies," one of the boys said as he put some chicken in a big cast-iron skillet and set it on the wood-burning range stove.

Daddy grinned and replied, "Maybe we can find some herbs weeds fennel or something to take to keep us from getting the flu." Now it was time for us boys to name the baby, so we thought. But Mom informed us that she had already named him and had sent the name in by Dr. Caffey; his name was Henry Caffey Rollins. He was named after the doctor who delivered him. All Mom's and Daddy's children were named after the doctors that had delivered them, all except Margret and Irra. Margret was named after the lady lawyer that helped Mom get Daddy in the veteran's hospital, and Irra was named after someone that Mom would not reveal or boast about. So we never knew whose name he was carrying. Some thought it might have been someone that Mom got acquainted with in Anniston while Daddy was at work in the foundry. That worried the daylights out of the whole family, including Irra, but Mom would only grin and stop talking when the subject came up. And Daddy wouldn't talk about it either; perhaps he was named after who got burned up in the hot molten iron at the foundry while Daddy was feeding the furnace. That was one of the most not talked about things in Daddy and Mom's life. We all accepted little Henry Caffey and decided to call him Caffey. That didn't set too well with Daddy since his name was Henry Wessley. He thought that Mom could name one of the boys after him, but it just wasn't to be. He told Mom that would be the last chance she would have to name one of his boys after him, that he would see that she never came down with the flu again as long as he lived.

The spring, summer, and fall was filled with much hard work and also filled with a lot of grief and disappointment. We grieved because we were living in poverty and disappointed because we didn't have nerve enough to kill off the Rossier family and take over the big house. Daddy and Mom both agreed that it may be bad luck to kill a family during crop-raising time and the crops were still growing; however, they had not heard of it being bad luck if it was done after gathering time, not bad luck for the killers but plenty bad luck for the family killed. We all agreed to try to get along with the Rossier family, and maybe they would die off from natural causes such as snake bites, poisoning, or getting dog mange and scratching themselves to death from the disease. The chances of this happening was far-fetched, but it was about all the hope we had, for we couldn't tell enough bad luck and witch tales to scare them away. We all worked hard, played hard, and loved a little and made out the best we could for the rest of the year. In those days, there was no television, and only the higher-class people could afford radios or subscribe to the newspaper. The most of our pleasure time came from setting out on our small front porch and listening to the old pump organ dance music coming from across the field a little over a quarter mile away as the Durke family had their weekly Saturday dances. They pumped out such old dance tunes as "When the Saints Go Marching In," "When the Roll Is Called Up Yonder," and "I'll Fly Away," and songs like that. We could see a little motion on their porch, in their yard, and the lantern light traveling toward the big barn out back and up in the cotton patch and down behind the hedge bushes by the spring branch. That wasn't very much entertainment, but it was about all we had at that time.

At times we could see Betty Durke holding one of the boys and giving them a thrashing with a left-handed brush broom, or see her pull one of the girl's dress tail up around their waist, twisting it up like a rope, holding it with her right hand and busting their tail with the old left-handed dogwood brush broom. Sometimes we boys would almost cry to see such cruel and unjust punishment being dealt out on such lovely and beautiful behinds. We even felt that she was trespassing on our private property. But we only watched and kept our mouths shut lest Mom took up her left-handed brush broom and gave us a dose of the same medicine as the Durke girls got for us being concerned with the girls' punishment. We would also be entertained by the Rossiers, watching them steal corn out of our mule's trough, sack it up, and hide it in the rumble seat of his car to be taken to town or somewhere and sell on Saturday morning. If we had only had a telephone or had some gossiping neighbors, we sure would have accumulated enough to gossip about.

At times Mom and Daddy would take the Bible from off the mantle, dust it off a little, remove a few old letters and postcards, and read to us the family. We dared not ask questions about the Bible, for we didn't want to hear a long sermon form either of them. Many times during the fall of the year during cotton-picking time, we would place a few sacks of freshly picked cotton on the ground in the front yard and lay on them and look up into sky at night. We could see seemingly millions of stars in the sky. The whole sky was lit up by the stars. At times we would see shooting stars streak across the sky. I would often wonder why God made the earth, the heavens, and all the stars; maybe a few would have been enough, but here we so many. And where was God? Since we didn't go to church, we didn't know the answers to many of the questions that came to our minds. However, we all wanted to get close to him and to know him better. Our friend, Sam Jones, had sown a few seeds and they were still sprouting up and growing. And some of the seeds would sprout up to help develop our lives in years to come. Sam would have been proud if he had only known how we talked about these things and how we had a great love and respect for him and the few things he taught us about prayer and the Bible.

Sometimes not having much to do gives our minds time to think of the more important things in life, and believe me, we sure had plenty of time to think.

Many times during the first summer in Goose Neck Valley, we boys would go fishing down the small creek from our pasture. Three small branches came together and formed a small creek. There were several little fishing holes, some about three or four feet deep, and pretty well stocked with brim, red horses, bass, and mud cats. Somewhere we had gotten a few small fishhooks, perhaps Daddy bought them for us. Mom gave us some no. 50 sewing thread that we doubled up and used for fishing lines, and using the roofing nail heads that Irra knocked off the barn where we lived over across the river, and the new fishhooks we could go fishing very often and sometimes we even caught several fish. We set our size limit to about two inches long and up to as big as we could catch. We learned from our Indian grandmother that fish would bite worms better if the water was muddy and muddy enough that the fish couldn't see us on the bank trying to catch them with the old mean life-taking fishing hooks hidden in the body of a good-looking fishing worm, a grasshopper, or maybe a fresh cricket. Before we started fishing, if the water was clear, we would go above the first fishing hole and wade around, throwing dirt in the creek and making the water real muddy for a few minutes. Then we would follow the muddy water downstream from hole to hole fishing in the muddy water. It really paid off too. At times we would catch enough fish to have a fish-fry supper. Most of the fish were so small we fried them until they were as crisp as a potato chip and ate them bones and all. Mom said, "A small fish with bones is better than no fish at all." Some folk told us that crawfish tails were good to eat, but we never tried them.

People even said bullfrog legs were good eating, but the only time Mom tried cooking a skillet full, as soon as they hit the hot grease, they began jumping out of the hot skillet and into the floor. Mom ran out on to the back porch and passed out. We revived her, and she made us clean the kitchen of them old devil frogs that refused to die quick and be cooked like a decent law-abiding dead thing ought to be cooked. She said if it could jump out at her from a skillet of hot grease, she didn't want it on her stove, for it might bring bad luck. One pair of back legs jumped out of the skillet and landed in her apron pocket. She had us burn the apron outside the yard, and she swore to never cook a frog leg again.

At times while down on the creek, we would come upon a water hard-shelled turtle sunning himself on a log or rock sticking up out of the water. We boys would go in after that turtle! The turtle seldom got away. Now, Mom didn't mind cleaning a good clean turtle and preparing it for supper. The Good Lord only knows how many turtles came for lunch with us. After dressing the turtle, Mom would let us fight over the turtle's heart to play with for the next few days. It would slowly beat for about seven days and finally stop beating and we would then throw it out to the cat. Mom told us that she had always heard that bad luck would come to the person that had possession of the turtle heart when it stopped beating. We didn't believe it, but she told us that if we had the turtle's heart when it stopped beating, someday that turtle would come back and stop our heart from beating. Whoever had the turtle's heart the last day or two sure tried to give it to someone else on or before the seventh day. Neal or Irra even took one to school and showed it to his "sweet thing" girlfriend and convinced her that was his little heart that he had taken out so it could beat just for her. The next day the girl brought a note to the teacher from the girl's mother telling the teacher of the incident and telling the teacher to talk to the guilty party. Upon reading the note, the good teacher called the guilty party up before the class and demanded to see the beating heart. The "guilty party" took two beating turtle hearts from a small tobacco sack he had in his bib overall pocked and handed them to her. The teacher screamed and called in Mr. Johnson, the principal, who had a big laugh and said, "Well I guess boys will be boys, and will this heart keep beating for seven days?" The guilty party informed him that it would and told him that he could have one to take home with him and study it. And he had the "guilty party" to take the tobacco sack and hang it up on a coat hanger in the schoolhouse hallway for the remainder of the day. When the class let out for the day, Mr. Johnson came by and got his heart and took it home with him. He seemed to have greater respect for us Rollins boys after that.

There were two peddling trucks that came through Goose Neck Valley each week selling can food and other foodstuff to the people along the route. They carried cloths to make clothing, thread, shoes, socks, overalls, and shirts, and a lot of other stuff like tobacco products, sugar. They sold a lot of sugar during liquor-making season and canning season. The trucks were loaded with wash pots, laundry tubs, axes, saws, mule collars, and a lot of other stuff that a country family might need before going to town time came around again. The peddling trucks were about twenty feet long inside, about eight feet wide, and about eight feet high. There were shelves on both sides running almost the full length of the big box bed. Each truck had a narrow hall running down the center from front to back; each had a back door in the center of the back and a side door about the middle of the right side with a step so one could step up and see the merchandise without going inside the big rolling store. Howell and Turner's truck was called "the Rolling Store," and Mr. Bell's truck was known as "the Store on Wheels." Mr. Bell's store on wheels had a large secret storage compartment built overhead and taking up one shelf space all the way down the left side of the big box bed. On the driver's visits, a sharecropper could slip a little of the landlord's cotton, corn, and other stuff and swap it for groceries or other goods. After the first cotton was picked, anyone going down the road could see sharecroppers beginning to dress up a little more fancy, and just look at their feet—they were wearing new shoes, all made possible by the peddler man and the landlord's share of the cotton. Our first year there we ate well, dressed well, and would even get back some money from time to time. Mom and Dad even traded several bushels of corn they robbed from Rossiers' plowing mule's feeding trough. Somehow the memory still haunts me about three little pigs and about a few dozen chicks that came up missing from the Rossiers' place. If they wanted to be mean and stubborn and not give up the big house for our family to live in—well they could pay the price, and their big old fat mule could pay too by being sent to his stable without his supper. The peddler man would weigh the cotton and corn that we smuggled to him and trade us what we wanted for it. We believed that when he would go to the Durke house that he would pull the big truck up in their yard and do some real trading with the oldest girl. Everyone dealing with him was taking a great risk, but we wore well and ate well and knew that he wouldn't tell anyone, for he would be in as much trouble as anyone of sharecroppers that he blabbed about. The first year we probably sold him a bale of cotton and twenty-five bushels of good corn. Somehow we didn't feel much guilty about it for we were trying to survive and keep well fed while living in that little run-down shack of a house while the three Rossier people had a big house with more rooms than they could live in.

We all worked very hard that first year in the small valley, farming, weaving baskets, making baby beds from hand-hewed hickory and oak timber, picking huckleberries, and Daddy and Irra cutting logs for Mr. Brown, a sawmiller. That summer Irra saved up a part of his log cutting money and ordered him a .22-caliber Winchester Model 27 repeater rifle. He learned to shoot small game very well, and he was very accurate. He could shoot both eyes out of a squirrel in the top of a tall tree and never scar the animal's face. He would take the rifle to the log woods and shoot several squirrels each day and bring home two or three and give some to the other sawmill hands who had a need for the meat but didn't have time to shoot the game. With Daddy's pay and all the money we got from odd jobs and berry picking and the stuff we sold to the peddler man, we had done pretty well that summer. We grew a lot of good corn and we raised and picked nine five-hundred-pound bales of cotton; half was ours and half went to Mr. Thrower, the landlord. He told Daddy that was more cotton than any farmer had ever made for him. Daddy just thanked him and grinned, knowing that if the peddler man had not come along every week, it might have been ten or eleven bales. Mr. Thrower had furnished us with groceries and other things that year for Daddy to pay for out of the money Daddy received from the sale of the cotton. Mr. Thrower settled up the charge account and gave Daddy back about seventeen dollars in cash. That was the most money that we ever had at one time in the last lifetime. At times we felt that the Lord had taken a real good liking to us again. Now we knew how to beat the system and take what really belonged to us, and maybe some things that belonged to others. We had learned to survive in a world that was unfriendly to people living below the poverty level.

Mom would sit by the little dirty window and look at the house that the Rossiers lived in and cry in deep depression because we were living in the most horrible conditions among our neighbors. We were all worried about her, knowing that she may commit suicide or something worse if we didn't move away quickly. What could be worse than killing one's self? Just almost killing one's self and leaving one's self in a state of incurable condition for others to care for the rest of their life that may be for many years to come. So we agreed to take the first house that we could find, no matter what conditions it was in. Just about a half mile further down the road from us lived a family that was renting from our landowner. Now, if we could get them to move, we could get that house. Their house had three large rooms built in an L shape, with a living room and a large bedroom on the front of the house and the large kitchen directly behind the living room, and with a medium-sized side storage room directly behind the bedroom. The living room and kitchen had ceiling overhead, but the bedroom did not. One could go to bed and see holes in the tin roof overhead. A few buckets were hanging on nails from the rafters to catch the rainwater while raining. The floor was much better than average for a farmhouse in those days. But there was a problem; the family, we will call them the Holt family, not their real name, lived in that house and they were happy there. We decided to use ghost stories and a little witchcraft to get them to move on. And within a few days someone caught them gone, stole their half-grown hog, their flock of about ten chickens, and their old puny hound dog, and used their water spring where they got their drinking water for a bathroom? Yes, they did. And a day or two later while they were in the wooded area cutting firewood to keep them warm, someone sneaked up and nailed two leg bones from their dog or perhaps their old hound dog in an X position over their front door.

When the family returned from the woods with a sled loaded down with freshly sawed firewood, the family was madder than before. Immediately, Mr. Holt and his oldest son grabbed their shotguns and started down the road inquiring from each neighbor if anyone had seen someone at their house during the time the stuff was missing or earlier that day while the family was away from home cutting firewood. Each of the neighbors told them that they had not seen anyone around the house. There was only one house in plain view of the Holt house, and the family was out working and didn't have time to be spying on us honest folk. After a few hours searching for the guilty persons who did such evil things just to make them get angry and move leaving the better house for some honest family to move into so some mother could find peace and happiness and quit worrying about the big house about a half mile away. After two days searching, Daddy asked him why he didn't go to Heflin and get the sheriff to come down there and try to unravel the mystery for him. Mr. Holt told Daddy that the sheriff was hunting for his son for breaking in a store in Edwardsville and stealing a lot of stuff and he could not take the risk of the sheriff finding his son and sending him to prison. This was not all the reasons for him not wanting the sheriff on the property. Mr. and Mrs. Holt seemed to be very nervous as Mom and Daddy went to see them on Sunday, the next day after the crossbones were nailed over their front door. Daddy ask them, "Who in the world hates you this much, and could it be a warning of some kind, warning you that something terrible is going to happen to you? If something like that ever happens to me, I'll be long gone and in a hurry, for it seems that they, whoever they are, mean bad business for you and your family. Mr. Bolt, do you have any enemies that you believe could do a thing like that?"

"No, Mr. Rollins, I don't have any clue as to who it might be. I know we have a few people that hate us, especially some of our sorry relatives, and some people that I owe money to. But we won't be able to sleep at night until something is done, and done pronto," he said as he began to remove the crossbones from above his front door. Then he dropped his head and said, "What would you do if it happened to you and your family? We sure don't need any trouble or anything like that." While he was talking to Daddy, his oldest son burst through the front doorway and almost ran over his father. He was carrying a small cardboard box in his left hand and a sawed-off twelve-gauge shotgun in his right hand. As he leaped off the front porch, he said that he had caused them too much trouble and that he was checking out of there in a hurry so his father could go ahead and get the Cleburnee County sheriff to try and find the mean person or persons who had tried to wreck the lives of the family. Mr. Bolt turned to Daddy and said in a trembling voice, "Mr. Wess, if any more of this stuff happens to me and my family, we will move to somewhere in south Georgia or somewhere where the guilty people can never find us anymore."

Irra had ordered a book from Johnjon and Smith on how to throw his voice and become a ventriloquist. While we boys were wondering in the wooded area a few hundred yards below the Holt house, we came upon something that we were not familiar with. It was some type of boiler tank about five feet high sitting over a trench in the ground. The tank had tubes or copper pipes running from it into another vat with creek water running from an old fire hose, with one end of the fire hose coming from the creek. Water was running through the pipe into the vat where an old car reader was submerged in the vat. We told Daddy what we had found. Now it began to make sense to us as to why Mr. Bolt couldn't have the sheriff come down and investigate the other stuff that had happened. Daddy told us that was a whisky still. Irra was getting pretty good with throwing his voice into any building or objects such as boxes or barrels or almost anywhere he wanted to. We thought up a plan to really get rid of the Bolt family. We decided to watch the still and see when the mash was ready for cooking. Since we had some kinfolk who knew all about whisky making, we asked one of our cousins who was about seventeen years old to come and stay with us on a weekend. About dark on that Saturday night our cousin decided for us to slip up near the whisky still while the Bolts were cooking it off. Mr. Bolt and his sixteen-year-old son, Randy, were firing up the boiler or cooking pot. We watched them from a good hiding place about seventy yards away. They had a lantern burning and had the cooking pot going full blast.

Now it was time for Irra to do his thing. Irra leaned back a bit, and with a rough voice, throwing it into a cluster of empty barrels, he said, "I am the devil whom you are serving, and I have come to take you to hell with me." And as the Bolts began to run, Irra threw his voice into some bushes a few yards away from the still saying, "I am the revenue officer and the devil can't have you until I'm finished with you. Come back here, come back here. When I'm through with you, the devil can have you, and what's left of you and your son." By now the Bolts were getting under way down through the briars, bushes, and trees while Irra kept throwing his voice a few feet behind them, saying, "I want him first," "No, I want him while he is living." Irra was altering his voice for each of the two, the devil and the revenuers. And he was throwing it a few yards behind them. There was a five-strand barbed wire fence about a hundred yards or so on the same side of the still that we were on. They passed us only about ten yards away from us. Just after they passed us running as fast as their legs would carry them, stumbling into bushes and trees, we started tramping our feet on the leaves and shaking bushes as loudly as we could while Irra kept on his work as a ventriloquist. Surely the two knew the fence was there, but they must have been so scared that they didn't think about the fence, hitting it at full speed in the darkness. They left their lantern behind. As they hit the fence, they both yelled some choice curse words while Irra threw his voice just behind them saying in the devil's voice, "I've got you now." But probably the devil himself could not have caught them. At that point they must have jumped the pasture fence, for we ran up to the road and watched them open the front door and enter the house and slam the door. We were about two hundred yards from their house, and we could see them fairly well from where we were in the road. We sure got a good laugh out of that caper.

Two days later, Daddy looked in the house on his way to work and the house was vacant and seemingly inviting us to move in. Two or three days later, Daddy hitched a ride on the lumber truck and went to Heflin and talked to Mr. Thrower about the house. He rented the Holt house from Mr. Thrower. We would still be sharecroppers but living in a bigger and better house. In our house we could not lie in our beds and count as many stars through the holes in the roof because we now would have buckets hanging under the holes to catch the rainwater leaking through the holey roof. For the next two days we cleaned the house and moved in using the same wagon that we rented to move us to Goose Neck Valley. The family was moved in and operating at full speed. None of us had to change jobs, schools, or neighbors, and Mom didn't have to set and look out the window at the Rossier house and greave because it was not for us to have that house. However, we might still be able to get the Rossier family to move out since Irra could use his voice throwing ability to scare the daylights out of the family.

After moving in the Bolt house, Daddy cleaned out the water well that was located on the side porch near the kitchen door. We could also carry water from a neatly kept spring located just across the road from the house. There was a wooden drinking trough just below the spring that was constantly kept filled with fresh water from the spring. We chose to get our drinking water from the spring rather than from the well. Mom was afraid that Daddy had spit baccer juice down in the well while he was down there washing down the wall and getting the cat and frog boned from the bottom of the well. Water standing over the rotting body of a dead frog or a dead possum or a dead cat sure does smell bad and taste even worse when you try to drink it. It was easier to drink water off a dead frog than to drink water mingled with a few spits of snuff or Brown Mule chewing tobacco, or at least it didn't taste "froggy." To most people there is nothing that taste or smells worse than a big dipper full of nice cool fresh water from down in the north corner of the well with a decaying frog leg floating on the dipper full of water. It almost makes one want to go drink from the mule-watering trough located down in the feed lot by the manure-smelling barn. There sure won't be any frog legs floating in it, for the mules and cattle had just as soon drink decaying frog legs as to not. A good God-fearing young mule might turn around and kick you in the rump if he sees you spit baccer juice in his drinking water. After cleaning out the well, we cleaned the yard all day Sunday and also repaired the hog lot and built the pigs a shelter to protect them from the winter weather. Daddy had managed to paint black spots on two pigs that he gathered up at the Holt hog lot just before they moved away in such a hurry. The black-painted spots kept anyone from identifying them and accused us of stealing their pigs. We made sure that they were sows, or "mommy-to-be" pigs. Now with two free sows, we could raise and sell pigs and make a little extra money. This was during the winter, and they wouldn't be ready to breed and become "mommierized" until about summer.

We soon settled down in our new house; it was almost the same size and built almost like the one that we had left near the river, except this house was far less quality than the river house. It seemed like we had fallen from paradise to hell and torment, and now we were lingering somewhere between. However, we decided to make the best of the situation and keep climbing up the ladder one house at a time. All of us boys were in school, and Daddy had a job cutting logs for Mr. Brown over in the Turkey Heaved Mountains, and Mom was looking after Margret and little Henry Caffey and looking out the living-room window watching a neighboring family going to and coming from their whisky still hidden in the nearby woods. She would watch the two men carrying large sacks of corn and sugar just before dark in the evening and watch them return a little after sunup carrying five gallon jugs of moonshine whisky and storing it in their four-stable barn. At times they would have a home cranked ice cream party and invite us over to eat ice cream with them and several of their menfolk drinking friends. Since this was about all the pleasure activity that the family had, we never turned them down. Some of the men would bring along banjos, guitars, fiddles, juice harps, and harmonicas to entertain us at the party. Since we didn't have a radio to listen to, we really liked the fire out of the music. They may have played off-key, offbeat, and without good harmony, but since we didn't know much about music, it really sounded good to us. There were a few young ladies that would attend each ice cream supper, but we didn't see much of them since they went walking up in the pasture with some of the men. The family that always invited us seemed to have a nice income, had a new car, wore nice clothes, and was always encouraging us to keep on climbing and telling us that we would be alright. We got acquainted with a few new neighbors living down the road from our new home. All our neighbors thought of us as truthful, honest, hardworking people. Well, they didn't know that we were eating Rossier chicken and pig meat, and about to begin a pig-raising farm using Bolt sows and start a poultry farm with Bolt-raised chicken. There was a certain part of the Rollins family's life that we didn't tell anyone about. Who knows, by next winter the Rossier family might have an accident and fall down a hundred or so feet into an old gold-mining shaft, or perhaps Mr. Rossier would accidentally hang himself with the rope plow lines on the mule harness, or his wife may get shot and he might commit suicide or some strange death overtake the family, and we could still get to move in the big Rossier house. But now we would be content to wait because some good things come to them who wait long enough, and sometimes bad things happens to people who push bad things too far.

It must have been just before Christmas when we moved in the Bolt house. We were much more comfortable living there; all the rooms were much warmer since the house was a few hundred yards further south than where we moved from. Now all we had to do to get firewood was to saw down the large shade trees right in our yard on all sides of the house. Well we didn't need them now since it was winter and the trees didn't seem to mind; they were probably glad to be sawed down and carried inside the house to keep them warm too. We never had much for Christmas, maybe a bag of about twenty marbles and always a simulated leather football. This year was no different except we got more candy, apples, and oranges than usual. That was because the peddling truck man stopped two days before Christmas and Mom bought about three Bolt hens worth from the peddler man. She almost bought her a new dress, but one of the chickens got loose and we couldn't catch the old hen in time to do the trading. O well, the peddler man would be back in two weeks, and Mom would just have to wait for her Christmas present, and maybe, just maybe, we could catch the Rossier family gone and raid their chicken pen so Daddy could get some new overalls too. Daddy's knees were sticking out through the holes in his work overalls, and we began to be afraid that his knees might frost over while he was out in the log woods and his knees might catch the flu or pneumonia or something like that. Sure enough the Rossiers' henhouse had a couple of vacancies. When the old rooster had the bed or roost pole check and roll call on one night the following week, and when the peddler man came the next trip Daddy got his delayed Christmas present—his new overalls and new shirt. Now his knees wouldn't stick out and come down with the flu. For the next few days, we didn't hear the big Rossier rooster crowing at all. He must have been grieving over his favorite hen being missing. Gosh, if we had known which hen was his roost-pole sleeping mate, we would have got two setting further back on another roost pole, for after all to us a hen is just another hen, but to that old rooster it was another feeling.

In a few weeks we could hear him burst out crowing from over across the small hill that separated us from sight of the Rossier house. The old red rooster must have taken up with another hen or something. Daddy was proud of his new overalls and shirt that Mom got him; he never knew where the money came from to buy them. Daddy would have worn us out with our new dogwood brush broom if he had learned that sad old rooster had go to roost without his favorite dominant hen. Mom was proud of her new dress, but she always regretted not getting another one of the rooster's favorite hens so she could have got her a new pair of high-top manure wading shoes to go with the new dress.

The winter was still hard on us. We boys kept on in school, and Daddy worked in the log woods every day that it wasn't raining or snowing, and Mom was left at home with Margret and Caffey. It must have been very hard on her having to carry drinking water from the spring, gathering in wood when we forgot to bring it in and cooking up the turnips, taters, making black berry pies and stuff like that. We boys usually brought in enough stove wood to cook all that good grub. At times when it was raining, we would have torn out the overhead ceiling and chopped it into stove wood, but the Bolt family had already took all the ceiling boards from the bedroom and burned them in the stove and fireplace, and Daddy wouldn't let us take down not even one board from the kitchen or living room. He said he didn't want to set in the kitchen and see large rats sitting up on the rafters and ceiling joist licking their lips watching us eat and wanting to be down among us, eating with us on our new plates we bought from the peddling truck man with money he got from trading a Bolt chicken, loaded down with Rossier ham and pork chops, buttermilk cathead biscuits, and homespun gravy. Sometimes after school Irra would go out and get a rabbit or squirrel to cook for supper. Somedays he would bring several robins or a crow or two so we wouldn't have to eat the same old stuff every day. When Daddy would get in from work, Mom could serve him crow meat, and he would be so hungry that he would eat it and never knew it was not one of the Rossiers' chickens. However, on those nights the rest of the family would each take a fried robin on our plates and maybe a fried crow leg or wing. Along with some corn bread, buttermilk, and collard greens we were living above some of the valley families. Some of the families living around us wouldn't work and tried to live on some federal relief program. We felt that was wrong to take federal help as long as we were able to raid henhouses, corn cribs, and pigpens we wouldn't take any more hand out. After all, we still believed in honesty and not sit and wait on the honest people to keep us up. At times we believed that some of the stuff that our neighbors were blessed with may have been meant for us, and somehow it fell in the wrong corn cribs, chicken coops, and pigpens and it was really left up to us to sort out our stuff and things from theirs. We felt that the people we were collecting all the good stuff from would have to pay it to the government in federal income taxes if we didn't take the shortcut and collect it first and save the feds a lot of collecting and give it back to us in a relief program. Man, just look at all the red tape we saved the federal government by collecting our share first, saving them all that trouble.

Soon it was spring and that brought a lot of relief for the family. We boys dropped out of school about a month early to begin farming. However, we never failed a grade in school for a lot of students had to do the same, but since we had made good grades up till the time we dropped out of school we never failed a grade. Some of the students that didn't seem to try and had barely passing grades and dropped out were left behind and were not allowed to be promoted to the higher grades. As soon as we dropped out of school, we hit the fields, cleaning off the creek banks, cutting and burning cornstalks, cleaning the fields of last years cotton stalks, and beginning to plow the open fields, getting ready to start planting the crops. There were a few weeks of preparation for planting before the planting began. Mom and Daddy would sit at the dining table at night and draw off a sketch of the fields on a piece of wrapping paper and name each field according to what we would plant in each field, such as corn, corn and velvet beans, corn with coy beans, sorghum cane, cotton, oats and vetch, and some other crops, such as potatoes, okra, turnips, watermelons, and other stuff. It always gave all the family a great thrill to take part in planting the crops on paper before the actual planting began. The plowing of the fields was the hardest part of the work. All the farmland had to be turned with a turning plow to put the top surface about eight to ten inches on the bottom and the raw soil on the top. After this was done, we would tie three logs about eight feet long and about ten inches in diameter with chains and drag then across the field in a horizontal position to smooth down the fresh turned soil.

The field always looked well groomed and smooth so one could lay out the rows about three or four feet apart before planting the crops assigned to that field. The planting was no fun, putting in the fertilizer first and then the seeds. The cotton was planted with a cotton planter, but the corn and other crops had to be planted by hand, the seeds properly spaced depending on the type seed planted. Planting the cotton came first and planting the other crops came in line as to what they were, however the corn planting came last, about June first to June tenth. This way some could be chopping cotton and hoeing out the weeds and grass while we were getting the other crops planted. There was never a resting time until the crops were "laid buy" about the first week in July. Then we would have a few weeks of breathing and resting from our labors before gathering time. But we never got to rest very much—berry picking time was at hand, so we had something to do all the time.

Daddy was real proud of the sows that he obtained from the Bolt's pig lot one windy night while the Bolt family were sleeping, the ones Daddy painted black spots on so no one could lay claim to them. He had two beautiful spotted sows that were ready to be bred to the Rossiers' big white boar, or male hog. Two of the Durke boys were passing our hog pen and saw that the sows were in heat and ready to be bred by a male hog. They told us boys that they would like to "get with the sows" if we would let them. Well since we had picked berries and traded them to get with their sisters in a more than friendly way, now we could return the favor. They agreed to pick a gallon of blackberries or a half gallon of huckleberries for the price to "associate" with a sow for a few minutes. At first we traded for about three gallon of berries and the sows went back to normal. Now, if we couldn't get them interested in breeding or in heat again, we would have to go back to picking berries again, the berries that we were bringing in was "traded" berries, and Mom didn't know that we didn't pick them each day. We would go swimming down in the swimming hole below our pasture while the Durke boys picked the berries and traded them to us for a time of pleasure with Daddy's two sows. One of the boys said if we fed them some hot pepper, they would go back in heat. While he was talking to us about this, he opened a large paper bag and pulled out a long string of red peppers that he swiped from the wall out in the hall at his house. He threw it over in the hog pen, and they began eating it. The sows ate the whole string of hot peppers and began drinking a lot of water. Well, it worked. We were in the business of sows for berries the next day. Within a few days, Mom had canned about one hundred ten quarts of blackberries and told us to stop picking any more. We let the boys come acourting the sows for a few days sort of on a free basis, but they were to bring their two sisters over to a broom sage field on a Saturday while Mom and Daddy went to town. It seemed that was one of the best trades that we boys had ever made. All the trading ended rather quickly, for Mom must have found out something for she lined us up and just about wore us out with the old dogwood brush broom, but she wouldn't tell us why. We all had a deep-down feeling as to what it was all about, for she told Daddy that night to butcher the hogs or sell them quickly. That Saturday he butchered one and salted it away in his big meat box. He agreed to sell the other one if he could find a buyer. But that never happened. He kept the other one until the first cold weather and butchered her. We boys seemed to have lost our appetite for pork.

As the summer passed, Irra seemed to get disgusted with the farm life and wanted to climb higher and become something other than a sharecropper farmer. For part of the spring and summer, he got a job with a surveyor who was surveying cotton fields for the government. The world was flooded with cotton, and the market had reached a low of seven cents per pound. The farmers were allotted only so many acres per farmer, and the other had to be plowed up and destroyed. The farmers were paid for the cotton plants that had to be destroyed. Irra helped the surveyor measure and map out the fields that were to be plowed up. The farmers got wise quickly. They would plant as much cotton as they had land, and the agents would make the farmers plow most of it up and pay them for what was plowed up. Then they would go back and plant corn in its place. This was about the same as growing two crops each year on the same fields. Irra was good at artwork, and he made the plats for the main survey team and wrote how much was to be plowed up. We caught on fast too. We plowed up rows in our pasture and planted cotton and later got paid for plowing it up. It seemed that Irra made a small error in his plat and showed our twelve-acre pasture as a cotton patch, and we had to destroy the cotton and turn it back over to the cow and mule, and we made more money for doing it than we could have made had we kept the cotton crop. We were not the only ones taking advantage of a good thing; people all over were planting acre upon acre of cotton in pastures, broom sage fields, and land that had not been cultivated for years.

Irra was now seventeen years old and had finished the sixth grade and wanted to move on with his life. Mom and Daddy signed the papers for him to get in the CCC camp and leave home to obtain a better life. It was a sad day for Irra and the rest of the family when we all went to Heflin and saw him leave. There was hardly a word said as we got on the wagon and watched the Greyhound bus disappear around the curve in the highway that ran through Heflin. For the next few months life was not the same for the family. One had left the nest, and just how long would it be before another would go? In about a month, Mom and Daddy got a check from the CCC for about $17.50, which was the money that they would receive each month while Irra was away in camp. And every week or two we would get a letter from him telling us where he was, what he was doing, and how well he liked the service. Many times Mom would cry when he read the letters, and she said that she wished that she had never signed the papers for him to go. However, when that big check would come in, she was all smiles. She would take the check and buy some store-bought clothes from J. A. Owens store in Heflin, and pay some on the doctors' bills from Dr. Caffey. The Rollins family was never the same after Irra left. It seemed that most of the laughter and joy were gone forever—and it was. There was a blank spot in the family in everything we did together. That blank spot would never be filled again except when he would be with us for short visits down through the years to come. After about seven or eight months, one day Mom looked up from her chair as she sat in the living room, and there stood Irra in his CCC uniform. She almost passed out. Mom never hugged us kids much; however, she broke out with the huggies that day; her firstborn son had come home. We all took off from the things that we were doing and had a holiday for that day, that night, and the following day. We rounded up one of the Holt fat hens and one of her store-bought Rhode Island red hens and prepared for us a real feast. We had some choice spareribs from our freshly butchered sow, and the sow meat tasted good by now. Irra told us stories for the next few days about his life in camp. But he said the thing that he missed most was the home cooking that Mom always had on the table for us. However, Irra would never settle down with us again. The following week, Uncle Shug Crain, who owned a heating company and a sheet metal shop in Anniston, heard that Irra was back home, and he came over and hired Irra to come and work for him doing heating and sheet metal work. Irra boarded with another uncle who worked for Uncle Shug. Irra liked that work so much that he never again walked behind a mule plowing or working in the cotton fields for the rest of his life. The rest of the family were not so lucky. We had to farm another season there and do some farming after this.

One day after about two in the afternoon, Mom called Daddy in to the living room and told him it was time for him to go get the doctor again. One of us asked him what was wrong with Mom, and he said she was coming down with the flu again. Daddy walked about a mile over to a neighbor's house and had him call Dr. Caffey. In about four hours, Dr. Caffey arrived. It was getting dark. Daddy told us boys to get our pillows and each of us to take a quilt and go up in the barn loft and make us a bed in the hayloft for the night. It was pretty warm that night, and we could not have any light except the lantern that the Bolts had dropped at the whisky still the night we scared the daylights out of them. Daddy hung the lantern on a post in the hayloft and turned it down pretty low so it would burn all night long. We laughed a while and went to sleep. About daylight the next morning, Daddy came down to get us for breakfast. When we got up on the front porch, we could hear a baby crying. Daddy took us in and introduced us to baby number seven, Baby Georgia Innus. They had named her after Daddy's mother Georgia and Mom's mother Innus. We were all thrilled to death, but why did Mom keep catching the flu and the doctor keep leaving a baby every time? We had already "flued" out of a place to sleep and now another flu baby! It probably meant that a bunch of us would have to sleep in the barn or pile up on the bedroom floor.

Each year when the cow would have her calf, Mom and Daddy would give one of us boys a calf. Irra and Neal had already got theirs, and it was my time this time. I had fallen heir to the little bull calf this year, and he was about three months old. A man had asked me if I would sell him the calf for fifteen dollars, and I had turned him down. But now we were desperate; we needed money for a new bed. Daddy got in touch with the man, and he paid me seventeen dollars for the calf. That night Mom took down the Sears, Roebuck catalog and ordered me a nice new all-metal headboard and footboard bed complete with springs. Three days later the postman came over the hill honking the horn on his Chevrolet coupe automobile with a bed frame tied to the top of the car and stopped in front of our house, got out and untied the rope that held the bed frame and set it in the yard. He laughed together so as to make a big bag; this was filled with wheat and oat straw from our barn loft to make me a straw mattress. We closed the end after filling with straw by sewing it together with a needle and heavy thread. We set up the bed and put the mattress on the bedsprings and jumped up and down on it to level out the straw inside the mattress. It looked and felt good. That was my very own bed; however, Margret slept with me on my new wheat straw mattress and new bed. We put two old quilts on the straw mattress to make it soft. I really enjoyed that bed for years to come.

That summer we farmed very hard and fast, for there was another member of the Rollins family. Mom would have me stay in the house and look after the three kids while she would go to the fields and help with the farmwork. Neal and Lewis plowed some, and Daddy helped with the plowing when he was not cutting logs for the sawmill. Mom had a large garden where we grew many types of vegetables. We always grew more than we needed and gave some to the neighbors. However, most of our neighbors wanted us to gather the stuff and bring it over to their house. We decided not to go that route anymore, if they were too lazy to gather the stuff and take home with them, we would let it rot in the garden. Mom always canned about nine hundred quarts of fruit, berries, and vegetables each year. This year was no different. She made me do most of the preparing the things for cooking and canning. From the two big apple trees that we now had, we peeled and dried about two bushels of fresh dried apples. The dried apple slices sure were good to put a few in our coat pocket to munch on at school, and they even taste better inside the big half-moon pies that Mom made for us each week. We also dried and canned a lot of peaches from the three peach trees standing in our side yard. If a family will just take and save what the Lord provides for them, they will not starve in America. The reason so many people in our country are in absolute poverty is because they are too lazy to take what the Lord has provided for them. It has been said, "Give a man a fish and he can eat for the day. But teach a man to fish and you are feeding him for a lifetime." Some might say, "Give a man a pint of whisky and he will be drunk for a day. But teach a man how to make whisky and he can stay drunk for a lifetime." By living close to some people, one can learn to believe both. Everywhere we lived we saw both sayings come to pass many times. I am so glad that my parents taught us to be honest and not to steal more than we needed at that time. They said it was always a good thing to borrow a few chicken, a pig or two, or a few sacks of corn from your neighbor if sometime you kindly meant to pay him back.

One day a neighbor girl, I'll call her Pearlie, came over while I was alone looking after the younger three kids. She was about a year older than me and was very beautiful. She was tall and just a little bit chubby and had full-size breasts. She and I hit it off real well together. She got up close to me and rubbed her body against mine. She put her little lovemaking arms around me and asked me if she could give me something good. As I was blushing real good, I said, "I guess so if you won't tell Mom about it." Then she smiled and reached her hand in her little pocket on her beautiful flowered short-tailed dress and pulled out a chocolate cookie and handed it to me and began laughing. We were standing by the bed in the living room, so I started laughing and pushed her over on the bed; and as I pushed her, my hand sort of pushed her dress up around her hips. Lo and behold, there staring me in the face was the prettiest sight that I had ever seen! At that time she pulled me down on her and held me closely while I lay on her and trembled. Then she smiled and said, "Frank, it is all right. Go ahead and do it to me. My two brothers do it to me almost every day, and Mommy and Dad don't ever care. I believe I want something different today." Without saying a word further, her dreams and also mine began to be fulfilled. Margret and Caffey were in the floor playing, and little Betty was in the playpen asleep, and Frank and Pearlie were lying across the bed having a good understanding of each other. It seemed that all the whistles and bells and all music of the world were going off at the same time. After a few minutes, we got up and she pulled her short-tailed dress down and hugged me real tight. And she said, "If you want me to, I'll come back tomorrow."

"Yes, please come back, just make sure you see Mom over across the creek in the cotton patch with a hoe handle in her hand. And make sure you don't tell anyone about this, for I want to see you a lot, but if Mom and Daddy find out what we did, they will beat me to death and bury me in the manure pile down by the barn and I can't ever get any more of your love," I told her as I felt of her big breast. Then I pulled her dress up around her neck and got both eyes full of the most beautiful person that I had ever seen. I had seen one of the Durke girls from the waist down, but it was not near as beautiful as Pearlie's body. This stuff could go on forever as far as we both were concerned. And we kept seeing each other once or twice each week. She would come over and get few tomatoes, a cucumber or two, and a few large onions to have an excuse to come over. This was a dream coming true; it was something that most boys think and dream about but only a few obtain. And now I had it all, just for me and her two brothers. But they didn't matter to me, for she was worth having close when we could be together—about three or four times each week. However, most good things come to an end. Our romance lasted for the summer and well over in the winter and ended when we had to move away.

Daddy had to walk about one mile each day to catch a ride on the Brown's log truck to get over to the logwoods near the sawmill. There were three other men that worked for Mr. Brown that waited there with Daddy. They were always laughing and joking with each other, it was about all the pastime they had. One of the men was a younger man that lived on a small farm, whose name was Roy. One morning Roy asked Daddy, "Mr. Wess, what can a person do for a mule that has eaten too much green clover and is bloated with gas and can't hardly stand up and can't eat or drink anything?"

"How long has this been going on, Roy?" Daddy replied.

"I think it started about three days ago, and I've done everything I know to relieve her of the gas and clover but nothing seems to help."

"Just what did you give the mule," Daddy asked.

Roy looked at Daddy and said as he stared at the ground, "Somebody told to give her some kerosene, and I made her drink down about a pint bottle full, and it didn't seem to help at all, her sides are so bloated that it seems that she will bust."

Daddy quickly replied in a very professional voice, "Roy, you have got to get that kerosene out of her in a hurry or you are going to lose a mule." Then Daddy stood up and walked away from Roy a few feet.

"But just how am I to get rid of the kerosene in her stomach?" Roy replied as he jumped to his feet.

At that time Daddy replied in a very firm voice, "The only thing that I can think of is for you to get a soft cotton towel and cut off one end of the towel about twelve inches and roll it up in a good tight roll and hold up the mule's tail and stick it up the mule's rectum and use it like a lantern wick, then light it and burn the kerosene out." Roy began chasing Daddy up the road because he thought Daddy was joshing or making fun of him. At that time the log truck came by and picked up the men. The other two men were laughing so hard at the remedy that they almost fell off the log truck. Roy had nothing to say to Daddy for the rest of the day, and the next day Roy was madder than an old wet hen. Daddy ask him if he had done what he had suggested, and Roy said, "Yes, and I almost burned the barn down. When I lit the wick, the mule jumped up and circled the lot about four times, ran through the hall of the barn passing gas very loudly and lost the wick in the hallway then jumped the rail fence gate and ran off into the woods above our house. By the time we got the fire out in the barn it was getting dark and we waited until daylight to check on the mule. And there she was grazing on the grass outside our garden. Mr. Wess, I'm sorry I got so mad, but I nearly burned my barn down, but you saved our mule, and that is all that really counts." They shook hands and had a good laugh, and as Daddy walked away, Roy picked up a pine cone and threw it at Daddy while both were still laughing.

Daddy took a great liking to Roy. Roy was young, about twenty-five, and a hard worker. Daddy had no patents with a person that was lazy and wouldn't work. Daddy chewed Brown Mule plug tobacco and always carried a big plug in his overall bib pocket. The tobacco was always wrapped in brown paper torn from a grocery bag. Roy wouldn't buy tobacco for himself but always bummed it from Daddy. Daddy decided to teach him a lesson, and maybe stop him from always asking Daddy for a chew of tobacco. Daddy had part of a plug of sweet tobacco that he didn't like because it was too sweet for him to chew. He wet the sweet tobacco and sprinkled a little salt on it, wrapped it up like he always did and put it in his bib pocket and snapped her down. The next day Roy asked him for a chew of tobacco. Daddy unsnapped the bib pocket and handed Roy the sweet tobacco. He took it and bit off a large chew, and began to look funny. Then he said, "Mr. Wess, does this tobacco taste salty to you?"

"Yes, Roy, it is supposed to, that is what makes it so good. That is my little secret," he replied. Turning around, he unbuttoned the fly of his overalls and urinated all over the plug of sweet tobacco, shook it off a little, wrapped it back up, and put it back in his bib pocket. Roy didn't say a word; he just walked a few feet away, and while he thought Daddy wasn't watching, he spit out the tobacco and headed for the water bucket and washed his mouth out real good. From that day on he never bummed another chew of Daddy's baccer. Roy didn't know that Daddy had his regular tobacco in his hip pocket that day. A few days later, Roy was seen pulling out his own plug and biting off a big chew. The other men working with them saw the change but never knew why. There are some things that one does to teach another a good lesson in life, and probably this was one of them.

That year the federal wage and hour law was passed by the congress and signed into law by our president. Immediately Daddy's pay was raised from seventy-five cents or a dollar for a twelve-hour day to about two dollars and fifty cents for an eight-hour day. About all the manufacturers and sawmillers said that the new wage and hour law would put them out of business. But it didn't. All they had to do was to set higher prices for their goods and prices. This meant that we could buy our own meat and stuff and stay out of the other people's chicken coops and hog pens. Our lifestyle changed a lot. We began wearing better clothes and eating better food. And now we could quit hiding stolen stuff behind the three big rosebushes by the road in front of our house, waiting for the peddler man so we could trade it for something to eat and other stuff. We now had cash to buy our stuff. The peddler man had rather kept trading for the stolen or "borrowed" stuff, and things because he could make a little profit for himself when he sold it. Mom and Daddy said that they had rather pay than steel or "borrow" as they called it from our dead-beating, lazy, good-for-nothing neighbors.

That was one of our better years yet. The Good Lord must have taken a liking to us for some reason. That year we picked and ginned seven bales of good clean cotton besides about a bale we sold to our friend, the peddler man. We grew and gathered in a crib full of good corn, also a lot of potatoes, beans, peas, pumpkins, turnips, and other stuff. Yes, the Lord had been good to us in spite of our borrowing and not even going to church. We believed in God. However, to see how we had to live, one might not be able to tell it. Daddy didn't have to weave cotton baskets and bottom chairs anymore unless he just wanted to. His wages were enough for us to live on pretty well. We boys hired out to help other farmers and made a little money and Mom raised and sold a few chicken too. And one of the best things that happened to us was that since she could not see the Rossier house, it didn't seem to matter anymore. That year Daddy finally decided to trust us with his twelve-gauge shotgun so we could hunt for game since Irra had deserted us and left us to find his peace, life, and fortune elsewhere. We shot a few doves, quail, rabbits and snakes as the year went by. But to shoot a bird at close range, about all you had of the bird was a mess of mangled feather held together with a bits of skin. And since the shells cost so much, Daddy made us only shoot big stuff like rabbits, squirrels, crows, and maybe a neighbor's chickens if they were out of sight of the neighbor's house.

A week or two before Christmas, Daddy came in and told us that Mr. Brown had bought a large section of land near Edwardsville. The land was covered with pine timber and had no farmland on it. There was a nicer three-room house with wood ceiling in every room. He told Daddy that we could move up there and live in the house rent free and Daddy would keep cutting logs up there for him. We boys could keep going to school in Heflin, riding the school bus from Edwardsville. We were all real happy to have the opportunity to move again. After all, we had moved about everywhere, why break the cycle now? The biggest drawback with us boys was that we would have to leave our occasional girlfriends, my Pearlie and their Durke girls. They would be hard to leave behind, but one gotta do what one has gotta do. When we told the girls about what we were going to do, they were real upset and almost cried. They all said that we made them feel better when we were with them than their brothers did and that life would never be the same again. Pearlie would have come with us if we had invited her to. But we both were far too young for anything like that. We began to make plans to move in January. We decided to butcher Daddy's old worthless sow rather than have to build a special hog hauling crate to move her up there. And besides we were ready for a lot of fried ribs and pork chops. Christmas seemed to bring more joy that year. We boys got a good imitation leather football, we had been playing with a blown up hog bladder. The girls got store-bought dolls and Margret got a set of play dishes. Mom and Daddy got some new clothes. This was the best Christmas that we had ever had together. Daddy's salary raise had really taken over now, we could almost live like the uptown Heflin folk except they had cars and we didn't even have a mule to ride.

About the middle of January Mr. Brown started moving his sawmill up on the Edwardsville location and told Daddy to go ahead and move. He loaned Daddy his large log-hauling wagon with its high bed to move with. He loaned us two beautiful mules to pull the wagon. This time it took two trips to move up there. The first trip we moved all the furniture, clothing and house hold things. We got that moved in and set up for the night, setting up the stove and kitchen stuff first. While Mom and Daddy fired off the stove with a little stove wood that we brought along with us, we boys set up the three beds and got ready to do some real sleeping in our new house. We built a fire in the large fireplace in the living room. Since the house had ceiling all through the house, a little fire gave us a lot of heat, even all the way to the back of the bedroom. It was pretty cold, but even the kitchen and dining area was real warm because of the heat from the wood-burning stove. After about an hour of cooking and setting up the beds, it was time to eat. Daddy even said the blessing and Mom was happier than she had been in years. She was extremely pleased with our new home. It meant no more looking at the Rossier house, no more farming and stuff like that.

Well, the next day Neal and Lewis went back with Daddy and got the cow and chickens and the wagon filled with corn. The chickens were in two large wire-mesh coops, and the wash pot and washtubs were hanging from the sides of the wagon. The freshly butchered sow was in Daddy's neatly built meat box and placed under the corn. The cow had been moved around so much she knew just what to do; she gently walked behind the wagon tied to it with an eight-foot rope. It was late in the afternoon when the second load arrived. Mom and I had slaved all day getting clothing arranged and getting everything settled in where she wanted it. We had put nails in the wall to hang clothes and things. Supper was ready soon after the wagon had landed, and the mules were fed and watered and turned in the lot by the barn. This time Mom really fixed a good gob of real nice food. We had brought all our food on the first load except the fresh butchered hog, but she brought some of the choice meat along. Again we stuffed ourselves with a great happy feast. As we sat at the table and ate, we were a real happy family again. It was like going from the wilderness into the promised land. Edwardsville may not hold much for us, but at least we didn't know it yet. We now lived in a much better house and had no danged old cotton fields to have to work in. We moved on a Friday and Saturday and rested a little on Sunday. On Sunday afternoon Daddy drove the mules and wagon over to Mr. Brown's place, which was about two miles away. That afternoon we cleaned up the yards pretty well, the people who moved left the house real clean, and the yards were even swept with the brush broom. Now that was so much different from what we found in Goose Neck. This place even had a two-holer outhouse with a shelf full of old magazines and there was an old Sears catalog on the shelf. Boy, this was almost like living uptown in Heflin or somewhere else. There was a water well in the backyard, but all our drinking water and cooking water had to come from a nice cold spring about one hundred fifty yards down a wagon road from the end of our house. We never used water from a well unless Daddy cleaned it out first, and now we were all big enough to bring water up from the spring except to do washing of our clothes. We built a wash bench between two trees down by the spring and carried our wash pot down there and set up our very own laundry department. We boys did the laundry once a week either one evening after school or on Saturday. Sometimes if the weather was real bad, we did the washing with water from the well and inside the kitchen with no wash pot privileges, just cold well water and bare hands and no battling stick, just bare knuckles and an old metal rub board. This was probably the way the west was born, but it sure was hard on our cold "snow white lilies" in icy cold weather. But we had been doing it this way for years with Mom to help us; now she graduated us and promoted us to the position of "washer boys."

Down by the spring we sawed down a big tree about three feet in diameter, leaving the stump about two feet high. The stump was our new battling bench or in our case-battling stump. We cut the tree up for wood for the fireplace and stove. This was like killing two things with one tree. Mom was real happy with our laundry arrangement; it meant that her older hardworking hands could take a vacation from the washtub, and we boys didn't seem to mind too much for the wash place was completely out of sight from the house and we could goof off and go fish a little in the larger creek about a hundred yards away from the spring and wash place. We would leave one to do the washing and two to do the fishing, taking turns as to who would do the fishing and who do the washing. Somehow we figured out that Mom probably knew after she saw us digging worms out behind the barn, one digging worms while two were carrying the laundry away. However, she was smart and didn't let on to knowing our secret, for after all she didn't have to do the washing and we were not breaking any of her rules. She had learned long ago while she was a little girl "not to rock the canoe" so you won't get so wet. By keeping quiet, she got the laundry done, and we seemed glad to do it. She had always said, "There is always a better way to skin a cat rather than use your butter knife," or something like that.

Within a few days after moving, we decided to meet the Thompson family that lived about a quarter mile further down the dirt road.

There was no one living beyound their house, there was an empty run down farm house a little further down the road but no one had lived there in many years and it was about rotted down and was covered with briars and vines. That was the very end of the road. Mr. Thompson, his wife and son, Neal were very kind, gentle country folk who had lived there for about all their lives. Neal was about ourage or maybe a year older. Re was a very nice boy and we got along great together. We boys fished together in the big creek that ran thru the Thompson's pasture and corn field. Mr. Thompson told that several years back after moving there that there was no running stream thru the pasture and field but the middle of the field and pasture seemed to stay wet for a long time after a big rain. He decided to dig a ditch thru the middle of the corn field and pasture. After digging the large ditch he never went down to the field for a week or two. When he did go just before reaching the ditch he could hear something that sounded like running water coming from the ditch. He walked over to the ditch and discovered a large stream of beautiful clear, cold water just rounning down the ditch. Appearently the water was running under ground all the time just looking for someone to dig its way out so it could run freely like all good water wants to. He said that the water looked happy to be out and alive to raise fish, frogs and turtles. After the water found its way out the pasture and corn field dried out and seemed to rejoice to have the water in the ditch which offecily became Thompson's Creek. It was his creek because he created it where no creek had been before. He must have felt proud to help God with his creation.

Daddy had the truck driver hauling lumber to Anniston to drop him off at a credits radio and appliance store where he bought a nice radio and six volt car battery. The truck driver brought him home with the radio held tightly in his arms and the battery held between his feet. He got out of the truck and we strung up the antena wire between the house and an apple tree and hooked up the radio. Daddy turned it on and tuned in on some music broadcasting station that was playing country music. There it played until about twelve or midnight. We had found a new way of life. About four the next morning Mom got up and turned on the radio to hear the news for the first time in her life. That radio went full blast until about ten o'clock that night. And on again about five the next morning. This went on for about a week and the battery went dead. After lugging the battery to a service station to get it charged a few times Daddy ask someone what to do. They told him to take it back to the store and swap it for a radio that had a power-pack battery that would last for about twelve to fifteen hundred hours of playing if played only about six to eight hours per day. The next day he carried the radio and battery to town and made the swap. The power-pack radio played even better than the six volt one and was louder and a clear as a bell with hardly any static interferiance. I dont think the tubes inside the radio ever cooled down for the first six months. That contracpion brought us into another world that we never realized existed before. Now instead of sitting around grumbling, fussing, cussing each other and calling each other old dirty words we could sit listening to the other world out there while we hardly spoke to each other and when we did speak it was in a soft tone of voice. Yes, the air waves had made us a changed family for sure. From that time on we all wanter a higher type of life, especily us children. We would nevwe be satisfied with working on a farm as share croppers and as porpers. We all wanted a better type life and if it was out there we were determined to hunt it down and get it. Isn't it amazing how one small thing like a radio with a power-battery can chang the lives of a whole family! One of the things some of us liked best was the quortet singers and the good preaching on Sundays. The preachers told of a different type life rather than stealing hogs and chickens. But that didn't help us much because we had already stopped that when we moved away from the valley. Where we now lived we didn't have any one that we could trust that we could steal from. If we had heard that type preaching while we was still living in the valley we might have just about starved to deathie. We could listen to it now for Daddy was making enough money for us to live only a little below a normal life. At one time we thought about getting a good rabbit dog, but Mom wouldn't let us get it. She said that it would scare all the bean eating rabits away from our garden, and we wouldn't be able to shoot as many of them while they ate her green beans and she had much rather have a good fried tender rabbit than a bowl of boiled green beans. So the rabbits kept on eating beans and we kept on shooting fresh fried rabbits. However we only shot about forty or fifty rabbits that spring and summer and still had plenty of green beans and peas. And almost everyone will admit that a fried rabbit is better than green boiled beans. So we never got the dog.

After school was out Daddy told us boys to scout around town and try to pick up a little part time work. That we did. The first thing we found was for a Mr. Bennett living in Edwardsville in a large white house ajointing a lot of farm land. He paid us a nickle per hour to saw fire wood and stack it for his winters use. We cut for several days sawing, splitting and stacking fire wood. It looked to us like he was starting a public wood yard fer to sell wood to others. He must have been selling it because after a few weeks during the hot summer he came over and hired us to cut a few more big stacks of wood. We was glad to sweat a lot and make a hand full of nickles for it. We saved up several dollars from our wood cutting and bought a Benjum Franklin pump air rifle. It was a "hum dinger" of a gun. If one pumped it ten strokes it would shoot a twenty two caliber lead pellet almost at the speed of a regular twenty two caliber rifle. It was so powerful that you could set up an empty tomato can on the top of a garden fence post and shoot a hole thru both sides without the can ever moving or shaking. That was one of the bird huntingous, snake shootingous, and hawk scareingness rifles that we had ever owned. Buying that air rifle made us want to stay in the woods and creek banks shooting birds and snakes about every day. But that had to slow down and we had work to do. Mr. Brown had a lot of farm land that us and his boys were farming on while he was home from the saw mill. He hired us to cut the bushes and briers off hi creek banks and around his fields. While we helped his sons do all this dirty hard work we always carried our air rifle along. His boys really liked our air rifle. They liked to walk up and down the creek bank hunting and shooting birds, snakes and fish. While they were hunting with our rifle they would let us walk behind the one that carried the air rifle, being very quiet as not to scare away their target. During this hunting period each day we didnt get much work done but we made the boss's sons happy and kept us from swinging brier blades and axes. Our old Indian grandma Crane had told us, "Kids, always be smart and always think 'wise'" and that was just what we were doing. After the goofing off and hunting snakes for about all day we would tell the Brown boys that we all had to work real hard and fast for the rest of the day or their Daddy might fire us and then they would have to do all the cutting and trimming alone and that without the use of our air gun and hunting previlegles. They didn't want us to get fired so they really worked to make a good showing for our days work. Each morning while we worked down by the creek we would let one of the Brown boys shoot the first snake that we saw sunning himself on a limb over the water. The snakes always rested on something hanging up above the water so if danger approached them they would just slide off in the water below. But that didn't always work if one of us was carrying a Benjum

Franklin air rifle. That snake had better have said all his prayers and get ready to wake up in snake heaven if there is such a place because the Brown boys were dead accurate with a gun. Many snakes and birds have died for their hunting pleasure. And a few have died to keep Neal, Lewis an me from having to clear the creek banks.

One morning we walked over to Mr. Brown's house to see if he needed us that day hopeing he didn't. To get to his house we always walked about a half mile down the rail-road track that ran from Edwardsville to Heflin. As we walked down the track we saw a box of rail road warning torpiedos lay on a cross tie near the steel rail. Well, we thought that to take two or three would be all right since there about forty or fifty, so we took three, put then in our pockets and proceded on to see Mr. Brown. When we got there he was out in his black smith shop doing some horse shoeing for a friend of his. His oldest son was helping him. Lewis showed one of Mr. Browns younger son the torpiedos His name was Joe. Joe told lewis to break off a small piece of the torpiedo, lay it on the big anvil and hit it with the large shop hammer. Lewis ask, "How pig a piece should I bresk off?" as he pealed the paper back oft the end of the torpiedo.

"A piece about the size of a pea" Joe replied. Well, there are shelled peas, peas in the hull and then there big cow peas. Lewis, not knowing which size pea he meant, broke off a piece about the size of a large unshelled cow pea, laying it on the anvil, drawing back the hammer and getting ready to strike the explosive. At that time Joe saw the size of the exploxive and jelled "Lewis don't—." Put it was too late. When the hammer hit the explosive a loud bang like a dinamite going off came from the shop. Mrs Brown was out in the garden a few yards from the shop hoeing okra plants, hearing the loud bang she looked up quickly, seeing a large shop hammer breaking thru the shop roof and going agout fifty feet in the air and landing in her okra row only a few feet away from her. She ran out to the shop to see what had happened. As she opened the garden gate the horse that Mr. Brown was shoeing ran past her, almost knocking her down on his way back to his own barn. Joe was on the Floor rolling and laughing so hard that he could not tell his Daddy just what happened. Lewis was sitting on the ground floor of the shop speachless. Lewis liked to talk a lot but this time he couldn't speak for a few minutes. Mr. and Mrs. Brown was very pale as they entered the shop. They didn't say anything for a minute or two then we all got a lecture in the fullest kind. After the Chewing out we boys went down and fetched back the scared mule which wasn't too happy to return to the shoe shop to finish getting his new horse shoes. We had to walk the mule around the shop and yard for several minutes before he would come near the shop door. After all had settled down and the mule decided to let Mr. Brown go ahead and fit her with a full set of horse shoes or horse moccisons if she was a wild Indian mule, Mrs. Brown went back to hoeing in the garden, but before going back she said to Lewis, "Lewis Rollins, if you ever expload some of that stuff in our shop again you had better use enough to blow you clean out of Cleburne County so I can't find you, for if I do I'll tie a whole stick of that stuff and tie you to the hammer handle and hit it myself." From that day forward we boys decided that we would leave the rail road torpiedos to the rail road nen after we had cut the lead strips from them. We needed the lead strips to make fishing sinkers to use down by the creek.

Down behind our house about half mile away was a large creek, the same creek that ran thru Mr. Thompson's fields and pasture. There were three smaller streams that ran into it just above our only corn field. The creek had some rather large and deep fishing holes that were well stocked with several kinds of fish. One day we boys decided to make some fish baskets or fish traps and get some of thes fish. We went to an old abandoned saw mill location and gathered several wood strips about the size as the frameing rails of Mom's quilting frame, about 1" X 2½" inches, And then sawed them in pieces about 36" long, nailing them together, making a box leaving one end open for the enterance. We took burlap sak material and made funnel shape cones reaching inside the boxes about eight inches with a hole about five inches in diameter at the little end of the funne. With this design the fish could funnel themselves in the box but could not funnel themselves out, when inside they just couldt find the front door again. We put the trap boxes in the large holes in the creek and put rocks on top to weight them down. Before lowering the traps into the creek we put some of Mom's left over corn bread in an old sock and put one in each of the four fish traps. Now all we had to do was wait until the next day to check our fish traps. That night was a long night for us, Would we find our boxes filled with fish the next tay or would be sadly disappointed? The following morning when the sun was about a hoe handle high we headed for the creek, it must have been about eight or eight thirty. As we approached the fishing holes our minds were wondering—had we wasted all those strips, nails, feed sacks and stale corn bread or would we have a flour sack weighted down with fresh live fish. Well, to our amazement, each box had several nice fish, the smaller ones swam thru the cracks between the side strips and would live to maybe caught another day or to live to be an old retired fish. That day we retreaved about twelve to fifteen pounds of brim and other fish. We had trapped or caught about twelve to fifteen pounds of fish the very first day. We kept the baskets in the creek for several weeks catching practally all the larger fish from each fishing hole. Fish restock year after year by raising babies or coming up stream to lay eggs and start new families. We didn't want to take all the fish—onlt the the ones large enough to cook.

We noticed that Mom had begun setting by the living room window and staring out into space. Now, that means only one thing, that Daddy had better start looking for us another house, and there was little time to waste. In a few days Daddy wouldn't get any rest or sleep at home until Mom's wants were granted. Once Mom made up her mind for us to relocate, all hell would break loose until we rented another place and relocated, and the new place had better be to her liking. Daddy had learned from past experience just what to do. He could stall her off by telling her that he was asking around for another job and house, but this would last for only a few days, and he had better come up with some offers on a house or new job. Mom wanted Daddy to rent a place where we could farm as sharecroppers just so we boys would not run loose hunting and fishing and maybe getting close to some girlfriends. She thought that since we were innocent of such things, keeping us slaving would keep us that way. However, it was too late for that. We all had been around the corner a few times even to look at us; we were not guilty of any such carrying on. She never knew about Pearlie or the Durke girls over in the Valley. But before she could come down on Daddy, he agreed to take a Saturday off from work and start looking and asking questions about a new place to live. It might mean that he would have to find a new job and leave Mr. Brown. That was something he didn't want to do at all, for he now had the best job he had ever had since he left the pipe shop in Anniston over twelve years ago. Daddy went to Mr. Brown early on that Saturday morning and told him of his plans to move and get another job. That was just what Mr. Brown wanted to hear. He had just bought a large section of good pine timber in the hilly country near Old Davis Town that was south of Heflin between Heflin and Anniston, in Calhoun County. He told Daddy that he had already asked about a place for us to move to, and someone told him that a Mr. Bob Faulkner had a large four-room house setting on about twenty acres that he wanted to rent to a sharecropper family. Mr. Bob, as he was known by, was a large landowner in the valley stretching out from Old Davis Town to the Choccolocco Valley. He had hundreds of acres of farmland and several rental houses and was always looking for honest hardworking families to do sharecropping for him.

Mr. Bob was a big man and was not afraid to work himself. He was friendly with everyone that he met. Daddy approached him that Saturday afternoon, and they got along very well on their very first meeting. He took Daddy about three miles from where his big seven-room house was located to some farmland bordering the hilly wooded area of the Talladega National Forrest. The land leveled out to almost level farmland, and setting in the northern part of the farm was a large plantation-type house. The house was in good repair but needed painting. There were four large rooms with an eight-foot-wide hall running through the house with two rooms on each side. The living room and kitchen was on the north side of the hallway and two large rooks on the other side. A large brick fireplace was in the living room and also one in one bedroom. The house must have been built by a plantation owner many years before Mr. Bob Faulkner bought up most of the land in the valley; perhaps some of his ancestors had built the house and lived there during their lifetime. Even the kitchen and dining room was as large as the large living room and had a large storage room attached to it on the back. The storage room had shelving all along two sides, and there was a grease floor where the previous owners had a meat box where they salted down their hog meat and stored it for their use all during the year. Daddy really liked the place and the house, for it was bigger and in better shape than the big Rossier house in Goose Neck Valley. Now the Lord must have taken a liking to us again since we had just about stopped stealing hogs and chickens and some of our part owned cotton Daddy quickly made a deal with Mr. Bob for the house and farmland. Mr. Bob agreed to let Daddy come over and pick out a good mule to do the plowing. He told Daddy to move in at any time he desired. Daddy got out of Mr. Bob's truck when they got to Highway 78, which was about a mile from our newly rented farm and home. Daddy hitchhiked a ride to Edwardsville and quickly walked to where we lived. Mom met him at the door and said, "Well, Wess, what is the news this time, what excuse do you offer me about you failing to find a place to move?" Before Daddy could answer her, she started crying, wiping her eyes with a rough guano sack towel as she waited for him to tell her of his failure. Then he began grinning and said, "Lee, start packing, for we are going to start moving tomorrow. You will like where we are going to move to."

Then he told her all the whole story of what had taken place in the few hours that had passed since the time they had last talked. As Daddy told her of his dealing with Mr. Bob and the big house and Mr. Brown's new sawmill location to near Old Davis Town, Mom started smiling and kept her mouth shut and let him do all the talking, which was a rare thing for her to do. But this time he brought her good news and much joy. It is needles to say what a good supper she prepared for him that night. We even had thick slabs of lean ham, big soft hot biscuits, along with two kinds of gravy, hot coffee, and plenty of cow's milk; she even let us boys drink our fill of fresh warm sweet milk. That supper meal was one of the greatest that we had ever had together. It was cooked and put on the table with great love and respect for Daddy. Mom was a great cook and she loved to cook when she was happy, and this was one of those rare moments in her life. While we lived in Anniston and Daddy made good money working at the pipe foundry, it was like living in paradise. Then the Great Depression hit and hit hard. Daddy was forced to leave that good money and move over to Cleburne County and live in a big eighteen-by-eighteen-foot canvass tent. His wages dropped to about 13 to 20¢ per hour, and at times he made only about 75¢ to $1.00 per day cutting logs for sawmillers all over the county, averaging moving almost each month. Yes, it was like being thrown out of paradise and landing in the torments of hell for Mom and Daddy.

Now we seemed to be beginning to climb back to a better life, but very slowly. To us boys it wasn't so bad, for we had never been growing up in paradise. Living in old run-down houses was all that we had ever known. Irra was only about four years old and Neal only two and I was only two weeks old when the gates of paradise was opened, and we were bumped out into the hell of poverty. Now with the new wage and hour law taking over and us boys being old enough to work, we were beginning to climb out of the worst kind of deep poverty and into a better life; after all we now had a radio to listen to and Mom had three new china plates and a new big cup for her coffee that she loved to drink each morning. However, Daddy's big cup had its handle broken off, and he had to let his coffee cool a little so he could hold the hot cup with his bare hand to drink it, so he would have to let most of the "hot" escape before he drank it unless he wore a sock on his right hand to hold the cup and not get burned. Sometimes Daddy would watch Mom drink her hot coffee from her new cup with its big cool handle and wonder what evil thing that he had done to prevent him from having a cup like that. But if they were not mad at each other and fussing back and forth at each other, she would let Daddy borrow her big cup that still had its handle so he wouldn't have to wear a somewhat dirty sock on his left hand to drink his coffee. Sometimes as I observed how much happiness that big cup brought Mom, my mind went back to the time we were living in our second house in Goose Neck Valley.

One day Mom gathered up some coupons that she had been saving that were in the coffee cans and ordered her a beautiful clear glass dinner plate with them. When the plate arrived, it was the most beautiful clear glass plate that we had ever seen; it had flowers etched in the glass and colored flowers painted on. It was a collector's plate and not to be eaten from, but she didn't know that. That night Mom sat down at the table and took out a large portion of very hot turnip greens and a slab of sowbelly meat on her new glass plate and began to smile. She had stepped up in life—a little. In a few seconds the plate went *clink* and broke in half, the turnip juice fan out on the table. Mom was so disappointed and began crying. She refused to eat her supper for a while, but the turnip greens and the freshly boiled sowbelly smelled so good she cast aside the new broken glass plate and got back down to earth and got her old cracked white china plate and joined us as we were finishing up our supper. We had left her some good stuff still in the serving bowl. We tried to get her to glue the two pieces of the plate together and set it on the dresser to look at, but she threw it out in the trash and said, "If a plate won't hold its self together long enough for me to eat my turnip greens, I don't need it laying around in my way."

The next day Mr. Brown sent one of his flatbed trucks with high side bed over to the house to hall our things and stuff over to our new home. After about two or three hours, we were loaded and ready to go except for the chickens, the hog and the cow. We would get them the next day. About lunchtime and after the twelve mile we arrived at our new home. Boy, were we all surprised! The house was larger and more beautiful than we could even picture in our minds. Surely we had moved up to the rim of paradise. However, there was a lot of cleaning to be done. The house had been used for a barn and grain storage for a year or so. The house was filled and infected with rats, not the little mousey kind, but the big squirrelly kind. We cleaned and swept up the floors as we moved the furniture in two rooms and kept cleaning and sweeping for the rest of the day while Daddy went back for the cow, hog, and chickens which were already boxed or caged up and ready to load. This time the cow would get to ride in the truck for the first time in her life. I bet she was riding high class. As the cow went down the highway, she would raise her head and seem to say, "Cows and bulls, just look at me riding and not walking to my new pasture."

However, if the cow had only known—the pasture was a rocky hillside with nothing but scrubby bushes and trees with no grass at all. That night we worked late and had done enough cleaning to set up the beds, stove, and dining table; after all, this was enough for a tired out family for one night. We ate mostly canned stuff with a pan of corn bread that Mom had cooked the day before and brought along for our supper. That wasn't very much, but we were so tired and hungry that anything tasted good to us. After we finely went to bed, the large rats came out to serenade us for the rest of the night. They ran across the floor, squeaked, jumped up on our bed, and did a lot of other things all night long. The next morning we looked up all the holes that they had chewed in the walls and doors and nailed boards and sheet tin over them. We pretty well rat-proofed the main living part of the house from the two hundred big rats and little mice that were serenading us. After Daddy arrived with the live things, we put the cow in the big barn, closed the gate, and turned the chickens loose in the big wired-in garden and left the young hog in its crate until morning. Early the next morning, we ran the stove pipe up above the roof, got out and gathered up enough old stove wood, and fired that old black cookstove off. As it heated up, the whole family cleaned up the kitchen and put the new oil-cloth tablecloth on the dining table and set up the bench on one side of the table and four wood split-bottomed chairs on the ends and on the other side of the table. Here we had plenty of room to our kitchen like Grandma's large kitchen. We all lived it. There would be no more crowding to get our place in the large kitchen. Daddy helped Mom prepare the breakfast that morning, and what a breakfast it would be. We had hunks or slabs of ham that one couldn't even get in one of the finest eateries in town. We had three kinds of gravy: good, better, and worse, and a lot of good soft cathead biscuits almost as large as a small bucket lid, canned peaches, and even blackberries that we had obtained from the Durke boys over by our sow pen. There was a lot of other stuff on the table to go with all this. Boy, when Mom was happy, she sure could cook up the good stuff. It was a wonder why she didn't catch and kill Daddy's big red rooster and cook him up and serve him that day. Daddy stopped her just in time that afternoon by telling her that if she killed his rooster, we would become cannibals and serve her fat butt for breakfast the next morning. At that point she smoothed down the old rooster's feathers and pretended to kiss his big head and gently put him down beside the chopping block and watched him run for his life. It was about three or four days before we saw that rooster again; he was out practicing how to stay out of Mom's big rooster-killing hands. Sometimes it is amazing how an animal or fowl can detect whether one is holding them with kindness and love or you are holding them for their execution and preparation for an invitation to dine with the Rollins family in a late-afternoon supper. At least that rooster sure was lucky that Daddy came up just in time to stop the execution. It seemed that after he finely showed after three days and joined his hen friends, he could crow louder than he had ever crowed before, and that made Daddy very happy just to hear his favorite rooster crow again.

After breakfast we decided to get our water from a spring locater across the cotton patch flowing at the foot of a small mountain about two hundred yards from our house. The water was crystal clear and very cold. This was the best water supply that we had ever had. There was a well on the south side of the house but, the well curb had rotten away, and when one looked down in the well you could see trash and rotten boards floating on the dirty water. We decided to start filling the well with our trash and anything lying around. And Mom said that the water wouldn't be real cold because the well was located on the south side of the house, and everyone knows that it is warmer in the south than it is in the north. For about a week we all pitched in to clean the house real good and to clear all the weeds and debris from the yard and garden and cow lot out by the big barn. It was late February and was still cold, so we went to the woods and chopped and sawed a lot of firewood and brought it into our woodpile that was located about fifty feet from the house and under a big black walnut tree. By the end of the week, one would not recognize the place; it looked like a caring family lived there.

Mom was more proud of this place than she could have ever been living in the big Rossier house over in Goose Neck Valley. And we could live here with a clear conscience, for we got here without witchcraft or maybe murder to obtain the house.

We had rented it fair and square from Mr. Bob. We knew that we could live there for at least about one year, and if things worked out well for us, we might be there for two or three years or perhaps longer. Mr. Bob wanted us to work for him for about fifty cents per day working on his large farm and the days were about twelve hours work time each day. However, we just wouldn't accept that low wage for such long hours. We had become liberated, and we wanted fair pay for a fair day's work. And with Daddy making good wages working for Mr. Brown, we wouldn't have to stoop for that low pay. We had stolen meat in the meat box, and a few confiscated neighbors chickens and Daddy's old twelve-gauge shotgun to kill rabbits and squirrels and some fishing stuff, so why not be liberated and independent for a change. At this point in our lives we really began to live. Here we had large cornfields below our house that were covered with wild onions and what we called "cresses." However, the cress might have been dandelions. The entire family liked cooked wild onions and boiled cress. All the rest of the winter, we boys would go down in the cornfields and gather large pans and buckets of these delicious and rare foods. We might be liberated but we still liked our old way of eating what the Lord had allowed to grow in the fields below our house. We gathered and ate this stuff until Mr. Bob came over with his big tractor and plowed up the cornfields and replanted corn again.

After about one week after we moved in the Faulkner house Neal, Lewis, and I had to report to the White Plains grade school and enroll for the rest of the school year. After one week of school, the teachers advanced Lewis and me from the fourth grade to the fifth grade. They said that the Cleburnee County school was advanced one grade higher than the White Planes school system. So it meant that we stepped up one grade by moving to our new home. Daddy said if we moved a few more times, we may be able to finish high school and even get a degree in college without very much book learning. Then we could be about as dumb as some of the well-educated people that he knew. We always seemed to have to walk about a mile and wait in the cold winter weather to catch the school bus. Here was no different. We walked over to Old Davis Town, a small thickly settled community and wait for the bus at Mr. J. C. Lett's small grocery store and filling station. Mr. Let was a kind gentleman, small in size but with a great big heart. He would let us wait under his canopy of the store in rainy weather and even let us wait inside when it was real cold. Mr. Lett sold us groceries and other supplies on credit and let Daddy pay for them each week after he got paid by Mr. Brown. Mr. J. C. Lett had a wonderful family. James became a chiropractor, and his daughter Irma married Dr. Walter Foster, a chiropractor, and Mr. Joe Lett, his older son, became a banker and a preacher. I'm sure Mr. and Mrs. Lett were very proud of their children. With all the kindness, Mr. Lett going to school was no picnic. However, with all the hardships and struggles of going to school, life would be most miserable without an education. We hung in there, and each of us boys was promoted to a higher grade that year. Lewis and I were promoted to the sixth grade, and Neal was promoted to the fifth grade. That year Neal came down with bronchitis and dropped out of school and was not able to go any further in school. The following school year Lewis and I completed the sixth grade at White Plains.

Mr. Walter Wade Robertson owned a hideaway resort camp about a half mile up in the woods above us. It was located on a small hollow, between two steep hills. He had graded out room for a rather large cabin, a big storage building, and a large swimming pool. He had a water-powered generator to furnish power for his camp grounds and cabins. In his storage building he had several 6-volt storage batteries wired in series to furnish 110 volts of current to everything that was electrical. The 110-volt generator furnished plenty of juice to keep the batteries fully charged at all times. Mr. Robertson owned and operated the Calhoun machine shop in Anniston and was a very smart electrical engineer. Mr. Roberson had to drive by our house to get to his cabins. Soon after we moved there, he invited us boys to the camp to show us what he had built near us and to see if we would help him do a little work. He mostly wanted to know if we were honest or if we would steel him blind when he was away. He asked us if we would clean his main cabin the next day while he would be at his business in Anniston. He promised to pay us a dollar to clean it a little and sweep the floor. After showing us where the key would be hidden, he showed us his large marble-lined swimming pool which was eleven feet deep and with a diving board twelve feet above the water. He told us that when the weather got a little warmer, we could go swimming without any cloth on when we liked. The camp was remote from civilization and out of sight from everyone.

The next day we went up to clean his cabin. As we entered, we saw silver coins lying scattered on the floor. We gathered up the coins and put them in a neat pile on his nightstand table by his bed and proceeded to clean the cabin. On a kerosene heater, he left a big pan of boiling peanuts. Boy, did we want to get into that pan of peanuts, but we didn't even steal one single boiled peanut. After he got in from work and came up to the camp, Mr. Roberson got in his car and came down to our house to pay us for cleaning his cabin. He went in and sat down with us for a few minutes and got acquainted with the family and paid us for our cleaning. He then said, "I was glad to see the money that I left on the floor was stacked on the nightstand. Every bit of it was left, and I didn't count the boiled peanuts but they were all there too. I put one dollar in change on the floor to see how honest you boys were, and now I know if you won't steal my money and won't even eat my boiled peanuts, I can trust you with my cabin and things while I'm away. And now I'll pay you a dollar each week to kindly look after it for me while I'm away maybe check on things now and then. And you boys can go, up there and go swimming anytime you like. You have proved to me that you are an honest family and I feel that I can trust you now." While he was talking, I got up and closed the kitchen door to keep him from seeing the leftover stolen chicken and ham scraps on our dining table.

As the weeks went by, Mr. Roberson introduced us to his two sons, Walter Wade and Wilks. They were so glad to go hunting with us and go swimming with us in their big marble-slab-lined swimming hole. The creek water running in the pool was always crystal clear and never had to be treated with chemicals. Walter Wade and Wilks really liked to come out there and spend the weekends and hunt and fish with us. They were the nicest and most wealthy boys that we had ever spent time with. They were a year or so older then us and just enjoyed being out of town and out in Gods country. And best of all, their father pretty well knew that we wouldn't be leading them in the wrong direction, into a lot of trouble. Mrs. Roberson told Mom that it was a great relief to know that their sons were hanging out on the weekends with good people. As long as we lived there, the two families were good friends.

In the spring, Mr. Roberson bought us a real good used bicycle and gave it to us just because he cared for us, and he wanted to do something to help us a little. We never did anything to make him mistrust us in any way. We didn't steel his pigs and chickens for he was pigless and chickenless. Mr. Roberson never at one time indicated that he was above us in any way. He always took time to talk to us as if we were one of his own boys. That kind of a relationship made us want to climb up the ladder of success a little higher. There was no way that we would wand to make him trust us less. He had turned our family loose in his camp to enjoy it at any time, and we sure did. We kept the grounds and his cabin clean, and we cleaned any leaves or other thing from the marble swimming pool. He lived in town in a big brick and painted house with indoor outhouses and running water and electricity, but he seemed to be just a common working man when we were together. That was what made him so great in our eyes. He had become one of us, and there was no way that we would ever steal from him or disrespect his property.

In the summer that we lived on Mr. Bob's farm, the U.S. government decided that everyone in the nation needed a nice new cotton mattress to sleep on, and since cotton prices were at rock bottom the government put in a new program. Anyone who wanted to make their own mattress the government agents would meet in schoolhouses and help design and oversee the mattress making. Some people would put cotton in the floor of the schoolrooms and beat it with a big heavy stick while others would cut and sew the mattress covers. The next step was to stuff the mattress cover with the soft fluffy freshly beaten cotton to the proper thickness and with a big curved needle sew it in and make turfs every foot or so all over the mattress. This made the mattress lie flat just like the ones we bought today. We made three new mattresses and burned the old ones that we had that were filled with wheat straw and grass hay. Neal said that we ought to feed the straw to the cow, but when she smelled it, she ran in the barn and refused to come out until she smelled the smoke as we burned the straw. No respectable sweet-smelling cow wants to be fed with old dirty foul-smelling wheat straw that dirty old humans have slept on for years. Somehow I believe that that old heifer respected us for not making her eat that dirty stuff. At this point in our lives, we really began to feel like we were on our way up the ladder. We were somewhat better off than we ever were before, but we had a long way to go. With a new radio, Daddy had two extra pair of overalls, a meat box half full of borrowed sow meat, and about twenty borrowed chickens; and our old cat had three new kittens, and Daddy had saved back seven dollars, and now we had three new cotton-filled mattresses for to sleep on. Yes, we were coming along pretty well. And to make life more pleasant, I had saved up about four dollars and ordered an Aladdin kerosene lamp, the one that has a silk mantle that glows as bright as an electric bulb. One night we sat down at the table after supper and listed what we had gained in the last few years, and we were gloriously surprised. We came to the conclusion that if we lived for about twenty more years with this same rate of success, we might be even driving an old car or at least own our own mule and wagon. Well at least we were making forward progress and not slipping further behind.

About two or three weeks before school was out, we boys had to drop out of school to start the farming thing for the summer. After talking with the teachers, we were told that our grades were high enough that we would pass on to the next grade anyway but to be there the last day of school to get our report cards. We had done this before, so it was nothing new to us. Mr. Bob let Daddy have an old clubfooted mule to do the farming. The mule could not walk very well and limped along every step that she took. Daddy didn't like it, but we decided to get one more summer out of the old mare. That summer we planted about seven or eight acres of cotton and several acres of corn and about an acre of sugarcane to make a few gallons of syrup. We had a small peanut patch and a large garden. Within a few weeks ole Nellie, the mule and we boys had most of the ground prepared for planting, and most of it planted. Old Nellie was slow, but she kept right on agoing and a plowing. I know there was great pain every step that she took on that clubfoot, but she never complained, at least not to any of us. By the first of May we had most of the planting done except for the corn. Daddy always waited until the first of June to plant the corn.

Just after dropping out of school to start farming, we all agreed to do something about our water supply. The old well was not fit to get our water from; it was just worn out. So we decided to dig a new well. We boys wanted to cut a hole in the back porch and dig it there so we could draw water without getting out in foul weather to get the water. But Mom would not even listen to us about the location of the well. Mom said that the further north we went to dig the well, the colder the water would be when we would draw it up. After all we all knew that the further north one gets, the colder the climate. So she made us go about thirty feet north of the house to start our new well so the water would be a little colder. Daddy said it wouldn't make much difference to move north about fifty feet, but Mom won the argument because she had two months more education than Daddy, and that gave her priority over Daddy's decisions. So we began digging out by the garden fence on the north side of the house. She even wanted us to move the garden to the south side of the house so it would be in a warmer climate. However, we agreed to just a day or two later to plant the garden stuff until the climate got right for the north planting. I agreed to do the digging the well, and Lewis and Neal would draw out the buckets of dirt that I sent up. On the first day we went down about six feet deep. The second day I only dug about five feet because in a forty-two-inch diameter well, one doesn't have a great deal of room to do the digging and shoveling up the dirt and putting it in the two-gallon bucket. Daddy had dug many wells, and he kept close watch on us to see that we didn't dig the well so crooked that when we was done, we couldn't see the bottom. He had us to take a string and tie a little rock on the end and use it as a plumb bob or plumb line to keep the well going straight down. He said that he had gone to clean out some well that were so crooked that even the sunlight had to carry a reflector mirror to shine down to the bottom, and he sure didn't want our well to be that crooked.

On the fourth day at about eighteen feet, I saw water coming in at the bottom bank of the well. It wasn't much, but it was water, the same water that we were digging for. We had to work fast for the deeper we dug the faster the water came in, and it was clear and cold. While I was getting wet with the cold water, I began to wish that Mom had let us dig the well on the south side of the house so the water wouldn't be hardly so cold. But it was too late now. We finished digging the well. Late afternoon that day we had only worked four days, and we had a good northern cold water supply. After I came up from that hole in the ground, we moved the windlass rig from over the well and covered it with two pieces of old roofing tin. The next day was Saturday, and Daddy had brought a few boards home from the sawmill where he worked, and we all built a well curb and windlass and began to draw out good cold water. It was good and cold, and Mom was extremely happy. We were all sure that she would cook up a good supper including Daddy's big red rooster, but Daddy had caught him and hid him in the corn crib for the day for his own security, the rooster's security—not Daddy's. However, a couple of Mom's fryers met their doom and paid the supreme price in celebration of our cold water well. After finishing the curb Daddy tied a wood strip of good wood to the well rope and let it down until it hit the bottom of the well and brought it back up to measure how deep the water was. The wet bottom part of the strip was up to Daddy's eyeballs, which meant that we had about six feet of clear cold water. Now we would not have to tread through the cotton field to get our water from the spring during rainy, cold weather. Now we could just stand out in the rainy cold weather and let the bucket down and draw out the supply of water. We boys quickly could see the real advantage of the new well; instead of Mom yelling for us to go to the spring for water, she could go out north and draw it for herself. We never were able to put a shed over the well, but it could fend for itself while we stayed in out of the foul weather. This was the first time in many years that we had good clean well water that we could trust to be clean with no toads, frogs, or snakes down there in the clean water.

One day Mom's brother, Hubert Crain, came over to see us on a Saturday afternoon. He told Mom that since she used to like to go to all day church singings, he would take her over to a church in Iron City the next day, which was Sunday. Mom worked the rest of the day and way into the night cooking large four layer cakes to carry to the singing. The next morning we all got ready for church and the singing. We boys had rather stayed home and went swimming in Mr. Roberson's big marble swimming pool, but we were not about to let Mom take four good-looking cakes off to feed other people and us not getting to eat our part. So the whole family went to the singing and stayed for lunch or the "dinner on the fround." After we boys were full, we decided to walk the two miles back home and go swimming. Uncle Hubert had a motive for asking Mom and Daddy to go to the singing. On the way home, he talked to them about letting one of us boys work for his farming that summer. He would pay fifty cents per day and board for five days per week. Mom and Daddy really needed the money, for Neal had developed a bad lung disease and had to go to Anniston once each week to be treated by Dr. Spearman. They agreed to hire me out to Uncle Hubert for the summer.

Uncle Hubert lived only three miles from where we lived, but I had to walk about one mile through the woods on a trail in heavy woods from the new CCC road to our house. I didn't like the idea at all, but since Neal was sick and Lewis refused to go, I took on the responsibility of the job. That Sunday afternoon we packed up some of my clothes and stuff, and I went with Uncle Hubert to his house. He lived in an older house by Grandpa's house, the same house that we had lived in at least twice before. Going over there was not so bad, for it was kinfolk and not like living with strangers. My room was a little side room off the front porch, the very same front porch that we four boys rolled around on the day that we got drunk on Mr. Dempsey's blackberry wine. And this was the same house that I had lived in when as a small boy. And I had learned to hunt birds with a slingshot and go to the small creek below the house and fish. The place brought back so many pleasant memories. But now I was fourteen years old and had to take on the job as a man. For a little while I went around to places where we had played at an earlier time in our lives and remembered all the good times that we had together. It was not the same now; Irra had gone to Atlanta to work for another uncle, our Uncle Hughes doing heating and metalwork. And now Neal, Lewis, Margret, Caffey, and Betty were all living at another place. Man, one can come to certain realities and real life so quick. Just two days ago we were all living together, and now it seemed that a huge gulf was created and stood between me and my family. The main thing that kept me from walking back home was that what I would be doing would be helping with Neal's medical expense.

I think I cried a little that night after going to bed. However, the next morning I settled down with the task of working with Aunt Luella and Grandpa's brother Green. They were all happy to see me and show me the ropes of farming mostly by myself. To have me there meant there would be less work for them to do on the farming. Uncle Green was a very hard worker and did all the wood chopping and looking after the livestock and most everything else that a man would do to keep a family going. Really he was Grandpa's slave. Although he was Grandpa's brother, he was really Grandpa's slave. Uncle Green got up every morning and fired off the big wood burning stove, built a fire in the fireplace, brought in fresh water from the well, fed the mules and cows, and did most everything else that no one else wanted to do. He did more before breakfast than Grandpa did all the rest of the day. Some relatives believed that Old Uncle was taking care of some of Grandma's needs while Grandpa was out scampering around with the other girls living over in the little cabin in the woods nearby. Well, he was always handy and Grandpa wasn't. Everyone loved Uncle; that was the name he always went by in the family. Many families would have liked to have a live in like Uncle to work and keep the womenfolk happy. After getting settled in that Sunday night of my arrival, I couldn't sleep very well while listening to the squeaking and rattling of the bedsprings just on the other side of the wall from my bed. Things were going on! And there was I to wonder just what was going on in their bed. But morning and daylight were bound to come, and come it did. Before good daylight, Uncle Hubert woke me up and told me to go up to Grandpa's well about three hundred yards away and bring back two ten quart buckets of fresh well water. As soon as I got back, he had me to start a fire in the old woodstove so Aunt Foy could cook breakfast. It seemed that I would really earn that fifty cents per day's wages. It seemed that maybe he wanted me to be somewhat the slave to his family that Uncle was to Grandpa's family. However, Uncle Hubert worked five and a half days for Uncle Shug in Anniston doing heating and sheet metal work. Sometimes I would go in to work with him on rainy days and on Saturday and work for Uncle Shug helping in the sheet metal shop. This I really liked for there I was paid ten cents per hour for my work.

Uncle Hubert wanted Uncle Shug to pay him for my work so he could take half of it but Uncle Shug told him that if he took any part of my pay that he would be fired from his job. So my ten cents per hour pay came straight to me.

After the first day or two getting used to my farm job, the plowing and farming started. Grandpa's mule was named Kate. She was medium sized and very gentle to work with. She took a liking to me and I took a liking to her. She would be like my own mule for the farming season. Kate and I began plowing the fields and getting it prepared for planting. Uncle and Aunt Luella helped me put down the guano fertilizer by hand and plant the corn and other stuff. We didn't plant any cotton, and boy, was I glad. Cotton is easy to raise but hard to pick. However, Daddy was raising cotton, and I would be there to pick it with Lewis and Neal. After working all week, I would go home on Saturday evening, to walk home would take only about an hour to walk the three miles. It was always a joy to get back with Mom and Daddy and the rest of the family. The hardest part of working away from home was not the slavery but missing the family. Back in those days, the children were not chomping at the bitts to get away to live somewhere else, but they usually wanted the company of their family as long as possible. However, I didn't mind it so much for I was helping to pay Neal's medical bills so he could breathe easier. The corn came up and stuck it little heads above the furrow rows and waved its little leaves or blades in the breeze. That sure was a pretty sight to see. Just to think that I had the biggest part in its being. I had to generate new life in the large fields and it would be my responsibility to keep it happy and growing until harvest time. I began plowing it with carefully selected plowing equipment to carefully cover the little grass that had poked it mean little heads up all around my young innocent corn plants. Uncle helped me to select the proper moldboard side plow to cover the mean old grass and not cover the corn plants. Upon his years of wisdom in killing grass, I was able to become a professional grass executioner. By careful plowing, most of the grass was covered and dead-dead-dead. Now my little cornstalks could grow and live a normal life without the torment of that dirty old grass. I just kept on a plowing, and the corn and stuff just kept on growing.

After I had been farming for Uncle Herbert, I went in to work with him at his job one Saturday. I had been farming for about a month and walking home on Saturday afternoon. When I got to the shop that day, Uncle Shug rolled out a good-looking Road Runner bicycle into the shop from his office. "How do you like the looks of this bicycle?" he asked me as he leaned it up against the workbench.

"I think it looks very good; someday I may buy me one but maybe not that nice." I said as I walked over and took hold of the handlebars.

"Why not just take this one, and you won't have to worry about buying one. I thought that it would keep you from walking over to work on Sunday evening, and it would take you home on Saturday, and since you are working now I think you should have a bicycle." Aunt Nell was standing in the office door grinning very happily at the whole deal. I rolled the bike around the shop floor and for me to work that day for I wanted to load that bike on Uncle Hubert's pickup truck and head for his house. We only worked a half day on Saturday; however, it was hard to keep working knowing that a practically new bike was leaning up against the workbench and staring at me and seeming to say, "Ride me, Frank, ride me." After working for about four hours, we loaded the bike and headed for home. When we got there I got the bicycle off the truck and "ride me" I did. After Uncle Hubert paid me my two dollars and fifty cents, I put my dirty clothes in the handlebar basket and tied them down with a string and headed for Daddy's house over in the valley. It was an exciting ride, two miles on a good gravel road with no traffic and then a mile on a well-beaten trail for a mile through the woods. The Road Runner bicycle was the easiest riding bike that I had ever put my rump on and peddled away. It rode like a dream, and it was my very own and it was free. After arriving at Daddy's house Neal and Lewis just had to ride it some. It seemed that they would never get off it and let me ride it again. After a few days they told Mr. Robertson about my bike. He had two older bikes that his sons got tired of and got newer ones. The following Saturday he brought one bike and gave it to Lewis and Neal. They were very proud of their bikes and offered to clean up the camp grounds to pay for the bike, but Mr. Roberson told them that the bike was a gift and said he would keep paying them for all the work up in the camp. It was hard for Mom and Daddy to get a full day's work out of them again that summer. My new bike was a real blessing for me; it was a way for me to go to and from Grandpa's house to our home in the valley three miles away.

That summer was very hard for me for it was the first time that I had a job away from home, and at the age of fourteen, I had the full responsibility of farming almost by myself with only a limited amount of help from Uncle Green and Aunt Luella. They helped, but all the plowing and most of the other work was left up for me to do all by myself, and I had never had all that responsibility shoved on me before. Each night I wished that I could just sneak off and go back home to Mom and Dad and the others, but then I would remember that Neal needed the medical care that the money that I was making would provide for him. The next morning I would get up and face the rear end of Old Kate, the mule, for another day under the broiling sun for another ten to twelve hours. As I think back over that year of hardship, I believe that the Lord was hardening me for the years ahead. If I had never gone through that year and the next year, surely my life might have been wasted and I might have chose to go the easy road. All summer long and into the fall I kept the farm going until the crop was gathered in and stored in the barn. After that was done I went back home to go back to school at White Plains. That school year seemed easier for me because I wasn't looking at the rear end of an old mule named Kate. And also maybe I just may learn enough to not have to look a mule in the rear year after year for the rest of my days. Somehow I believe that look at the south end of a north bound mule day after day was sort of like going to college, for I was learning what not to look forward to for the rest of my life.

That winter was hard on us boys attending school and doing all the things we had to do at home like cutting firewood and carrying it on our shoulders from the wooded area about two hundred yards from our house. After school we would have to get the cow and calf from the main pasture and feed and milk the cow. This had to be done rain or shine whatever the weatherman had to offer us for the day. Daddy had to do his work at the logging location for the sawmill. That winter wasn't as hard on Daddy as the winter before because we boys were old enough to take most of the load off him at home, and he didn't have so far to walk to get to his job. Daddy was really living a life of ease a lot of the time. About all he had to do was to get up in the morning, build a fire in the large fireplace, fire up the cookstove, break the ice off the water bucket, wash his face and hands in the icy water, and help Mom cook the ham, eggs, and biscuits, eat breakfast with the family, and take himself to work carrying the eight-pound lard bucket filled with chicken legs, ham slices, large biscuits, and a big slice of Mom's coconut cake wrapped in a page from the farm magazine or an old newspaper that we had picked up at the trash dump and saved for such occasion or something worse. He often said that he could turn the bottom of the greasy biscuits up and read some of last month's news off the bottom of the biscuit, plainly printed in black and white and hog lard. However, Daddy just kept on a working and we just kept on eating and living.

After the hard winter was over and school was out Daddy went over to get the old clubfooted mule and start farming again. Mr. Bob refused to let us have a mule, the clubfooted mule was dead and he blamed the mule's death on us. The old mule died while in his care and probably because of starvation and old age. Mr. Bob told Daddy that he wanted us to move out of his house within ten days. We refused to go. Mr. Bob took Daddy to court before a justice of the peace, who was his cousin. And of course, Daddy lost the case and the justice of the peace gave Daddy five days to be out of the house and off the property. The next day Daddy and Mom walked over to Grandpa's house where I had lived the summer before to see if they could rent the old house where Mom was raised up in before Grandpa had built the large plantation-type home that they now lived in. Mom and Dad rented the older two-room house that was now being used for a corn crib and farm equipment storage building. Since living there, Grandpa had built two mule stables on to the back of the house and a small mule lot with a rail fence around the lot area.

The next morning at the crack of day we all left for Grandpa's farm to clean out the old house and get it ready for us to move in. Uncle Green and Aunt Luella pitched in and helped us. During the winter, Uncle Shug had hired Daddy and me to build Grandpa a new barn up on the other side of his house. For the next two days, Daddy and I worked very hard to finish the barn and corn crib and the two new mule stables. As we were finishing the building, the other members of the family were hauling hay and corn up to the new barn. The old house was cleaned out and the floors were scrubbed with Grandma's corn shuck mop, using fine sand and lye soapy water to clean the floors. After three days, long days, the house was clean enough for us to move in. Daddy hired Uncle Hubert to move our stuff and things on his flatbed pickup truck after he got off work. After we had loaded the final load on the truck, Daddy left two of us to do some final "things" at Mr. Bob's house, sort of like putting two wheel barrows full of fresh cow manure and dumped it in the well. We destroyed all the living plants in the garden and tore down the garden fence we had built and threw it down in the well. We wanted to burn the house, but Daddy told us not to go that far.

After we had done that, it was beginning to get dusty dark, so we set out walking over to our new home which was about an hours walk. When the darkness got heavier, we sure did walk fast. We cut the hour down to about forty-five minutes. When we arrived, Grandma and Mom had us a lot of good stuff to eat. After supper Neal and I joined the others and got our beds up and ready for some good sleeping. Old Kate the mule was still sleeping in the stable just behind us in the stable joining our bedroom. We were in such a hurry getting set up that we had not noticed a hole the mules in the past had chewed in the wall to get to the corn that had been stored in the room. Our bed was pushed up against the wall where the hole was. Shortly after we had gone to bed and blew out the kerosene lamp, Old Kate stuck her nose through the hole and started nibbling at Neal's foot that was almost against the wall. Neal yelled out, "Daddy, I think the devil is after me! He grabbed me by my foot, and I saw his big shiny eyes through the wall!" Daddy ran in to see what was wrong, lighting the lamp he could see two big shiny eyes staring through the hole. He got a board from the well house outside and nailed it over the hole so the devil couldn't get any of us that night. We could not get all our furniture and stuff in the house, boy was it crowded. We put the stove outside with the table and chairs. The stove went under the big well shed, the well curb had been removed and the well covered over with huge four-inch-thick timbers. The kitchen cabinet and the table and chairs were also set up under the well shed, with the edge of the table and our kitchen dining bench sticking out under the eave of the shed. When it rained, we had to drag the table in and place it against the front of the stove and cabinet. After the rain had ended or slacked up, we could drag it out and eat again. Since I was going to work for Uncle Hubert farming that summer, I was allowed to eat and sleep up in the big house. After living in this condition and since we boys were old enough to do work outside to help out we finally decided to try to buy us a place somewhere nearby. Having to live under these conditions helped us to decide very fast, about three weeks was enough decision time for the family. So we began to ask around with friends, neighbors, and relatives. Daddy's brother, Dave, owned thirty-two acres and a pretty good three-room house about two miles away on Highway 431. Dave had moved to the Coldwater area near Oxford. He was renting the house to a bootlegging, whisky-guzzling family that wouldn't pay rent and wouldn't move either. So he was our first try.

The next Saturday morning Mom and I got Uncle Hubert to take us to Oxford, about fifteen miles away, to see Uncle Dave. After the usual greeting we got down to business. Mom said, "Dave, we have practically no place to live, and since you have moved away from your place over on the highway, Wess and I wondered if you would sell it to us and let us pay you something each month like rent. We are tired of moving every year and fixing up some old house and being kicked out or having to move so Wess can find a new job."

"Lee, Arnold and his wife, and I have talking about selling the place since we don't really need it anymore. And since need a place I had rather sell it you and Wess than anyone else I know. If we don't get that whisky-guzzling family out of the house, they may chop the house down and use it for stove wood if they have anything to cook," Dave said as his son Arnold had walked into the room where they were sitting, sat down, and was listening to them talk. He began grinning and said, "Daddy, that will get that whisky-drinking whore out of there along with her 'shack-up' friends. If you and Uncle Wess buy the place, we will know it will be taken care of."

"Lee, what would you be willing to pay me for the place?" Dave asked as he sipped on his cup of black coffee.

"You are the owner, just would you be willing to sell it to us for and how much would you want down and how much each month? We don't have but about ten dollars, but with Frank working and Wess a job somewhere real soon we can pay you some each month."

"I could sell it to you for three hundred dollars, with the thirty-two acres on the highway, and I'll throw in the house to boot, and I'm willing to take ten dollars per month down and ten dollars each month thereafter. If you can't pay me each month just pay me as often as you can. I know you and Wess won't beat me out of the place, and I'll be glad to help you own your own home and land," Dave said as he sipped on his cold coffee.

"How soon can we get a deed and move in?" Mom asked Dave. Dave replied, "I'll write you on right now, all I have to do is write you a deed wording it my old deed and sign it over to you. You won't have to sign it. That is all there to it. You don't have to sign a mortgage for Wess is my brother and he won't try to mess me up." While he was speaking, he was fumbling through papers in a big shoe box that he had retrieved from the bottom drawer of a large dresser. He then pulled out a large envelope from the bottom of the box and took a single sheet of paper from it. Picking up a large school tablet to the kitchen table, he began to write out the deed, the wording the same as on the deed except he wrote Lee and Wess's name, signed it at the bottom, and handed to Mom. She handed him a ten-dollar bill. Somehow I believe the angels in heaven began to rejoice over us crossing the river and having a piece of the promised land. Well, we sure did. We now owned our own home for the first time in any of our lives. That was worth rejoicing about. Mom had Uncle Hubert drive us to Heflin and get the deed recorded at the courthouse. We didn't want Uncle Dave to back out on the deal. For the first time in her life, she, Daddy, and the family owned our very own house and thirty-two acres of good land and not off in a wooded jungle but right on Highway 431. The house set about seventy feet from the highway. Now we could see the cars and truck whizzing by. It would be like living pretty close to paradise. After returning home, we celebrated a little. Grandpa and Grandma and all the others were very happy that we now owned a drunkard-infested house. The next step was to get them out.

After we had been home for about an hour, we all put on some better-looking clothes and walked over to our new house which was about two miles from where we were now living. It took us about forty-five minutes to make the journey from the "wilderness" to the "land of promise." The house where Daddy's parents lived and died in was just across the highway from our new house. As we approached our new home Daddy looked over at his old home place and wiped tears from his eyes, perhaps remembering that he was unable to be at their bedside when they died and did not get to attend their funeral. When we walked up the dirt driveway to the house, the family who lived there (we will call them Smiths, not their real name) was out on the back porch resting the rest of their life away. Daddy told them that we had bought the house and asked them how soon they could move out. We were quickly told that they would move when they got plenty good and ready and for us not to come back asking them to move for they were not moving. Then Daddy told that if they were still there Wednesday, he would get the sheriff of Cleburnee County to come over and put their things on the side of the highway. The Smiths got boiling mad. Daddy told them again that he might have the sheriff there on Monday rather than Wednesday. We walked around for a few minutes, eyeballing all the orchids, outbuildings, and garden. As we were beginning to walk down the driveway, Mr. Smith came out and began running his mouth off his, at us at which time Daddy told him that he had been told that whisky was sold there and the county revenue officers would come along too. Mr. Smith called Daddy a dirty name and went in the house and slammed the heavy wooden door. At that time we just turned around and walked up the highway home.

Early Sunday morning, Daddy, Lewis, and I decided to go over there and check the pasture fence and repair it if needed. There was about ten or twelve acres in woods and pasture on the north side of the property, about ten to twelve acres in farmland, and most of the remainder was almost level wooded land on the east side of the property. Our house, garden, big yard, and orchard took up the remainder of the acreage. There was a pretty large toolshed and workshop with a small barn and cow stalls just beyond the work shed. When we left out for the place that morning, we carried Daddy's double-bladed ax, a claw hammer, wire pliers, and Daddy's twelve-gauge shotgun and a pocketful of high-power shotgun shells, just in case we saw a snake or rabbit or some other creature that might be good to eat for supper. About the time we began to get out of sight of the house, we watched the Smith family flatbed pickup truck back up to the back porch. The loading began. The family was throwing and loading stuff on the truck just as fast as they could. We walked all the way around the fence, repairing it in a few places. Neal shot two rabbits in the edge of the field about two hundred yards from the house. It was about lunchtime when we got back to the barn, repairing the complete fence.

As we got back in sight of the house, we saw the Smiths driving off in the big flatbed truck loaded down with furniture, bedding, and stuff. It was tied down with wire, heavy cord, and ropes. When they hit the highway, they were going so fast the truck almost turned over on its side; however, the driver managed to keep it upright and sped away as fast as the old truck would go. When we saw them leave, we laid everything down and quickly went in to inspect our new home. It was a mess. The looked like a miniature city dump. Apparently, they had poured out a lot of moonshine whisky through the cracks in the kitchen floor. It smelled to the high heavens, and it is a wonder that we didn't all get high or drunk from just smelling the whisky fumes. Daddy left Neal, Lewis, and me there to start cleaning up the mess and burning all that would burn and piling up all the rest out near the barn and woodpile while he walked back to get Mom and let her see the inside of the house. In about two hours, Daddy and Mom came in with a large bucket full of big biscuits and fried chicken and a half gallon of sweet milk. They had eaten at home while Mom got dressed for the two-mile walk. The two of them were so happy they cried a little. Mom really liked the house. She had been there some years before but had somehow forgotten how the rooms we situated. Looking at the house from the front, there was a large sixteen-foot-by-sixteen-foot living room on the right with a front door and a fireplace in the end. To the left there was a large bedroom the same size with a front door and a window in the end of the room. There was a door joining the rooms together. The kitchen and dining room were the same size as the living room and were setting behind the living room with a door going from the living room to the kitchen, and the kitchen had a door going out on either side, one going out to the well and the other on to a back porch built in the L of the back part of the house. We all liked the layout of the rooms and the yard and surroundings. And it was the first time we could say that it was our very own.

After a few minutes we boys washed our hands in an old bucket we found inside the house and set down on the edge of the back porch to eat our lunch that Mom had prepared for us. We were tired and the chicken and biscuits sure were good along with the glasses of sweet milk. While we ate, Mom and Dad walked out toward the barn with their arms around each other, returning in about twenty or thirty minutes grinning at each other. They must have been very happy about the new house to do a thing like that. Daddy and Mom had brought a broom, shovel, garden hoe, and garden rake back with then. Now we could do some serious sweeping and cleaning. We all swept, raked, and cleaned the house and yard the rest of the day. The house was cleaned pretty well by the end of the day except for scrubbing the floor which would have to wait until the next day.

The next day was moving day; however, Mom had always heard that it was bad luck to move on Monday, but we got around the "bad luck" by having moved the cleaning tools there on Sunday. We borrowed Grandpa's mule, Kate, and his one horse wagon to move our stuff into the new house. Early that morning two of us borrowed Grandma's corn shuck mop and came over and began scrubbing all the floors while Daddy, Mom, and Neal loaded the wagon and started moving. By the time the first load arrived, the floors were cleaned and almost dry. But wet or dry, we were moving in our very own house, because it is better to move in on wet floors in one's own house than to move in on dry floors in a rented run-down shack. That day we moved load after load until all the household stuff was moved in. Daddy put a rope around the cow's horns and tied her to the back of the wagon and brought her in on the second load. Our chickens would have to be caught that night and brought in the next day. All this moving was a great task, but it would not be repeated for many years to come. The wondering family had been wondering from place to place for fourteen years and now had found a roosting place with our own roost poles to be ours until all the children were married and gone from home.

Here we put three beds in the big bedroom and one in the living room and the dresser and chest of drawers set in the living room. We drove large nails in the two by four-inch wall studs to hang most of our clothes in the bedroom. Boy, this was the most room that we had ever had except over at Mr. Bob's place. The kitchen was spacious with plenty of room for Mom to cook our ham and eggs and biscuits and gravy and never having to stumble over Daddy's big feet while he was getting his early-morning coffee. After supper that first night there, we all sat around the table for what seemed like hours laughing and talking and planning on what we were going to do in and around our new home. Part of the plans would never be carried out, but we sure had fun planning them. As I now look back on that night, I believe that there was more love, joy, and excitement there that night than most brides and grooms experience the first night of their honeymoon, well except for the X-rated bedroom stuff. Now that we had our own home life would never be the same; truly we had come from wandering in the wilderness to the land of promise. There would be no more sharecropping just to have a run-down shack to live in. We now had farmland of our own! Soon we would begin hiring out and making money to help Daddy keep the bills paid and help us to eat steaks and good stuff instead of ground hogs, rabbits, squirrel, and other varmints of the wilds. While the rest of the family settled in the new house, I had to live with Grandma and Grandpa and farm for them. Uncle Hubert paid me seventy-five cents a day and my board. And if I decided to, I could ride my bike over and spend the night with the rest of my family, which I did at times.

It was time for me to start farming for Grandpa and Uncle Hubert. It was late April, and the plowing and planting had to be done. But it would be a little easier this year. Uncle Hughes's wife Rosa had died, and they had five children that he let Grandma keep for the summer. There was Alonzo, Ealene, Elenor, Margie, and Buster. They ranged from about fourteen down. Ealene was about my age, and was she beautiful! We got very well acquainted and even smooched a little behind Grandma's back among other little accommodations and other little nice things when we knew no one was spying on us. Boy, was she beautifully built. If she had not been my first kissing cousin, we might have wound up getting married or something like that. Well I'll just say that we were well acquainted, and that relationship lasted all summer and well into crop gathering in the fall. The boys and girls helped us out on the farm doing all they could do with all the work. I even taught Alonzo the pleasure of plowing the fields, and he really liked it. However, I had to stop letting him plow when the corn got up pretty high because he would get careless and let the plow plow up the corn and stuff at times. They did a lot of gardening and other things that they could do. Ealene seemed to always want to bring me water when I was working out of sight of the house. Grandma encouraged such action, and I fully believed that she knew what was really going on between us. At times she would arrange for Ealene and me to be working together or to be together while no one was around. Somehow Grandma seemed to take a great liking to me and wanted me to enjoy one of the better things in a young person's life. She sure hit the nail right on the head this time.

At times after supper she would make the other children go to bed while Ealene would clean up the table and do the dishes while Grandpa and Grandma would go across the hall and go to bed. Ealene and I would then sit on a long bench behind the table and read the paper. Instead of reading, I would gently slip my hand under the table and push up her dress and start playing around. She would not be wearing her panties so we could have a little party. After we felt that everyone was asleep, we would slip upstairs where Grandpa's coffin used to be and get on a pile of old quilts and get on with the fun, making sure that we were very silent and not making a sound. However, that is sometimes hard to do when the pleasure has reached the boiling point. After the fun party was over and finished, we would quietly sneak downstairs, making sure there was no telltale evidence left behind. Then each of us would slip into our beds, lying there wishing we could be in bed with each other. Oh well, there will always be tomorrow, and perhaps she can bring me some water while I'm plowing down in the tall corn or near the wooded area where we can get close together again. All summer long and into the fall we enjoyed each other so very much. It was hard to break away from each other when the summer farming was done. Fall would soon be here, and the fun could begin while we gathered in the crops. And on certain days and on Sundays, I could ride my bike over to get some horse apples or something. We had a lot of fun gathering horse apples and even going out in the woods and picking huckleberries. What was so funny about all this was that while everyone thought I was the cream of the crop and a little angel dressed in Frank's overalls, I was really a fun-loving, pleasure-seeking, and pleasure-finding young man. I was not really that little innocent baby that was moved out of the foundry housing project in Anniston fifteen years earlier. But now I was a growing up! That fall Uncle Hughes took the children back to Atlanta so they could go to school, and I never saw Ealene again until I attended her father's funeral in 2002 and only for a few minutes. At that time we were strangers to each other. A lot of water had gone under the bridge in both of our lives, and perhaps we had best not remember that summer many, many years ago. However, the sweet memories of that summer will be with me the rest of my life. Someone told me she died last year, and I didn't know it until after the funeral.

That summer, 1939, Uncle Hubert and Aunt Foy bought about two acres of land on Highway 431 and decided to build a home on it. Their two daughters were growing up to school age, and the school bus didn't come back in the backwoods where they lived. Aunt Foy's brother Larry came down from Stone Mountain, Georgia, to live with them and help build the house. He lived with them that summer, and I lived and stayed at my grandparent's house. It was a little crowded that summer; however, we all found a place to bed down. While I farmed Uncle Hubert's crew hammered on the house. Each Saturday I would go in with Uncle Hubert and work until about noon for Uncle Shug doing heating and sheet metal work. I didn't know it then, but I was beginning to learn a skilled trade that would take me through the rest of my life. There were a few bumps in the road, a few detours, a few failures, but finally I got in the middle of the road and stayed there until I retired from heating and air-conditioning in 2002 at the age of seventy-seven.

Now at the age of seventy-nine, I am writing this book mostly to keep my wife, Margie, from running me out in the ninety-five-degree weather and make me cut the grass. I just think that grass would be very angry with me if I abused and cut it out in the hot sun. It might even decide to grow faster just so I would have to cut it more often or maybe it might decide to die on me so I would have to get out in the heat and plant more. That grass is cantankerous stuff when it gets mad. I'll just tell you how bad it gets: When we lived on Mr. Bob's farm, Daddy plowed up a field of Johnson grass and planted watermelons. The grass didn't like being disturbed, so he plowed around melon vines disturbing the Johnson grass again. Well, the grass got so mad and frustrated it grew up so fast and thick that we were afraid to go in that wilderness of Johnson grass to gather the watermelons. As well as we all liked watermelons, we just let the Johnson grass have them, and they rotted in the grass wilderness. I sure don't want to get the grass mad at me again. And besides I told Margie that It was always considered "bad luck" to cut grass except when the moon is full and it is sprinkling rain. I'll probably know if she believed me as soon as she gets back from the beauty shop and her dentist. If this is the end of my book, you will know she didn't believe a word of the "bad luck" story I told her.

There has been a delay in my writing since I wrote you about it being bad luck to cut grass in the hot weather. Well now I can tell you that sometimes it is "bad luck" not to cut it while your wife Margie is gone to the beauty shop and dentist. My head still hurts a little from my bad luck.

In June of that year, the Reverend Arce Haywood and Preacher Lovell were holding a revival at the Liberty Hill Methodist Church. Uncle Hubert and Aunt Foy invited me to go with them to the services, which I accepted and went with them to church all week long. On Friday night that week when the invitation was given I accepted Christ into my life. When the invitation was given I could not hold back any longer so I went forward and settled the salvation matter forever. After the services that night, Uncle Hubert stopped the truck and let me out at our new home. I rushed in and told Mom and Daddy what Had happened. Boy, were they proud of me. Mom asked me, "Frank, do you feel any different now that you have been saved?"

"Yes, I feel a lot different and it seems that I can hear a large choir singing." I replied as I went to the kitchen to see if there was some of Mom's good cooked food left. And there sure was, some chicken, cold biscuits, gravy and milk. After supper we talked for a while and then I went to bed. The next morning Uncle Hubert picked me up so I could go to work with him like I had been doing each Saturday all summer. That afternoon I went back to our freshly bought house to stay there for the rest of the weekend. That Sunday morning I attended Liberty Hill Church for the services. Life would be different now since I had accepted Christ into my life. My life wouldn't be perfect now but wouldn't be lived in sin without hope and without Christ as my partner and guide. Life would never be the same from that day forward. Now I had settled that age-old question that most everyone has to face, "What about Jesus?" That was the greatest decision that I ever made or will ever make. I joined the church and began to take an active part in all its functions and services.

The week of the revival Brother Haywood's daughter Kathrene accepted Christ and was saved and joined the church. She was about four years younger than me, however, we became good friends and we were baptized together in the Chulifinee Creek about a mile from the church. I can still remember the nice white dress with small flowers. Her shoulder-length light brown hair was dripping water as she came up out of the water and seemed to sparkle in the evening sun. She seemed to be the loveliest girl that I had ever seen in all my days. I think that I even asked the Lord if he could give her to me to be my very own. From time to time she sang solos in church while her mother played the piano. It was like an angel had come down to visit us each time she sang. The night that I was saved I felt the call to preach the gospel. Now I felt that if the Lord would give her to me, we could make a lovely couple to go forth and spread the gospel to other churches and maybe someday I could pastor a church of my own. She and I talked to each other at church, and we looked forward to seeing each other each Sunday. Kathrene seemed to enjoy being with me as much as I enjoyed being with her. There was a great feeling of love in my heart for her, and I'm sure she felt the same. Even until this day I believe God wanted Kathrene and me to belong to each other in the holy bonds of marriage. We were too young to date each other, but I sure did want to. Our church-time romance continued the rest of the summer.

After all the plowing was done that summer, I came back home to be with rest of the family. Margret and Betty were growing up along with Henry, my younger brother, and they were all living at home. However, there was just enough room for one more in the three beds in the bedroom. For the rest of the summer I worked for Uncle Shug and rode into work with Uncle Hubert. Working full-time, I was now making twenty-five cents per hour, which equals two dollars per day. That was pretty good wages back in those "good old days." When school started, Lewis, Neal, and I started school at the Hollis Cross Roads Grammar School. Neal was in the fifth grade; he was held back because of sickness. Lewis and I were in the seventh grade. Lewis liked to challenge the teacher on some of the subjects. Mr. Morris was our history teacher, and Mr. Alton Campbell was our geography teacher. Some of us boys would buy Lewis a Coke to get into a lengthy discussion with the teacher during class so we could goof off in class and not be lectured to so much. Lewis could keep the discussion going for almost the entire class period. I believe Lewis would have been a good lawyer. He sure could get us out of a lot of lecture time. We would be let off the school bus almost an hour before class started so the bus could pick up another load of high school students and take them to Heflin High School. Kathrene rode another bus and got there early too. She and I would stand side by side in the hallway and look out the window at the playground. We didn't touch each other, but it was the pleasant smile that made my heart skip and beat fast. She seemed to enjoy being with me as much as I enjoyed her. My love for her helped me keep going when the going got rough. We both had a great love for each other which was never spoken about.

Kathrene never told me that she loved me, and I never told her that I loved her; however, when we stood side by side at that window, and many times not saying very much, we both could feel a great love between us. It was there and in great force. Some days we would set our lunch boxes on the windowsill and eat our sandwiches and biscuits. She would always bring loaf bread sandwiches with peanut butter and jelly or other things and I brought large biscuits filled with ham, cubed steak, and pear preserves and stuff like that. Sometimes we swapped some of our good lunches with each other. If you have never had a lovers' lunch-swapping ordeal, you have missed out on one of the greater joys of life. When we were together, there was no lust in my mind at all. It was love and a great desire to hold her close to me and tell her that I loved her and wanted to spend the rest of my life with her, standing side by side no matter what came or went. I suppose that is what one could call real true love.

That year there was another beautiful, sweet, kind girl just one year younger than me going to Hollis. Her name, well I'll just call her Sally. We had met about a year earlier, and I had sort of put my claim on her as my girlfriend. That was before I met Kathrene. Sally rode the school bus with me to school each day, and sometimes she would save me a seat so we could sit together on the bus. That was very sweet of her. She was in the eighth grade, and we didn't attend classes together. She seemed to like me a little and even claimed me as her boyfriend; however, we never dated. Well, we did attend a Christmas party together. I gave her a gold necklace with a gold heart on it. The heart-shaped locket opened, and I had placed a picture of me on one side and I put a picture of her on the other side of the locket. Up until the time Kathrene and I became such close friends. I thought about perhaps Sally and I might get married or something. As Kathrene and I grew closer together, Sally and I somewhat seemed to drift apart; however, we kept sitting together on the bus and talking to each other on the play grounds at school. Perhaps I Was enjoying life at my age. I had just had a good summer with a favorite cousin that had moved away and left me alone in this cruel world of sweet kind women or girls. Well, I just had to face each day and make the best of a good situation.

On a Sunday morning, December 7, 1941, I went to Sunday school and church as usual. As I walked back home from church the mile seemed a little shorter, for I was hurrying home to get in the big bowl of fried chicken and biscuits and other stuff. Mom met me at the door and said with a rather loud voice, "Them lame old Japanese has bombed Pearl Harbor and she probably never done a thing against them. I don't know who she is, but the people on the radio shore are mad at Japan for bombing her like that." Mom was so upset she was shaking and crying. She was about as mad as an old setting hen when you are trying to steal her eggs to take to Mr. Brown's store to swap for coconut candy.

"Calm down, Mom, Pearl Harbor ain't no person, it is a place out in the ocean somewhere where there is a harbor that ships pull into to let the sailors get off and get drunk and do other stuff," I replied as I looked under the guano sack tablecloth to see if the rest of the bunch had left me any chicken and stuff. At that time I was able to salvage three chicken wings, a half of a chicken leg, and about a biscuit and a half in all and some mashed potatoes and some gravy. Mom dried he eyes and accepted the fact that some poor widow woman named Pearl Harbor was not bombed and probably hurt or killed. This was the beginning of a turning point in all our lives, as well as a turning point as a nation. We were being forced into war with a country that some of didn't realize existed before that day. A few weeks earlier in Mr. Campbell's class, I had to make a speech on Japan, being made up of over three thousand islands. Or at least that was what I told the class and no one argued with me or corrected me. All of a sudden, our nation went on full-time wartime emergency work. Daddy got a job doing work at Bynum, just out of Anniston, handling bombs and other ammunition. The whole nation was upset and trying to do what could help end the war. We children finished that year in school, but never returned to school again. Lewis and I went to work at the Adelaide cotton mill in Anniston packing and shipping large cones of cotton yarn to be used in uniforms for the military. In May of 1942, one of Sally's brothers came over to our house to see me. He told me that Sally wanted to see me very much. Later that afternoon I went over to see her. Her mother and stepfather had gone to work; they worked the second shift in another cotton mill. Upon arrival, Sally took me around to the back of the house to talk to me. She asked me if I would marry her. I thought about it for a minute or two; these decisions cannot be made hurriedly, one must take some time. She was fixed up so pretty and looked so beautiful I really didn't need a long time. Although we had never dated or even held each other or even kissed, love and lust took over. My mind began to take over. If I said yes, all the beauty and all the good things could be mine in a matter of a few days. After about two or three minutes, I said, "Yes, and just how soon?"

She looked at me smiling and said, "Just as soon as we can."

"Can I hug you and see how soft your body is?" I said to her as she turned to me and gently put her arms around me and drew me close to her for the first time we had ever held each other. It seemed like heaven itself. I felt her in places that I didn't know she had.

She asked in a low sweet voice, "How soon can we get the license and get married?" I was ready to get on with it right then. With her soft body pressing against me, I knew it would be like heaven to have her for my very own and to be able to hold her any time I wanted to. And I was more than sure she felt the same about me.

"It will take a few days to get the license and then we can get hitched," I said to her as I looked into her smiling face. Then I asked her, "Are you sure that is what you want to do?"

She smiled at me and said as she pulled me a little closer to her lovely body, "Yes, I'm sure that is what I want to do as soon as we can. I think about you day and night and I really do want to marry you as soon as we can arrange it." At that time we put the plan into action. I went home and talked with Mom and Daddy about it. They agreed with me that if that was what I really wanted, to get married, go for it.

The following week Sally and Mom and I got in my Model A Ford coupe and went to Heflin to get the license. Sally told the county clerk at the courthouse that she was eighteen years old, and I told them that I was sixteen, so Mom had to sign for me to get the license. When we got back over to our home, Sally and I decided to go over to a Mr.

David Roberson, a justice of the peace, and let him tie the knot. He lived about a half mile from us. He did the marriage very quickly after we arrived at his house. He was a poor man and needed the five dollars that I gave him for performing the marriage ceremony. We walked over to his house and returned as married as we could be. Now we could explore forbidden territory with each other. There was an old empty house about halfway between our house and Mr. Roberson's house. Sally and I stopped to explore the old house but wound up exploring a lot more! We got into things and stuff that we had never knew existed before. We spent our honeymoon in the bedroom with three of my brothers and two of my sisters. Well at least we had a full bed to ourselves. About midnight Sally's mother and stepfather drove up in our yard in his pickup truck and yelled, "Sally, are you and Frank in there?" She got up and went to the window and yelled back, "Yes, we are in here and we are married, so go away and leave us alone."

"We will be back with the sheriff tomorrow," her stepfather said, and they backed down to the highway and drove away. However, they did not come back the next day. The following day after they had gone to work, Sally went over and got her clothes and things and had me pick her up in the car and bring then over to her new home. We lived there for a few days and then rented the old empty two-room house that we had visited the day we were married. It was run-down and really not suitable to live in, but we gathered up enough furniture and things to live there. I had my own bed and Mom and Daddy gave us a cookstove that they had stored in the barn and someone else gave us a table and two chairs. We bought a few odds and ends, enough to make out with and moved in. It was a hard life, but a hard life was all that we had ever known. I kept working at the Adelaide Mills, and Sally just kept on living with me. But after a few weeks, we decided to move to Anniston so I would be closer to my job and we could be around other people other than my relatives. We rented a big room in Oxford from a distant cousin that had a gas stove and a bathroom. It was all the space that we needed. And since I had sold my car I could ride the city bus to work and back each day.

We were very happy in our marriage, and we really loved the little apartment. It was cozy and perhaps the best place we had ever lived in. The winter was coming on, and it was getting pretty cold. The apartment was heated with a fireplace grate and burning coal. I had never burned coal before, and we both enjoyed the open fire at night. Since we didn't have a bearskin rug to lie on in front of the fire, we just lay on a quilt bare. Gosh, all the things and stuff that we thought of and did on those cold nights with only the warm fire to see us. If our mommas could have seen us, they would have skinned us alive, or something like that.

We had enough money to live on, for we didn't have any bills or utilities to pay, the money I got for the car bought about everything we needed for housekeeping in our new home. My pay was about thirty-six dollars per week, which was more than enough for us to live on real well after paying our rent. We attended the Calvary Baptist Church in Oxford, only about five blocks from where we lived. We paid our tithes to the church and really enjoyed our church life. At times we would catch the city bus and go to Anniston and attend the Noble or Calhoun theater. In those days, we didn't have a radio and TV had never been invented. Sometimes I wonder how we ever got along without TV. A newly married couple can only talk so much. Then comes out the old quilt spread in front of the open fireplace, off with the clothes and things, and a night of pleasure begins. Today I wonder if those "couch potatoes" realize just how much they are missing watching TV instead of roasting their nude bodies in front of an open fire. Today when I see the TV judge shows and hear the men talk about their wives not giving them the sex they need, I just want to tell them they both need to roast a little on a quilt or blanket in front of an open fire with nothing covering their bodies except the light of the flickering flame coming from the warm fire. The warm glowing ambers and the soft light of the flickering flames of a lovely fire could solve many marital problems. There is just something magical about an open fire and a soft blanket! Perhaps our fast way of life today, and TV, radio, and other cares of life have robed many of our real pleasures, so we head for the divorce court, each one blaming the other of neglect in the bedroom. About all we have to do is build up a big fire and get a big soft blanket and let your imaginations run wild a few times each week or month. In those early days, Sally and I loved each other very much, and we showed it each day and night. She didn't have to work, and I loved my job at the Adelaide Mills. All day long I would sing, inspect, wrap, and pack yarn for shipping, remembering that blanket or quilt folded and placed in the corner of the room just waiting for the night shadows to fall.

The war was going on, and I was about to become eighteen. After a young man's eighteenth birthday, he was required to register for the armed services. Just before Christmas, we rented a room from my Uncle Earnest and Aunt Lola about three city blocks from the Oxford Lake. The Oxford Lake was a recreation center with Ferris wheel, different rides, paddle boats to ride on the lake, and there were many other things of interest to keep people entertained. There were many people attending the lake every night. Soldiers from Ft. McLellan located just out of Anniston would come there every night to find a little happiness before being shipped out to war. The loud music from the dance hall kept us awake at night, but we didn't mind. Young married couples can always find something to do. We set up housekeeping in a large eighteen-by-eighteen-foot room. At the end of January, I had to register for the armed service. About a week after that, I came down with the measles and scarlet fever. During the weeks following, I received a letter from Uncle Sam ordering me to report for duty. When I reported for duty, I was peeling my skin like a snake. I wasn't pleasant to look at. I was a bright red and as scaly as a fish. I was somewhat embarrassed to walk around necked before all the doctors that were examining us men. I had to explain my condition over and over to all of the doctors, even the two women doctors. One woman doctor asked me just what was wrong with me. I replied, "There ain't nothing wrong. I'm part Indian, and I belong to the little red scaly tribe." I heard a few chuckles from the doctors; however, I passed my examination. After the second day of examination a doctor asked me a lot of questions about my left knee. It was what we call a "trick knee," that jumps out of joint when any pressure is applied to the outside of the knee. It was an injury that occurred when I was in the seventh grade of school when I hit a softball while playing at school. It was never treated, and the ligaments in the knee never healed in their original place. After the doctor talked with me for a few minutes, he picked up a "rejected" stamp and said, "You could never stand the army with that bad knee, could you?"

"No, but I think I could stand the navy," I replied. He just looked at me for a moment and picked up the navy stamp and stamped my papers and sent me on my way. Later that day many of us were loaded on a train and shipped of to Norforlk, Virginia. That would be my new home for the next six weeks, at the end of which I was given a few days off to return home from boot camp to see my family and friends for perhaps the last time. It was a very joyous and happy time for me. I was again with my wife, whom I loved so very much. All the time that I was away from her the love for her was so very great. All my waking time, the thought of her kept going through my mind, day and night. It seemed as if I and she were talking to each other. All the thoughts were lovely thoughts because I loved her so much. The week we now had together might very well be our last time to be with each other, so we enjoyed every hour of the time. We visited our friends and relatives, letting them see me in my navy uniform. We made a lovely couple together, and our love for each other just seemed to burst out and bloom like a beautiful flower in springtime. Every time I looked at Sally, she looked so beautiful to me. I was so proud that we were married and that I had a reason to go to war, just to fight for her and our home together. This thought kept me going and doing my best.

The week at home went by so fast. It was time to get on a train and return to Camp Perry, Virginia. On the morning, I left for camp I hitchhiked or caught a ride from Anniston to Birmingham and boarded a train for Camp Perry, just out of Norfolk. After arriving at camp, we were all given a battery or series of test to see what we were best qualified for and where we would be sent next. The navy chose me to be sent to the University of Illinois to be trained as a signalman for the navy. I had been tested for reading and recognizing colors because of my work as a yarn inspector and color inspector in the yarn mill. Upon arriving at the University in Urbana—Champaign, Illinois, we who were selected for this training was placed in the large athletic building with the swimming pools and race tracks and all the other training equipment. Here I was in a university with only a seventh grade education. Most of the men that were shipped out there with me had had at least finished high school, and most of them had some college. I wondered, "Just how can I fit in with these men and learn as fast as they do?" Well, they were learning all new stuff just like me, so it was easier than I ever thought it could be. The navy personnel marched to the dining hall and ate with the other university students. We were in our uniforms and wore our navy hats. Boy, did we look sharp. And the food was so much better than that other navy chow.

After being at the university for about a week a navy person came to the classroom where I was and called me out into the hall and informed me that my wife had come up to see me and I could be dismissed from the class to go meet her at the main barrack building. I immediately marched out in a column of one alone to meet her. Boy, was she beautiful! It had been two weeks since we last held each other. I was given the rest of the day off to find us a place to live and settle down. It was easy to find a room in the home of a retired Methodist minister and his wife. They rented rooms to help with their living expenses. Our new home would be only one block from the barracks building. We who lived out with our wives had to be in the barracks by six each morning and we could leave each evening after chow or at five o'clock. However, we had to live in the barrack two nights each week, and on those nights we had to be in the barracks by nine for bed check. For the first time in my life, I had two beds but I only enjoyed sleeping in one of them. Since the navy pay was very little, Sally took a job nearby at a dry cleaners making a few dollars per week. My food was always waiting for me at the college dining hall, so I always ate there. From five on Friday to six in the morning. Monday, we were on our own to play around and do stuff and things. These months there were the happiest and most carefree time of our lives. It was summertime, and we went swimming and went to the movies often. And we just enjoyed walking around the campus. It was an old campus, and the buildings and trees and other thing that make up a campus were beautiful. As well as I can remember, the large trees were somewhat like the large trees in downtown Savannah, Georgia. Once you get acquainted with them, you never forget how beautiful they are. Here Sally and I spent perhaps the most joyous months of our lives. Here in the university, Sally and I meet a new group of people unlike the type that we had been around in our earlier life. These were mostly young people that were in college and were preparing for a better type of life. Back home most of our relatives and friends had no knowledge of college, nor did they have any desire to better their lives by going there. But here it was different. Most of the students that we met had a greater expectation in life other than just taking whatever life handed out to them. Just to be around such people helped change our way of thinking about our future. All the navy personnel around me were high school graduate or had from two to four years in college. It was nice to rub elbows with that type people. While it may have seemed that I was dragging them down, they were helping me to rise to a new way of beliefs and thinking.

When our time of training and schooling finally came to an end, it was time for testing and graduation within the naval session. I was proud to stand and receive my grading scores along with the higher educated naval students. To many others' surprise, my grades were up among the rest of the class. For the next day or two, we were assigned to our place in the navy. Some were assigned to battleships, some to destroyers, some to torpedo boats, some to submarines and some to naval shore signal forces. Perhaps because of my knee problem I was assigned to shore-based duty somewhere in the Pacific. That would require more training, but where to next? After the graduation service, we were dismissed from the campus for seven days, but we must be present on the eighth day at 6:00 a.m. to be shipped out to some unknown destination. Sally and I packed up and boarded the train back to Alabama. We wanted to see our families and home friends again. After arriving home we spent the rest of the week visiting family and just relaxing a little for a change, trying not to think of what would come next is us being separated again. We had learned to love each other more than ever before, with no family around to grab our attention away from each other. During this week at home, I had the chance to show off my seaman third class strip that I had one of my aunts to sew on my white shirt sleeves. Boy, was everyone at home proud off me! I even felt a little proud myself. I hadn't counted how many stripes it would take to be an admiral, but I was really trying to get there. We had never had a high-ranking military officer in our family, and I felt that I may be the first one. Irra was now in China and in the air force. I sure was hoping that I could be the first commissioned officer in the armed services. I could just see General Irra Rollins and Admiral Frank Rollins coming home and having dinner with our family at the same table. However, that would take a lot of promotions to get there, but I had taken the first step. As they say, wherever we are going, we have to start with the first step. Irra had made staff sergeant and I had made seaman third class, at least that was a first step.

On the seventh day of our leave, we all seemed to arrive at the barracks about the same time. We were happy and joking and most of us stayed up the night awaiting to be shipped out. Many of the boys spent the night in the bars, or with lady friends they had met in college. The only one left for me that night was a beautiful girl named Evelyn who had a room next to us in the rooming house. She was beautifully built and a very loving person. She was attending the college to majoring in education. That night we got very well acquainted to the fullest! We had a very lovely night together. But early the next morning we would have to say our final goodbyes, and I would go to the barracks with tears in my eyes, and she would wipe away the tears and go on with her schooling never to see me or hear from me again. I reckon she was just doing her part on the home front to keep our troops happy. Well, for one time she made me forget the past and just live one night for now. Many times since then I have wondered where she was and what she was doing. After about 0700 that Monday morning we began to get our orders as to where we were going. I was placed in a group and titled "Company Dog Two." There were about twelve of us, mostly country farm boys. We boarded a train to go to Oceanside, California. We were shipped in "cattle cars," which were rigged for troop transportation. It was a very long trip by rail and not a very comfortable one either. However it was something new to us, being almost like a hobo yet having makeshift food served along the way. For some of us it was better than we were used to at home.

Finally, after about three of four days on the rails, we came to beautiful California. Then we went on to a small naval base at Oceanside. It was really a marine base. Here we received about three months training in invasion-type warfare. We were trained to go in with the landing forces and set up shore-to-ship communications for the invasion. We worked closely with the troop carriers and the supply cargo ships. We told them when and where to go for men and supplies. To me it was more fun than a real job. And I didn't mind getting shot at so much; it was almost like being shot at while stealing chickens or Mr. Anderson's watermelons. Except here the enemy really must be mad or something, for they shot to kill. Here at Oceanside we were right on the rocky beach with steep mountains on the eastern side of our camp. The camp was small made up of about twenty-five or thirty Quonset Huts, each holding about twenty men. Some were used for cooking and dining and also classrooms. Here we got down to the real business of battle and war. It was here where I got my first sighting of a prairie dog, a little squirrel-like animal that burrs and lives under ground. I tried to catch one for a pet, but I reckon they didn't want to be caught so I failed. After about three months training there, it was time to be sent overseas to do war with the Japs. We were loaded on a troop train and sent to Camp San Bruno, just out side of San Francisco.

San Bruno was a horse-racing track with bleachers and a lot of horse stables, and a big office building and some other horse-related buildings. Some of us began to feel at home sleeping in the stables on a dirt floor and eating out under the open air shed. If they had some cows, chickens, and a pig or two, some of us would have felt right at home. The horse manure had been removed, but the smell was still there. Some of us felt that reminded us of what we were fighting for. We didn't have training at Camp Bruno; it was just waiting to be shipped out to our assignment over seas, and to get our final health shots before leaving. We were there for several days and were allowed to go into San Francisco at night and on the weekends. Then one morning we were ordered to get our seabags and satchels and board a big navy bus. We went across the Golden Gate Bridge and put in a big barracks for the rest of the day and night. The next day we boarded a big army transport ship. Here we were in the navy and having to ride an army ship. After getting under way before we had really gone under the Golden Gate Bridge, I was so seasick that I could barely stand up and walk. This lasted for most of the voyage to Pearl Harbor. On the second day of the trip, we were all ordered to go up top side and get fresh air and exercise for a while. I went up, but I was so sick I came back down and went to my bunk and lay down.

In a few minutes a soldier dressed in a khaki uniform told me to go up on the main deck. I told him that I wanted to stay in bed; then he ordered me again to go upon the deck. I rose up, looked him straight in the eye, and said, "Feller, I have wasted more navy ink signing navy pay slips than you have drunk army coffee." He turned up the corner of his khaki shirt, and there were two gold bars attached. Now I didn't know what army rank that was, but I immediately knew it was higher than a seaman third class. I jumped to my feet and ran up the stairs and tried to hide from the officer in a crowd. However, that hardly worked at all. The captain of the ship called a fire drill and we all fell into our positions on deck during the fire drill. The army officer, whatever rank he was, came over and singled me out and ordered me to go with him. We went down to my quarters, at which time he handed me a toothbrush, a bar of hand soap, and a two-gallon water bucket and ordered me to get the bucket half full of water. Then he ordered me to get up on the top bunks and scrub the black shoe-sole marks off the ceiling with only a toothbrush, soap, and water. The rest of the trip to Pearl Harbor, I only saw daylight when I was going or coming from the mess hall. I could go out at night and see the ocean in total darkness, for during the war the ships didn't run with the lights on at night. Someone said the light might scare the fish off or something. I sure did scrub a lot of black marks off the ceiling, and what made it even worse was that he was standing there watching me the whole time.

From that time on I never disobeyed an order before looking at the corner of the person's shirt collar. However, this misconduct was never put on my records, and I was discharged with a 4.0 discharge, the highest given by the navy. When we arrived at Pearl Harbor, we were sent just across the harbor to Airquis Point to receive more special training. Here we got down to real business. We were taught hand-to-hand combat warfare by the U.S. Marine Corps. After several weeks of this type training, Company D2 was put on another army warship. It had big guns and all kind of war stuff. The ship was equipped for an invasion somewhere, and we were going to be a part of it—finally. Some of us were real eager to see what war was all about, and we were soon going to find out. We sailed out of the harbor that day, and we could feel the ship vibrating all night long. The next morning I went up on the main deck to look around. No land was in sight. But in all directions were hundreds of warships, cargo ships, troop-transport ships, aircraft carriers, and the like for as far as the eye could see. I realized that whatever we were going to do, we had enough ships to carry out the mission, and I would get to be a part of it. This made me feel worth while and proud to be an American!

About a week had passed. On a Sunday morning It seemed that all hell had broken loose! The big guns on our ship were booming as fast as they could be reloaded, and all the boats and ships were doing the same thing. Well, if war was what we were looking for it had come that morning. We were invading Okinawa, Japan. And we were pouring it on them hard and fast. I wanted to see what was going on, so I sneaked up the stairway and out on the main deck. The whole sky was lit up with tracer bullets and shells being fired at the enemy shores of the island of Okinawa. However, my viewing quickly came to an end when a soldier or marine ordered me to get myself back to my quarters and stay down below. Since there were thousands of shells and bullets flying all around the sky, I felt a little safer down below. This shelling went on day and night. On the third day we were ordered to get on a landing craft and go ashore. The marines and army had been going in from the first day. By the time we went in, the beaches were secure and the fighting was a mile or so inland. But there was nothing standing on or near the beach except a few trees here and there, and they were all shot up. We built a signal tower about twelve feet high with a little room on top about eight by eight foot with a roof overhead and a wall about eight feet high with a roof over it, and the upper four foot left open so we could see out and communicate with the ships laying just off the beach. Life for us was very different on the beach than it was in training or back home. However, since most people in my company were off the farm or from other hard working conditions it seemed somewhat like a camping trip or picnic. But we can't escape—war is *hell*. One never gets used to all the shooting, bombing, and strafing around you. You were never safe day or night, but somehow I was never scared. There are many stories that I could tell you about my stay on Okinawa during the forty-five days of battle, but to write about them brings back hurt and sadness that I had rather forget. I made it back to Pearl Harbor to get ready for the next invasion, and I didn't ever get a scratch. Our company never had a single injury in the forty-five days onshore. Our Lord must have been with us real good.

When we arrived back at Pearl, we were given two weeks free leave to go where we desired in Honolulu or anywhere on the island. Within a few weeks, we were ordered to board ship again and go as occupation forces in China. The Japanese had surrendered, and the war was officially over. However, our job was not. We were ordered to go over to China as occupation forces. After leaving Pearl, we traveled for a few days and were ordered to go to Manila Bay and enter a debarcation camp and wait our turn to go home. After a few weeks there, we boarded the New York luxury line ship to be sent back home. We were crowded in the passengers' quarters of the ship. My bunk was up near the ceiling on top of a large stack of coffins. Each coffin was in a wooden box, so I put my mattress on top of a coffin and slept there. Now, I probably would have been scared or something, but I was used to being around my Grandpa's coffin that was stored in his attic room. We never knew if the coffins were filled with dead people, but I was not scared of the dead ones; it was the live ones that I feared most. At night I could smell an odor coming up from the boxes, and later I learned that the odor had the same smell as embalming fluid. At least the dead bodies were not carrying guns and shooting at me.

After arriving in New York and shaking hands with Miss Statue of Liberty, we were sent to Memphis, Tennessee, to be discharged and sent home. As I was handed my discharge, I had serious mixed emotions. I loved the navy, but I wanted to come home to my family and friends. I almost reenlisted that day, but the line was moving so fast I just moved with the crowd. Two days later I was back in Anniston at the bus station. I was expecting someone to meet me there, but not even my wife was there. I took a taxicab out to her grandmother's house where Sally was staying. She seemed so disgusted to see me; then she started crying. She seemed to have lost the love she had for me. After talking with me for a few minutes, she showed me a small wooden box or chest which had a lock on it, and I was told never to open it or even touch it. That box was a coffin to bury her love for me. I never knew what the box held, but I believe it held a secret that later would help to destroy our marriage. I could tell by her first actions that day that I had been away too long. I could tell that there was very little love left and that she was giving up some part of her life to be with me. We got a friend to take us over to my parents' home where we spent a few days. Everyone there was happy for my return from war without a scratch except for a damaged ankle from falling off a signaling tower on Okinawa.

After a few days, Uncle Shug offered to sell me Grandpa's big house and eighty acres of land, the old farm, for a real low price. Since I had my mustering-out pay from the navy, I took him up on the offer and bought the place. Sally and I moved in the big house with furniture that relatives gave us and some stuff that we had before. The place sat back about one mile in the wooded section; however, there was our old home about two hundred yards away where a good-for-nothing family lived, and about a half mile on the other side of us lived the Burke family. They were good, hardworking people. That was where Sally lived when I was farming for Uncle Hubert. She would come over and buy milk from Grandma, and that was where I first met her. I thought that she was the most beautiful girl on earth. I had been taught that all angels were in heaven and there were none on earth; well, I believe one sneaked out or jumped the fence for here she was! I made up my mind that I wanted her, and after some months I got her.

After moving in we cleaned up the house, big yard, and barn. In a few weeks we bought twenty-five baby chicks, a cow, and Uncle Hubert's old mule, Kate, that I was well acquainted with and began our way to success. I started farming, plowing the fields, planting, and all the other stuff. Sally got a job over at the textile mill where her mother

Leona and her stepfather, Sim Lewis, worked. They lived about a mile from our new home and they provided transportation for Sally. They worked on the second shift. In the summer when the farming was done I got a job with Daddy cutting logs for one of my cousins who had a large logging location just behind my land. With the one hundred dollars from the government each month, Sally's pay and the log-cutting money we had a pretty good living.

One afternoon I came home from the log woods and entered our home and found a short note pinned to the tablecloth. The note went like this, "Frank, I love you but not enough to live with you, so I'm leaving and I don't ever want to see you again." When I read the note, it was like a knife had pierced my heart. I knew that she didn't seem to love me like before my stay in the navy, but now this. It was hard to deal with. This had never happened to me before, but it would not be the last time. She left me once before while we lived in Anniston. We even got a divorce. After sixty days the day before the divorce was final she called me and wanted to remarry. The next day, we got married again. Things seemed settled between us and we were very happy together, at least that was what it seemed to be. But now this happened again. For about a week she stayed away. Then one afternoon I caught a ride to Anniston and went to the textile mill where she worked and talked to her. She promised to come back the next night. Sure enough she kept her promise. I was very happy again. However, in a few weeks she left me four more times, each time staying away about a week and then coming home. I thought it might be because we lived over in the wooded area. I owned six acres of land on my father's place that I had paid for. Sally and I decided to tear down the big house and rebuild a smaller house on these six acres over on the Highway 431.

The following week we started tearing down the big old house, making sure we didn't damage the lumber and framing material any more than we could. We removed the nails and stacked the building material, covering it to keep it dry. During this tear-down time, we lived with Mom and Daddy. I hired Lewis and Neal to help me some. I had a one horse wagon and a very fast horse that I had traded Old Kate, my mule, for. We hauled the material on the wagon the two miles to the new home sight. After all the materials were delivered and carefully stacked, I hired Monroe Rollins, Daddy's brother, who was a very good carpenter, to layout and build us a two-bedroom house. There was a large living room, kitchen and dining room, and a bathroom. It was a beautiful design. We really wanted a large picture window in the living room overlooking the front yard and the highway. Uncle Monroe built us a very nice house from the materials taken from the big house that we tore down. He finished all the outside, roof, and front porch. Now I had to hang the sheetrock on the inside walls and finish putting the fixtures in the kitchen and bathroom. The grooved overhead ceiling was beautiful. While living in the country we were attending the Calvary Baptist Church in Oxford. We were very happy now. I was working for Uncle Shug full-time doing heating, air-conditioning, and building metal awnings to cover windows, patios, and storefronts. I really enjoyed my job. Sally was working in his office which he shared with the owner of a car garage. She worked for Mr. Bob Newman and Uncle Shug. We had an old Nash car that looked good and ran good.

It carried us the fifteen miles to work and back each day without grumbling. Sally and I were working every spare moment finishing up the house. It was a labor of love; we really enjoyed it. We were paying our tithes at church and buying material for the house with what money we had left after living expenses. We had moved our stuff in the new house and moved it around as we finished the inside and painted the walls.

One morning we went to work and had a normal day. I came in the shop after a day working on a job outside. Sally was not there to go home with me. I ask Mr. Newman where she was. He handed me a handwritten note. It said, "Frank, I'm leaving you. I'm going and getting all my clothes and things. I have been pretending that I loved you but I don't love you anymore. I'm moving to town and I won't ever live with you again." The note broke my heart. That morning we came to work singing and laughing just like we always did. There was no hint of trouble in paradise. Mr. Newman seemed happy to give me the note, and I wondered why. Later that week someone told me that he and my wife were going to the Bevis hotel about two blocks away from the office to have coffee about every day. I had a .32-caliber automatic pistol that I began carrying with me in my pocket. It made some folk very nervous to see me coming to the shop and office. Uncle Shug told me that it would be better for me if I went to Atlanta with Uncle Hubert and got a job up there. The next Sunday I went up to Decatur, Georgia, to live with Irra and his wife, Dot. Irra got me a job working at Buckhead Sheet Metal Shop working for Mr. Crawford. Since I was good at hanging gutters and sheet metal duct work he started me at top pay and told me he was glad to find another "all-around" skilled man.

For a few weekends, I went back to Alabama with Uncle Hubert hoping to hear from Sally—but not a word came to me. This time I knew it was over for good. Irra and Pete Talton broke away from their jobs and started a new heating company called D & R Heating Company. I went to work for them. The shop was set up in Irra's basement. Irra and I could just walk down the stairs and go to work in the shop. Uncle Hubert went back to work for Uncle Shug in Anniston. I stayed with Irra and Dot and their two children, David and Carrol. It was good to have family around; however, it did not fill the lonely feeling in my heart. Every day I would work with tears streaming down my face. I loved Sally so much that it seemed that my life was over. There was no reason to keep going. I could not go to church or do anything but sit and grieve or cry on the job or at home or in the bed. I was ready to take my own life, but I had not decided how. I thought about hanging myself with a rope tied to Dot's high-strung clothesline, but what would I use to get my neck high up enough to stand on and then jump off? I thought of jumping off a high bridge, but I didn't know about a high bridge in that part of the country. Next I pondered poisoning myself, but that didn't appeal to me, for we lived by a family where a young man in the family had a situation somewhat like mine. He drank down eight bottles of iodine one night to end his miseries, and the next morning his stomach ulcers were cured, but he was doing just fine. Then I thought about shooting myself, but that just seemed too final. Once you pull the trigger, you just ain't gonna get a chance to back out.

One night I cried myself to sleep when at the hour of midnight I was awakened by a very strange sound from just outside my window coming from a small maple tree. It was one of the sweetest bird songs that I had ever heard. Being raised up in the woods and on many farms, I had heard many mockingbirds before, but not at midnight in total darkness. I believe the mockingbird might have been sent from God to bear a message to me. It was time for me to listen as *he* spoke to me, and spoke to me *he* did. Immediately I realized that while I was crying like a baby, the Lord had a job for me. Why consider destroying the life that God had given me just because an unfaithful woman had walked out on me! Immediately I fell on my knees beside my bed and had a serious talk with my God. After some time talking with him I became very sleepy and went to bed. I fell asleep at once, for I now had made peace with my Lord. That night I was carried back to my early life in a dream. That is where this story began. From this point on in this story, it started the next morning. It seemed that I had a new beginning, a new look on life, and a new desire to not die but live.

The next morning was Sunday and I had a great desire to go to church. I decided to go to the Rehobeth Baptist Church in Tucker, Georgia, about one mile away. David and Carrol wanted to go with me. They were little kids but Dot got them ready and I took them with me. We went in and sat down about six pews from the front. Everything was normal until the singing started. Tears began running down my face. I tried to hold them back but to no use. Something beyond my power had landed on me and I could not control my feelings and tears. The pastor Reverend Lester Buice seemed to know what to do. He preached love, peace and joy that day and the Holy Spirit seemed to take over my life again, and more than ever before. I could see clearly what the Lord wanted me to do. I had been licensed to preach, and now it was time to stand and take up my responsibility and get prepared. No unfaithful wife should ever block the work of God in anyone's life, especially mine. My wife liked to party and dance and attend the hellholes of sin, but now I could rise to new heights without a stumbling block to hold me back. It was her lifestyle; it wasn't mine. So I chose to live for the Lord, and become a messenger for him. After talking with Reverend Buice, I joined the Rehobeth Baptist Church.

Within a few days, I had Sunday school class to teach, and a week or so later I was placed as the director or teacher of a BTU class of young people. I worked very hard at these two positions. Brother Lester Buice took me into his care and helped me along. Soon he and I enrolled in to a Bible college classes in Atlanta. We visited the funeral homes and the homes of the sick of our church. Brother Lester Buice and I attended classes in a Bible college in Atlanta. He seemed to take me under his wing and love and guide me more than anyone had before. In a few weeks, I was elected to be the associate training union director for Lawrence County. During this time, I asked Brother Buice if he knew of a Bible college that I could go to full-time. He told me about a little Bible school in Chattanooga, Tennessee. The school was Tennessee Temple College and Bible School. I called the school that day and talked to one of the higher officials, Brother J. R. Faulktner. He asked me about my salvation and my church affiliation. I poured it on thich. Then I told him that I only had a seventh-grade education. He quickly informed me that salvation came first and my former education didn't matter, just send him a letter or postcard expressing my desire to come to Bible school giving a testimony of my salvation.

This I did at once. In a few days I got a letter of my acceptance to Tennessee Temple Bible School. This was by far the greatest thing that had ever happened to me other than my salvation. After receiving the letter and enrollment sheet, I filled it out and returned it at once, I was ready to go. However, I had to wait a few weeks until the spring semester started in January. The waiting time did not treat me kindly. Every night I would stay awake and wonder if something would keep me from entering Tennessee Temple Bible School and College. This kept on plaguing me until the day finally came for me to load up my suitcase and board the bus in Atlanta and leave for Chattanooga. I had not visited the college before enrolling; would I like it? This was a great step forward for me, and it didn't matter whether I would like it or not; I would be a student before the day was over and the sun had hidden its face in the west.

The bus driver let me off at the college. As soon as I stepped off the bus, a real good feeling came over me. There were no big tall buildings or large trees or a large campus like I saw during my stay at the University of Illinois. But rather I saw a large church and some educational buildings and a four-story men's dorm, which would be my home for the next three and a half years. I was thrilled to the depths of my soul. The Holy Spirit seemed to say, "Frank, you have just found the place of rest for the present and years to come." A Mr. Chastaine came across the lawn and introduced himself to me and offered to take my old roughed-up cardboard suitcase, and take me to Mr. J. R. Faulktner's office, where he introduced me to Mr. Faulktner, the vice president of the Tennessee Temple College, Bible School, and Seminary. Mr. Faulktner had me set before him at his large desk as he interviewed me for a while. I told him how I was saved, how I had worked in the church, and that I had been licensed to preach. As we were talking, it seemed that I could almost read his mind—"Lord if you have sent us this piece of dead wood to make something useful to you please send me some more serious instructions. If he is to us but mud on the potter's wheel, we've got a lot of rough pottery skills to learn. If he is timber to be carved into an ax handle, we sure have a lot of sawing, chipping, draw-knifing, and scraping to do. But, Lord, I reckon that is what you put me here to do."

After sizing me up for a while, Mr. Chastaine took me up to the top floor of the men's dorm. I reckon he felt that might be as high as I would ever get at Tennessee Bible School. After meeting Mr. David Lockrey and getting my paperwork done, I was shown to my room no. 406. I unpacked and settled down. I was content but very lonely. However, the loneliness would rapidly pass from me, for I was about to enter the rim of the unknown. I was but a bit of clay to be placed on the potter's wheel, and place me they did. I seemed to learn twice as much Bible the first day than I had ever known. Day after day, the teachers and instructors kept shaping and molding me into something that I had never dreamed possible. There we had some of the finest and greatest teachers and instructors in our modern civilization whittling at me, making me to be a vessel fit for the Master's us. As fast as they taught, that was how fast I learned. Dr. Lee Roberson was the founder of the schools and also the pastor of the Great Highland Park Baptist Church. I attended all church services there except when I went out to assist in Sunday school and church services in other churches. My life was beginning to take shape sort of like a great man once said. I don't remember who the man was and I have forgotten what he said, but by golly, I believed him! Whatever he said seemed to take hold of me and changed my life forever.

After a few weeks in Bible school, one of my relatives died and I came back home to help in her funeral arrangements. As soon as the funeral was over, I boarded a bus back to Chattanooga to college. After arriving, I went to the corner drugstore where we students often went for a Coke or something to eat, mostly just about dark time. As I walked in wearing my best funeral suit with a tiny pink rose in my lapel of my coat, a beautiful young lady about fifteen years old came up to me and introduced herself to me. Her name was Dottie, Dottie Roberson. She lived about one block from the drugstore in a very lovely house, one of the better-kept homes in the neighborhood. Boy, was she beautiful! In college we had been studying angelology, or the study of angels. Now, we had been taught that angels were all up in heaven. But now I believed that that theology was wrong. After seeing and talking with her for a few minutes, I believed that somehow while Saint Peter or some other great soul that had gone before who was guarding heaven's main gate had turned his back and at least one had sneaked out and escaped, Dottie.

For a few moments she had made me forget my past life and only believe in the present and in the future, perhaps my future with her or someone like her. But here I was studying for the ministry in a Baptist school where it was taught that a Baptist preacher should never be divorced and remarry for any reason. One could be divorced for the reason of adultery; however, he should never pastor a church. And here I was divorced and studying to be a church leader and perhaps a pastor, and here comes Dottie. Being with her and sitting across the small table from her some of my desires and plans were starting to take a different route. However, even being sitting at the table from an angel freshly escaping the joys of heaven and almost landing in my lap was not a valid reason for me to quit the ministry and try to win her over for myself, although it was something to think about. Had Satan sneaked her out of heaven and placed her in my path just to throw me off my main course and seek the wonderful pleasures of life with a lovely young lady like her? Could I just forget the ministry and marry a lovely lady and settle down to a normal married life? Oh boy, these divorces sure can mess up a man's life, especially if he been called by God and set aside for the gospel ministry. Although the divorce was none of my fault, it was ruining my plans for my life. But some of the main pleasures of life, such as having a loving, beautiful wife like Dottie, were not be. That evening sitting and talking with Dottie was a milestone in my life. Maybe God loved me enough to send me someone to comfort me in all my loneliness and despair, and disappointments in my past marriage life. Dottie seemed to take a real liking to me and we spent a lot of time together while I was in Bible College there at Tennessee Temple. I would take her to all the banquets and social gathering at the college. She always dressed nicely and always made me proud to be with her, and she seemed to always be proud to be by my side at these occasions. She remained as my best friend as long as I was in college there. Dottie married someone else during my final year there, and I was the best man at her wedding. Just before I left school there, she had a lovely baby girl, Jamie, named after he husband,

James Magathy. She came through Anniston one time on their way from Florida and spent the might in our home. I was married and had a baby of my own at that time.

During my second semester at Temple, I met a very lovely lady student there named Billie Wayne Ryan. She was a little heavy set and had rather long brown hair. She was beautiful and a very lovely lady. For a while I sort of wondered if Saint Peter had fallen down on his job guarding the gates of heaven again and was letting the lovely, beautiful angels escape at times. Well, you have to think about it, for here were two that I had met. Billie was lovely and we saw each other a lot, but we were not allowed to go out on dates together, for she lived in the ladies' dorm and the lady students were not allowed to date men off campus. I believe she really loved me, for we talked of maybe getting married someday and moving up north to her grandparent's big house and making a life there. I believe she was to inherit the big two-story house when her grandmother died and perhaps the large farm too. But that was not to be, for that would mean that I would be sidetracking and getting away from the main reason that led me to come to Tennessee Temple Bible School and College. Billie and I shared many good times together for the next three or four semesters. Then she dropped out of college and went home because she needed to go work awhile and get money for her schooling. At that time, it was difficult for one to get government loans and grants for schooling. Billie didn't come back to college there again while I was there; however, she did visit there one weekend while I was seeing someone else, and Billie and I only talked together for a few brief minutes.

A little later, on and further down life's road, a man that I was working with introduced me to one of his cousins. After talking with her for a while, I began to think differently about the study of hellogy or devilogy, for we are taught that no one escapes from hell, but after talking with Jane for a few minutes, I began to think that Satan had let down his guard at the gates of hell and Jane escaped, or perhaps she had crawled under or through the fence of hell or had escaped someway. She almost talked me into going out with her at night to a cave called Niccawaga Cave somewhere on the west side of Lookout Mountain. She began to tell me that she wanted a son just like me and I could be its father. Now that made me believe that she might be about halfway pregnant or something. And I was not about to go into a dark cave with a woman that I believe had escaped from down under and wanted a son "just like me." Who knows, she might have gotten me down a dark cave and hornswaggled me, whatever that means. And I gave her up in a hurry, for I had not come to Temple to get involved with an escapee from hell and help her have a son. Loneliness is bad but not all that bad, not bad enough to sneak off to a dark cave with a halfway pregnant woman who wanted a son like me. I didn't know much about pregnantology, but I knew enough to stay out of that cave with a half-pregnant woman that perhaps had escaped the torments of hell and had come up here to recruit me to go back with her. Maybe I needed to do further studies of "hellogy and devilogy," so I wouldn't get caught up with a destructive woman like her.

One day Dottie introduced me to one of her girl friends named Martha Pierce. Martha was sick in bed with a severe cold or something when I met her. She was very beautiful, kind, and a real sweetheart that day. Right then I knew that the Lord had better put someone else to guard the gate, for there were just too many escapees from heaven or maybe I was seeing and imagining things. Why would the Lord just let so many heaven escapees wind up in my life? I had prayed very hard for a new soul mate, but why so many prospects? Maybe, just maybe these were just plain lovely young ladies just waiting for a lonely Christian man to come along to sweep them off their feet and set them on my large white horse and ride of to a life in paradise. Martha and I hit it off real good, and she invited me to come over to see her the nest evening. Since I was still a stranger to her, I invited Dottie to go over with me. As we sat by her bed, Martha asked me to fluff up her feather pillow for her. As I reached down to fluff the pillow, she rose up and put her head on my arm and smiled ever so beautifully at me. Well, that did it! Before I left that night, we had become good friends, and soon we were dating and going places together, like ballgames and going out to eat every Friday night. I was beginning to love her very much by now, and I wanted to be with her about all the time, and we were together much of the time.

After a few weeks, I asked her if she would consider marrying me and spending her life with a bum like me. She threw her arm around me and said, "What do you think?" as she smiled and looked straight into my eyes. Well, that did it. We began to talk of marriage and stuff like that. At that time school was out and I was working full-time and making about five to six hundred dollars per week. I called a jewelry store and had the owner to meet me there after closing time. He did, and I bought her a beautiful diamond ring set for over two thousand dollars. Martha was so happy to show off the diamonds that she was wearing, and I was proud of her too. It seemed that this heaven's escapee had been captured by me and that I would reap a lifetime of joy and happiness as my reward. But that was not to be. It lasted for a few weeks or a few months. For some reason or another we broke up and didn't see each other anymore. It was hard on me. At that time I began to feel that I was getting to be sidetracked from what I came to Bible school to accomplish. To get married would defeat my purpose in my life's dreams and work. But must I have to do it alone? I felt that I was designed to love and to be loved. And it was a hard battle for me since I had been married before and had known a life of happiness for a few years to think of facing life as a lonely man forever. Unless a person has to face that problem, they can never know. The only way I could survive was to get into the Bible and to be in constant prayer day and night. I was daily reminded of the words of the country song, "I'll cry myself to sleep, but I'll wake up smiling and no one will ever know the truth but me."

It is said that God can take a broken vessel and put it together, and it will be the same as if it had never been broken. Well he had a lot of putting together to do for *I was really broken*. The only way that I could keep going on was to pray a lot and get lost in the work of our Lord. And that I did. I spent some of my evenings down at the Union Gospel Rescue Mission talking with men such as me who had lost all that was important to them and had given themselves to drinking and traveling over country as castouts. I felt that only by the wonderful grace of God I perhaps would be in their shoes and be just one of them. But I thank my Lord for the Reverend Lester Buice, pastor of the Rehobeth Baptist church, who realized my needs and took me into his care and helped me to get into Tennessee Temple Bible School. Had it not been for Brother Buice, I might have taken my own life. On that first time to visit his church, the Holy Spirit visited me, and I believe *he* visited Brother Buice that day too. It was because of his love and kindness that I am here today. I don't know if he has gone on to be with the Lord or if he is still living, but I feel that out Lord has a special place in his heavenly kingdom for him. When I get up there, I hope to get together with him and tell him how much he has meant to me and the input he has been in my life. So many times we neglect to tell the most influential individual how much they guided us in our lives. In many cases all our success or failure is due to someone else who has guided us along the roads of life. Somehow I truly believe that I might be pushing up daisies in some small cemetery if I had not gone to Rehobeth Church that Sunday and let Brother Buice's Lord get a hold on me. That was a great turning point in my life. All that I am or will ever be I owe mostly to the Lord, to Lester Buice, and to Dr. Lee Roberson and to Tennessee Temple Bible School and all its great teaching staff and to the college. And may I say to anyone reading my story that if you are mixed up and don't know which way to go, go and talk with your church pastor or church leader and listen to their advice. And I am sure you will be much richer by going.

At Tennessee Temple we had some time for fun. The boys and girls were not allowed to go off campus together on dates and such. However, between the end of spring semester and summer school, we had a week that we were on our own with no strict rules to guide our ever steps. The second summer that I was there, many of us were there waiting for summer classes to begin. Three beautiful girl students approached me and asked me to take them just out of Chattanooga to Lake Chattanooga, a large watershed lake on the river that ran through the city, to go swimming. I had a Jeep panel truck at that time. So the four of us loaded up with our swimsuits and headed for the lake. It was on a Saturday afternoon. We spent most of the afternoon swimming and riding in a rented boat. However, we were back at school for the evening meal. One of the very attractive girls said she wanted me to hold her around her waist in the water and let her learn to swim again. Well, I did, and the swimming lesson lasted most of the afternoon. Finally she told me she believed she could swim a little. I let her go and she swam circles around the rest of us. She could swim like that all the time, but she and I really enjoyed the afternoon lessons. All four of us lived on campus in the dormitories. We all went to Highland Park Baptist Church where Dr. Roberson was pastor. It was said that he always started his preparing his Sunday morning sermons on Monday to be preached the following Sunday. Well, that was not true the next day following our swimming party. He opened up on the four of us not calling us by name, but we knew very well he was preaching to and was it was about. That morning I didn't think he like us very much. However, it made us realize that we had really broken the college rules by going off on that swimming party. From that day on, we took our swimming lessons in our dorm showers away from each other. That afternoon was just an afternoon of harmless fun, but we were really breaking the rules of Tennessee Temple Schools although it was between semesters. From that time forward while I was at Temple, I never dated a student off campus again. I lived a victorious Christian life while I was in Tennessee Temple Bible School and College. It was a period of hard work, study, and pleasure all rolled together. However, it seems that many good times come to an end.

After receiving my bachelor degree I returned to Tucker, Georgia, to work there for the summer and return to Temple that fall. I decided to attend the University of Georgia Atlanta branch night school for the summer. There I took logic, psychology, and some other courses. Soon it was time for me to go back to Temple to start my studies working toward my master's degree. On Friday before the college was to start on Monday, I packed my bags into my '54 Ford car and was to leave for Chattanooga early Saturday morning to enroll in college and get started on work for my master's degree. It was an exciting time. However, about two o'clock Saturday morning I awoke with a severe pain in my right side. It was so bad that I got Irra, my brother whom I was living with, to take me to their family doctor. The doctor told me that my appendix was about to rupture and it had to be removed that morning. He sent me to the Georgia Baptist Hospital in Atlanta for the surgery. There I was rushed into surgery where my appendix was removed. I remained in the hospital until Friday. I went in the office to pay my hospital bill and was told that the operation and hospital stay was free since I was a ministerial student. On the following Monday, I had an appointment with the surgeon at his office. At that time he informed me that I was not healed enough to make the trip to Chattanooga. Perhaps that was one of the saddest times of my life. It seemed that the Lord had turned his back on me. My whole dreams were slipping away. The thing that I wanted most at that time was not going to happen to me. Going to Tennessee Temple was about all that I was living for. What was I going to do? While I was listening to the doctor and heeding his advice for the next two weeks, life seemed so unimportant to me.

During those two weeks, Irra and Dot decided to sell their house and move back to Anniston, Alabama. Uncle Shug had offered Irra and me a job working for him in his new business of heating, air-conditioning, and sheet metal work. Irra would be in charge of the main business, and I would be selling for him. Now that was something different for me. I was real good at working the trade, but selling was something new for me. I hit the road trying to sell heating and metalwork, but I was getting no sales. I could preach and teach the Bible, but I couldn't sell a life jacket to a drowning man. I had never had to sell anything before, so it was very hard. However, after losing about twenty-seven bids that I had placed with the builders, I finally made a sale. But in the process we had lowered our prices to about half the price that our main competitor was selling for. The news got to other builders very quickly, and we were selling one heating job each day. We had to hire new men left and right to install the jobs that I was selling.

After about six months Uncle Shug decided to sell Irra and me the new business. This was not anything close to what I wanted for my life. I decided to go ahead with the deal since I didn't have anything else to do. It was either to buy as a partner with Irra or look for another job. So we bought. Boy, was that a big blunder in my life. Now all the plans for me being in the full-time ministry were going down the tubes. But at that time I believed that at some point real soon that things would change and I could drop the business and go back to school. But every day I was driving more nails in my coffin as far as my dreams and great plans were concerned. We were getting more obligated to our customers and builders. We were supposed to stand behind our work for one to five years. That meant that we couldn't just close the business and we go back to school. So I decided to make the best of the situation and go on with the work for a while longer.

The Reverend Floyd Battles came by my office and invited me to come over to his church. Floyd was pastoring the Glenn Addie Baptist Church at that time. Floyd and I had been roommates at Temple for three years. He offered me the job as youth director and a Sunday school teacher in the church. I accepted the jobs and counted it a great privilege to serve under him and with him in the ministry. Floyd had a daily radio broadcast over one of our local radio stations, and at times he would call me up and let me have the broadcast for that day. My Bible was always on my desk, and since my office was only a few blocks from the station, I could jump into my car and be there in five or six minutes. And at that point in my life I was ready to take on the devil and preach the gospel of Jesus Christ on the spur of the moment anywhere and at any time. My preaching might not have been as good as many preachers, but it was plentiful. At that time in my life, I could read almost anywhere in the Bible and announce my text and soon depart therefrom and head straight to Calvary's hill and the cross. After being in the Glenn Addie Church for a few months, I started a Sunday-morning thirty-minute broadcast. Sometimes I would have members of the church come and sing for me. It went over quiet well. Radio time was hard to get on Sunday morning. After several months, Reverend Albert Johnson, a Temple graduate and the pastor of Ironington Baptist Church, wanted to get a spot on the radio station; and since I was not pastoring a church, I let him have my spot, nine on Sunday morning.

At that time my plans were to go back on the air as soon as another spot was available; however, that time never came for many months. So I never returned to my radio ministry. After a few months, Albert Johnson dropped his radio program, but he did not let me know that he was dropping it so I could get back on the station.

For the next few years, I remained at the Glenn Addie Baptist Church, working with the youth group, softball team and filling in where needed. I always had a Sunday school class to teach. During this time I was preaching at other churches and teaching Training Union classes when asked to. I reckon the Lord was good to me during these years, for he never told the pastors to overload me with their work. All this time I was just waiting for the time to be right for me to break away from my business and return to Tennessee Temple College. I had enrolled in Jacksonville University taking business courses and music classes. Somewhere during the first three years in business, Irra became dissatisfied with the business and wanted to go to Huntsville, Alabama, and get a job doing sheet metal work in the field of rockets. One of his close friends got on there and was making much more money than Irra was taking home. Irra was so worked up about the possibility of getting on there that he had a nervous breakdown and was put in a hospital in Birmingham for several weeks. Just before going to the hospital, Irra sold me his half of the business for three thousand dollars. His wife Dot was keeping books in our office at that time. She continued working while he was in the hospital. Irra was away and did not know that she was being paid on a weekly basis for his part of the business. She had collected most of the three thousand dollars and had not told Irra about getting the money. When Irra found out about the money that she had collected, he was very angry. They almost got a divorce over it. After Irra came home from the hospital, he worked for me for a few weeks and got a job in Carlton, Georgia, and moved to Carlton. After working for a Mr. Davis for a few months, he bought some shop tools and equipment and went into business for himself. He did real good. He divorced his wife, bought a home and built a big shop for his heating and air-conditioning business, and bought a new car and a new pickup truck. In a few years he divorced that wife and married another woman. After a few months, she talked him into selling me his truck, tools, and shop equipment, and into moving to Florida and working down there. However, after a few weeks, he moved back to Huntsville, Alabama, and went to work for Henry, my youngest brother.

While I was youth director at Glenn Addie Church, I sort of fell in love with a nice young lady much younger than me. She was Patricia Hopkins. She was brought up in a fine Christian home. After dating her for a few weeks, we decided to get married. We got married over at Reverend Floyd Battles's home. Floyd wouldn't perform the ceremony, but another preacher did. Floyd, like most Baptist preachers, won't marry anyone that has been divorced. But he was just as guilty as the other preacher, for he actually stood by and witnessed the crime. Patricia, who we all called Pat, and I were very happy in our marriage. Pat was finishing up his final year of high school and working in my office in the afternoon after school and working with me on Saturday. After getting married, we rented a downstairs apartment in a big colonial house on Eighteenth Street and Christene Avenue in Anniston where we lived for the next few months.

As soon as Pat's schooling was over, I began to make plans to sell the business and go back to Tennessee Temple College. Pat didn't want me to sell a good business and go to college. So she let herself get real pregnant by sleeping with her feet out from under the covers on a cold wintry night or something like that. I don't know just how it happened, but it did. When she told me, it was like a stab in my heart. Now that ended my dreams of going back to college and working on my doctorate degree in theology. All the planning that I had done up to that point went out the window. I could give up my business and leave my faithful customers stranded, but now with a baby, that was most unlikely to happen. Now I had driven a whole handful of nails in my coffin of my future schooling. It was all my fault; I should have put another blanket over her feet or turned the thermostat up a few more notches the night she got all pregnant, or something. Now that we were going to have a baby, we wanted to move out of that place for all the neighbor would know what was going on between us. We were even afraid to let her parents know what was going on between us. They thought that I was a very nice person—and now this!

I was doing a lot of work for Mr. Odell Bennett, who was building about fifty houses per year. He and I got together, and he agreed to build me a three-bedroom house up by the golf course on Johnston Court and McCall Avenue in Anniston. That was where a lot of poor rich folk lived. Mr. Bennett was a well-respected businessman and builder. He said he would build me the home, get it financed, and take a second mortgage for the down payment. Man, he must have me. We agreed and he began the building. Pat and I were the happiest people in town; we were getting a new home over where a lot of the poor rich people live. Within a few weeks, the eighteen-hundred-square-foot house with a full basement was finished and we could move in. And move in we did! By that time Pat was getting very pregnant, and her belly was as big as a barrel. I was very proud of our new home; however, I felt ashamed for our new neighbors to see Pat in that condition. They were bound to know what we had been doing at night while they were sleeping. Pat's father, Grady Hopkins, who worked for Frank Kerby, the owner of Anniston Electric and Appliance Store, helped us to buy a real nice used refrigerator, electric stove, washer, and electric dryer at a real employee kinfolk price. We furnished our new home with new furniture and stuff. Our new home was much more comfortable than the rental house. We had a new central heating and cooling system that my company had installed as the house was built. The builder Mr. Bennett also owned a furniture factory in Jacksonville. We bought our living-room furniture from him. Since I was doing his metalwork and heating and cooling on his many new houses that he was building, we traded heating and cooling for couches and chairs.

Finally it was time for the new addition to our love nest. One very cold morning about daylight Pat decided that was the best time for her to have the baby. That morning there were about eight inches of fresh snow on the ground and streets. There had been a car or two driven on Johnston Court, leaving two car tracks in the snow. It was so cold that the snow in the car tracks were frozen solid ice. As we were driving the mile to the hospital, we met a milk truck coming up Johnston Court. We were both driving in the car tracks in the snow. I saw him about two blocks away coming up the hill. He had tire chains, and I didn't and my car was going downhill. When I applied my brakes, the car seemed to get faster. I tried to steer my car out of the ruts in the snow, but it just kept sliding toward the milk truck, and it would not leave the two frozen tracks in the snow. The milk truck driver saw what was about to happen, and he managed to back up with his tire chained wheels. He got out of my path and avoided a nasty accident with a car full of a pregnant woman.

When we got on East Tenth Street, it was better driving, and we finally got to the emergency room at the Anniston Memorial Hospital. After a short lifetime, the doctor had me come into the delivery room and meet my new daughter. She was so beautiful and so active, waving her little arms and kicking like she wanted to run away. At that very moment in time I suddenly realized that this was really what life is all about. Life is made up of a series of happenings and this was one of the happiest happenings in my whole life. As the nurse let me hold our daughter, Vickie, I forgot about college and thought of about the joy of us having a baby together. I no longer hated the night Pat slept with her feet out from the blanket and caught a case of bad pregnancy and thought only of the joy of having our own little baby girl. This was something that they failed to teach me in Bible school and college, this was real, it was really real. The ladies of the Glenn Addie Baptist Church and the friends of the family gave Pat a baby shower about two weeks before Vickie was born. Pat was born and lived there all her life until she got married, and many people knew her and her family. This seemed to be the biggest baby shower that had ever taken place at the church. There were about two carloads of baby things given to Pat. Someone said that the large amount of stuff and baby things was because that I was not a quitter and that I was not about to stop now, and stop I didn't—there were three boys and another girl to follow. Pat had the five kids with a machine gun effect—*pop-pop-pop-pop-pop*—five times with only months apart. It seemed as if we missed a Sunday at church some of the congregation would see if Pat was going to the nursery with a new baby in her arms. After all five of the children got a little older, when we would drive up to an ice cream store or a hamburger joint as soon as the station wagon would stop rolling, the back door would open, and out would jump five kids. It reminded me of the horse-racing gates at the race tracks—the doors would open, and out came the horses, but in this case it was the Rollins family. As time went by and the children got older and larger, at times when Pat would have them all in her little Tempest car and she would stop for a red stoplight, people would stare at her and the kids. Many times she would roll down the window and say, "Really, they are not all mine." We just kept having them, and we just kept loving them. Those were the most joyous years of our life. Now that I am eighty years old, I just wish that we had had more, for everyone of our children brought us great happiness and joy. They came to us in this order: Vickie, John Frank Jr. Douglas, Michel, and Cathie. Vickie married Clayton Morris, and they are missionaries in Romania. Pat and I gave all the others some land here near us to help them have a mobile home or build a home of their very own. We helped them buy mobile homes, and Mike, Jay, and Cathie lives here today. Doug sold his lot to Jay and lives about two miles away. All the children have families of their own now; however, it is almost like having them live here with us even today. In July 1998, Pat died and went to be with the Lord, leaving all the children and grandchildren here for me to enjoy as long as I remain here.

The business went on as usual for many years as our children grew up. In or about the year 1960 or 1961, my brother Henry and I opened up a heating and air-conditioning company in Huntsville, Alabama. After about two years, I sold Henry my share of the business. The company soon became one of the largest business of that kind in that area. They did a lot of work for the government at the Redstone Arsenal. In 1963, Mr. J. O. Bennett contracted to build me a large building on South Quintard in Anniston. I was doing about one heating and air-conditioning per week for him, and we were trading out the work for the building. My business went along quiet well for a time after that, until I got careless with the way I handled the business. I let some building contractors get slow on their payment for my work, and I could not pay my bill as I should. During that time, I had branched out in a roofing company and was working over twenty men. That became more than I could look after. I hired Seals Corn to help me look after the roofing company and Roger to help me with the heating and air-conditioning part of the business. That ran my labor cost up so high that I was going in the hole financially.

After a few months, I had to file for bankruptcy with the companies that I owned. In the meantime, I had opened up Rollins Employment Agency, which was taking up a great part of my time. After the bankruptcy, I went into business with Roger Williamson, my brother-in-law. After a few months, Roger wanted to go on his own with the business, so he and I divided the tools and trucks and we both went our own way. The Rollins Employment Agency was beginning to pay off; however, I now needed to get back to the heating and air-conditioning business full-time. After I closed the agency, my other business began to build up fast, but it was like starting all over again. Roger took most of my good customers with him in the deal. But I was so glad to have the business all to myself that I would have done about anything to be on my own again.

I took my share of the tools and my personal truck and began work by myself. This went on for a few months, and I was climbing the ladder of success again. We still had a roof over our heads and were eating three meals each day and paying our tithes into the church where we belonged. I was teaching the men's Sunday school class, and my family was in church regularly. One Sunday after church was out, a man approached me wanting to buy into my business. I didn't want to sell any part of my business to anyone, no matter who he was or how much money he may have. However, after talking with him about all that afternoon, we finally made a deal. He would own half of the corporation. I would be president of the company with 51 percent of the shares, and he would be vice president with forty-nine percent of the stock. We would let his wife keep the books, and I would do the selling, installing, and collecting the money. This man would be the treasurer for the corporation. We had an accountant come by every Friday and do the main bookkeeping. This went on for a few months. Finally, some of our suppliers where we bought our equipment and supplies began calling me and demanding money for the stuff that they were furnishing us. Since I was collecting the money from our customers and turning over the money to the secretary and treasurer, I began to question where the money was going. I knew that we were making a reasonable profit on the work. I was keeping books secretly without my partner knowing about it. When my books showed that we owed several thousand dollars in the bankruptcy for the bills, *we knew it* would be impossible for him or me to pay. He gave up his stock in the company but never let me have all the company books. His secretary told my wife, Pat, that he took the money out of the money that I had collected and turned over to him to pay our suppliers and spent most of it to build him a home down on the river. After struggling for a few months longer, I finally filed for bankruptcy. Within a week or two, I formed a new company all by myself. However, it was costly for me to give up one company and start another. A few years before this, I had bought one hundred and nine acres of land just south of Oxford in Talladega County. We remodeled the house and had moved from Anniston to our remodeled home. We had managed to get several head of cattle and repaired the pasture and sowed it down in fescue and clover. My children had a few horses. We were setting good for a while, but we had to sell the cattle and horses to try to keep the other company from having to go into bankruptcy. But we ran out of horses and cattle before we could put the company on solid ground again. But that was not to be. Sometimes failure comes in spite of all one can do to make a success, so it was with me. Someone once told me that I accepted failure with a smile and never feeling bitter. He wanted to know how I did it. I informed him that was because I had never been defeated, maybe I had lost a few battles but I had never lost the war. I told him that one only suffers defeat when he gives up the fight, and I was not about to surrender while I was able to start over and go on.

After my second bankruptcy I decided to take a real estate course and get into real estate and do some home building. And so I did. After finishing the source and getting my broker's license, Pat and I decided to subdivide the farmland into building lots and do some home building. After laying out the streets and lots, we needed a builder. I don't remember how we got acquainted with Mr. Corvin Gaddy, a local builder, but we did. It was a good thing for us. We would deed him the lots, one at a time and let him build small houses financed by the farmer's loan association out of Talladega. I would sell the houses and get a real estate commission and the money for the lot at the final closing of the loan. The buyer only had to come up with three hundred dollars and buy him and his family a new home. Each house had about nine hundred feet of floor space which contained two or three bedrooms, a kitchen, a living room, and a bathroom. These houses were sold for a very low price from eight thousand and up, depending on the size of the house. I believe that I could have sold at least one or two houses every day if they were available. Within a few months, we filled up my subdivision and had to lay out more lots. In the mean time I went into heating and air-conditioning business again, and my business began to do real well since I had got rid of a bad partner.

Late one afternoon I had gone up to Jacksonville to collect some money from a builder who owed me for some heating and air-conditioning. Pat and the five children had gone to a little league football game where Doug and Jay were playing. As I drove down County Line Road when I got near my home, I saw the flames and smoke coming from my roof. There was a large crowd standing around and several Oxford and Munford fire fighters trying to save the home. However, the house had a corrugated metal roof, and it soon was totally engulfed in flames. Because of the metal, roof they could not save the house. This was about the worse thing that ever happened to my family. We lost our home, clothing, furniture, and all our personnel possessions. Pat and I could stand the loss better than the children. Each of them lost small personal toys and other things that could not be replaced. Vickie's sewing machine seemed to be her greatest loss, but all the children had lost all their clothing, toys, and, well, everything they owned. We placed the children in other people's home until we could buy a large Redman Mobile home and set it up in our front yard. After about a week, we rounded up the rest of the family and got new furniture and started a new way of life in the new home. Man, it took some getting used to living in close quarters. Vickie and Cathie had one small bedroom, Jay Doug and Mike had one larger bedroom, and Pat and I had the larger bedroom. The trailer had two full baths. We adapted to this rather quickly. It was worse for me. I would imagine that I was still riding on a troop train from Chicago to San Francisco, but as soon as I opened the front door, I would suddenly realize that I was standing still and not going anywhere fast. We started making plans to build us a large house up on top of our hill overlooking the valley, our subdivision, the airport and downtown Oxford and a large part of Anniston. The location was where Mike used to visit and sit under the large trees and enjoy the quietness of being alone; he said it gave him a chance to think. At that time Mike was only about eight years old, and the hill was almost a quarter mile behind our old home.

Pat and I began looking for a house plan that would be right for our family and that we could afford. We had received about sixty thousand dollars insurance from our burned house. We came up with house plan that had just what we wanted. It was a split-level containing twenty-six hundred square feet of floor space. There was a kitchen, dining room, living room, den, five bedrooms, and three and a half baths. There was a large game room, over thirty by thirty feet of floor space, and a basement under the remainder part of the house. Mr. Grady Vaughan drew up the plans, and after a few changes in the plans, he gave them to us so we could get started. We had already hired Mr. Jim Cooper, a real good grading contractor, to grade us a street and level the top of the hill and get ready to build. Mr. Cooper had graded down for the two level part of the house and graded further down for the basement. The basement, game room, bedroom section, and main living area gave a four-level home. We had the floor of the basement and the game room poured with extra strength concrete and contracted the foundation to a block mason which did a good job.

After the foundation was done, we let Phillips Manufacturing Company prefab the house and dry it in. I purchased the windows and doors and we contracted for Earnest Hall, a good local builder, to do the finishing up the house. I let some of my workers help me do the plumbing, the electric wiring, the central vac system, and some of the other work. The game room had a large steel beam running down the center with no visible post holding it up. There were several large plate glass windows four-by-six-feet windows on three sides and an entrance door. Leading down from our den to the game room was a seven-foot stairway. This made the den and game almost as one room. The way the home was constructed, a well-to-do businessman wanted to buy it to use as a supper club. But this was our new home and not to be used for a supper club. Mr. Foster, a well-known rock mason, contracted to cover the foundation wall outside and the game room outside with rocks. He built me a large fireplace and inside planters and a twelve-foot rock wall in our den. The children, Pat, and I spent all our spare time working on the house and building a large swimming pool or cement pond. It was built at an angle and was twenty by forty feet on the longest side and held thirty thousand gallons of sparkling clear water. We were unable to find anyone to build the pool for us, so we had to pour the floor and build the walls with twelve-inch cement blocks and put steel rods in the floor and also in the walls and pour the walls and pour a decorative cement top over the blocks. After finishing the wall and top, we poured an eight-foot-wide cement walk around the pool. The walls of the pool were covered with a half-inch coat of white King cement and marble dust. It was a sparkling sight until we got some swimming pool paint and painted the walls and rail around the top. After getting the Oxford Fire Department to hall a few tankers of water, we began swimming in the pool. The new sand-filtering system kept the water crystal clear.

Vickie and Cathie had a bedroom together and a private bath, and each of the boys each had a bedroom to themselves with a bath for the boys. Each one had the joy of selecting the color for their carpet and wall paint. The children were very happy to leave the mobile home and move up to paradise. Pat and I had a large master bedroom about fourteen feet by fifteen feet and a large bathroom with a four-by-four-foot tiled shower, and on the other side Pat had a sunken tub with a shower. Pat had a large walk-in closet, and I had a long closet with vented slated doors. Each room had large double windows with double-glass or insulated windows. Most of the house had wainscoted walls with a chair rail about halfway between the floor and ceiling. That was Pat's idea. It added beauty to the home and served a good purpose when she was confined to a wheelchair the last eleven years of her life. Our new home was really more than we had ever dreamed of having. In a few weeks of hard work, we were ready to move in our brand-new home. Each of the children chose their own furniture and furnishings, curtains, and carpet for their own room. It was great pleasure and fun to start living in the home while being completed. To the boys it was almost living camping outside while having the comforts of living in a home. It was like living in paradise or maybe a little better.

After a year or two, the children began marrying off. First there was Vickie, then Jay, then Doug, followed by Mike and Cathie. Pat and I let them live with us for a few weeks while we helped them get set in an apartment or home of there own. However, each of them bought a mobile home and moved it up on the hill beside us. They were very eager to get off and then live in our yard or a few hundred feet away. Pat and I liked it this way, for they were out of our nest and making nest of our own, and since we had about twenty acres of beautiful woodland up here, we enjoyed having them close in. Children always need help, and we were close enough to each of them to help them when they needed it.

Many years have passed since then and I am now eighty years old, and much has happened since the last paragraph in this story. My wife Pat had became disabled to walk and was in a wheelchair for eleven years and was on a dialysis machine for six years before going to be with the Lord. Within a few months after Pat's passing, I got acquainted with Margie Harrell, a former real estate broker and home builder, and shortly after we got married. She had a beautiful split-foyer two-story home about two miles from me. When we got married, she came to live with me in my larger home. It was hard for her to get used to living here, and frequently she would leave me and go live in her home for a day or two at the time. But finally she got used to my home and settled down here to stay. She is seventy-four years old and just doesn't get around so well. She is still active but slow active. She is still very beautiful after having to put up with me for eight years. We have been happy together, and we still are. While we were still able, we went fishing together, but not this year. Her health is failing her, and I have a serious heart trouble that may require an artificial heart valve installed, and a pacemaker, and only Dr. Camran knows what else. About three years ago, I had a triple bypass surgery on my heart. I was able to do hard work until a few days ago, and I had a light heart attack. Dr. Camran is planning to go in again and do an LMC three days from now. Because of this, I may have to cut my life's story short, for I might not have any life left. But before I kick the bucket, I will give you a little more of my story.

Shortly after Pat's death, I gave the company to Jay so he could keep it going. Mike and Doug were working for the company or for me. I deeded Jay the large sheet metal shop and the trucks all the shop tools and equipment. He agreed to pay off all the company debts and keep the company going. Since I was too old to do all the work required to run the company, and since he was the only one of my sons with the proper experience to take over the company, I let him take over and I would work in the office and help him sell heating and air-conditioning jobs to the builders and homeowners. Mike and Doug felt left out, but my back was to the wall at that time. Jay and his wife had already bought a business license and were going into business for themselves. I talked him into taking over my business and paying of a large company debt that had built up because I had taken money from the business to pay Pat's medical bills. The medication was over eight hundred dollars per month for the past eleven years. When he took over the business, there was about eighty thousand owed to suppliers and to the bank. I owed about sixty-five thousand on my home and land. I have to pay that debt myself. Our home and land was paid for before Pat's disability; I had to borrow money to keep going and paying drug and doctor bills. I'm so glad that we could take care of her medical bills by mortgaging our home and still keep going. All the children seemed proud of the way we did all that was possible for their mother until her death.

Jay and Debrah were able to keep my customers and keep the company going. I helped him for about four years, and then I dropped out and retired from the business. Since then I have built five apartment in the children's part of the home and the large game room downstairs. There are two apartments upstairs and two downstairs, another in the basement, and one in the two-room office space that I added to the back of the house. All in all, I have twelve apartments or rentals. The money comes in handy to live on and pay the utilities, and I have to the banknote of over a thousand dollars per month out of my Social Security check. The mortgage note will be paid off in July of 2007, which is only eight months away. And I am looking forward to that day. I may even take Margie over to the Waffle House and celebrate that day.

As I look back over my past, I am reminded of something I heard many years ago,

"Man's life is like the pages of a diary in which he means to write one story but always writes another."

The writer of the book of Psalms put it this way, "We spend our years as a tale that is told" (Psalms 90:9).

I never forget that "Tomorrow will always be different because of what we do today."

Do I have regrets about my life? *Yes!* And plenty of them. My greatest regret is that I never gave everything up and went back to Tennessee Temple University and received my doctorate degree and spend full time in the ministry.

Perhaps someone reading my writings won't make my mistake and give up their education for the same reason that I did. Perhaps do it for some other reason—you will be sorry when you are eighty years old.